To Sue

Hope you enjoy
reading this book

xx

Cover design and book design and setting by Neil Coe

First published in 2010

Ecademy Press
48 St Vincent Drive, St Albans, Herts AL1 5SJ
info@ecademy-press.com
www.ecademy-press.com

Printed and bound by: Lightning Source in the UK and USA

Printed on acid-free paper from managed forests. This book is printed on demand, so no copies will be remaindered or pulped

ISBN 978-1-905823-89-5

ACKNOWLEDGEMENTS

Thanks go to Morris Hogg (my business partner) who has stuck with and been highly supportive on this and all the various projects through thick and thin over the past 9 years and continues to provide unparalleled commitment to everything we do... he is a diamond.... One in a million.

Thanks also go to **Nicola Cairncross** (http://www.nicolacairncross.com) at the Money Gym for setting me on the path to understanding Internet marketing and for the support systems in place in those early days.

A big respect to **Claire Raikes** (http://www.claireraikes.com) for those long deep marketing strategy sessions, many of which were over and above the actual jobs which we set out to achieve. These 'chats' steadily knitted all the Digital marketing components into place and underpinned the understanding necessary to pull everything together for Step 4 of this book.

Thanks also to Claire for the hard work on bringing all the online blog / web sites together and her creativity even though it was all a bit lastminute.com!

A special thanks to **Suzanne Barnett** (http://www.kisstrainingonline. com) for the hours formatting and laying out the book (even with my amendments and additions highlighted in a myriad of colours) and for getting the book into decent shape for its eventual distribution.

Thanks to the team at Internet Power Systems particularly Otis and Livia for their patience and support whilst I abandoned them at times to seek solitude to finish a book which they must have cursed at times it was taking so long to complete.

Thanks also to those that took the time to read the various chapters as they were completed and provide positive feedback without which the book might have taken a few more years yet!

Thanks go to all those who unwittingly have contributed in one way or another through interaction with me over the past 30 years. This book is a culmination of many different experiences, and phases in running and managing businesses and would not have been possible without those who have been part of this journey.

Finally thanks to all those who believed in me and the Book, providing much needed impetuous to continue on whilst trying hard to fulfil a day job... you know who you are! ... and peculiarly thanks to those who lack belief too, for in my case this has often re-energized my drive and determination to see the job through.

FOREWORD

This book has finally come together after having talked about it for circa 6 months. I guess I'm not the first and I won't be the last who has struggled to find the time to write a book with everything else going on in our lives!

For all those people involved in running or managing a business today I am sure you will agree we live in exciting times! Some would argue, challenging times, and possibly this is true for many of us.

If we just look at what kids have to pick up and learn in today's modern world, mobiles phones, computers, gaming, iPods, the Internet, social networking, a decent education as well as looking cool and being popular we can see what we're up against.

As business people we have to contend with not only 'Running our Business' but we must be aware of all kinds of developments and how they affect our businesses. History books are littered with those who took their 'eye off the ball' and fell victim to more agile and flexible competitors.

No doubt about it, we are probably at the start of the biggest shake up in 'Business Management' since the Industrial Revolution. It is a bold statement I know but, the Internet will reshape the traditional 'business' definition and strip away the walls that surround our companies. The good news is that we still have time and we don't have to do it all at once! But… do it we must!

We have seen vast changes already with the adoption of Web sites, email, searching and the emergence of social media platforms… but the next generation of changes will revolutionise the very structure and operation of business itself. The 'normal office based' business will change to accommodate ways of working more in harmony with how we want to live. Connectivity will enable us to make choices about the work we want to do and with whom we want to work. This revolution will effect large and small companies alike and change the workplace forever giving birth to huge new markets whilst closing others. It is set to be a rollercoaster ride for sure!

This book contains a 7 step process to ensuring you have a business that you want and that it is engineered for the future. Each of us is different as are our businesses, so these 7 steps will lead to many destinations.

'... Even the longest journey, starts with a single step'

Your journey has already started, by opening this book you are already ahead of the game. This book will definitely ask you to 'rethink' many things and may present a case for 'changes'...

As Anita Roddick of 'The Body Shop' fame once said:-

'Learn to nest in the gale'

The only thing that is certain is that change is inevitable!

The next few years are likely to be revolutionary for many businesses. For those who get on board with some of the new ideas highlighted in this book, **more time**, **more money** and **more freedom** might just be your outcome!

ABOUT THE AUTHOR

Chris Ogle was born in Stanmore just outside London and now lives in Watford. Chris is a co-Owner and Managing Director of Internet Power Systems Ltd. Since leaving secondary education, Chris initially worked with Rolls Royce, Leavesden before moving on to a software house in London.

Chris has worked in the computer industry for over 25 years. An established programmer on a whole range of computer platforms Chris is equally at home with technicians as well as commercial and business professionals.

Although initially from a technical background Chris has helped a wide variety of companies to implement manufacturing and accounting systems. The interface between the system users and the technical development team is where Chris's major strengths lie.

Since 1992 Chris has run and managed his own SME businesses, primarily implementing and building business process solutions for other SME's.

In 1997 Chris recognised the impact that the Internet would have on the business world and was quoted as saying:-

'one day all business software will be delivered through a web browser'

From the year 2000 Chris began to develop solutions in the 'Software as a Service / Cloud computing' marketplace although these terms would not surface for another 8 years!

In 2002 Chris established Internet Power Systems Ltd. The company was set up to introduce low cost, flexible, trouble free business computing to SME's and take them through the 7 Steps to success outlined in this book. For the first few years IPS set about creating i-Tr@der, their Web based business platform that sits at the centre of the 7 steps. IPS work with a network of independent Implementation Practitioners that are so essential in providing high quality, individual support required to customers. SME's are now able to enjoy many of the benefits previously only afforded to big corporate companies.

'Small and Medium sized companies had been left behind in the Internet race' says Chris 'but speed of decision making, the necessity to streamline their businesses, and ability to adapt operations to the SaaS / Cloud computing model will enable them to compete at every level with the big boys'.

THE 7 STEPS – AN OVERVIEW

Step 1 – Mindset Management

This chapter takes a long hard look at why a business might have been started in the first place and revisits whether the original goals and objectives have been met.

If the answer is no, then we need to take stock, decide whether what is happening is what we want or not? And if not? that we'll probably have to make one or two adjustments to a few things.

Once we've established where we've been, where we are right now and what we want for the future we can set a course to get to the destination that works with the 'winds of change' that are upon each and every one of us.

Step 2 – Business Analytics – 'Doing Things Right'

In chapter two, we look in much more detail, introvertly at the business itself. Where are the bottlenecks? Where are the areas of indispensability (normally the business owner)? and how we can lay the foundation stones to creating a business that flourishes even if they key people there today were absent in the future?

Prising the knowledge and information out of the Business owners and Key peoples head's is often a difficult task and sometimes not that willingly undertaken, but it is the only way to be truly free.

Step 3 – Running a Business Online – Cloud Computing

In Chapter three we begin to evaluate the advantages of utilising latest technology Cloud Computing business platforms for our business.

Passing through the complete history of modern computing right up the latest Internet and Digital Age this chapter explains how and why we've arrived where we are and how important it is that companies migrate to the 'Cloud Computing' technology to retain their competitive edge in a global marketplace.

Step 4 – Increase Sales - Digital Marketing

The largest chapter in this book by far and for good reason. Digital Marketing and the implications are set to revolutionise how we find our future Prospects, Customers, Suppliers, Business acquaintances and Joint Venture Partners.

More than that though, the online world with Social Media such as Facebook, LinkedIn and Twitter changes the very fundamentals of the Business model as we know it.

This chapter explains in detail all the components of Digital marketing, what each component does, why you would use them, and most importantly when you would need them? Distributed throughout this chapter are carefully selected links providing access to all the most important online services in effect, a one stop shop... Digital Marketing reference book.

Step 5 – Outsourcing – You don't have to do it all

If you believe that Outsourcing is bringing in some Credit Clerk accounting cover whilst Joanne is away on annual leave, then think again!!

Outsourcing combined with Digital Marketing and Cloud Computing is set to instigate a revolution and complete metamorphosis of how we look at the shape and form of 'Business' in the future.

This chapter gives us some insight into how the Internet is empowering all of us to change our work habits and bring about a business management revolution on a scale not seen since the Industrial revolution.

Step 6 – Ideas – Getting new projects back on the table

Chapters 1 through 5 are about introducing Business Automation and releasing time whilst increasing sales.

Chapter 6 is about growing the empire! What else do you want to do with your life? What is your passion? and what other untapped projects are hidden in the cupboards? Having successfully automated one business why not do it again... but more quickly? But... this time no need to do things alone, why not enlist the help of a few Virtual Directors to validate and support the project as a mastermind team?

Step 7 – Networking – Business Support groups

Unless we are in a very specific industry sector, there are really only two ways we are likely to gain business in the future, either through online promotion through Digital Marketing (in its variety of guises) and through personal connection (networking).

Chapter 7 explores the 6 degrees of separation, the various Networking options available to us and how networking should become an integral part of everything that we seek to build.

Table of Contents

INTRODUCTION

Running a company today is a complex business. A few years back we could buy products, sell products, account for what had taken place and as long as we made a profit, pretty much things were ok.

Then along came computers and things got a bit more complicated. Business people had to introduce computers into their organisations to keep up! Few can argue that computers have transformed the information availability and enabled us all to make better decisions. But there was a price tag and a reliance on the IT people who assumed a position of great importance in our operations.

Nowadays it is incredibly complicated. Not only do we have computers, we have mobile (phones) technology, email, the Internet, websites and e-commerce to contend with. And if that isn't enough we have new terms such as 'Cloud Computing', 'Software as a Service', 'Digital Marketing', 'Online Social Media' and 'Web 2.0' to try and comprehend.

Then… it's not finished… after all of this we are encouraged (and would like) to comply with 'Green Initiatives' because we are all concerned about 'Global Warming' and want to do our bit for conservation, recycling and carbon emission management.

…and we have new rules about working conditions, family friendly work ethics and flexibility on where and when staff can work!!

This all adds up to a very different proposition compared to running a business in the 1960's and 70's.

The 7 Steps in this book will show you 'carefully but methodically' and in plain English how a business can adapt to the 'Internet Age'. Actually, much of what is in this book is non-technical and can, believe it or not, simplify our businesses!

Perhaps some of the 7 steps in this book are not wholly applicable to your organisation, but there is something here for every business. Just one of the 7 Steps has the potential to bring great rewards.

If the 7 Steps in this book have helped to take some of the mystery out of the changes that are upon us. If it has brought some clarity to the challenges of running a business today and a few ideas for dealing with them, then, it will have achieved its objective.

STEP 1

Mindset

Nothing has grown more quickly it would seem than the self development and personal coaching marketplace over the past few years. The holistic approach to getting your life in balance by acclaimed authors such as Anthony Robbins and Stephen Covey are without doubt essential reading.

Step 1 in this book is about getting yourself in the right mood for change. The future and the rest of our lives depends on what 'Decisions' and 'Actions' we as individuals take for ourselves and our businesses. How and what we think and how we deal with that inner voice does seriously affect our outcomes.

Has anybody ever heard the little voice in our heads in the morning persuading us to stay in the warmth of the bed for another 5 minutes when the alarm goes off?

How come we are never tired at 4am when we are getting up to catch a flight to go on holiday, but on work days we struggle to get up at 6am or 7am?

Any business owners ever asked why we are doing this? Is it all really worth it? after a particularly challenging day.

It's not the good days that underpin success, we can all stroll through those on a high. No, it's how we deal with the bad ones and the normal, routine days that makes us different. Much in the same way we can determine how good a business is, not by how they are when things go right, but how they deal with things when they go wrong.

'Having a bad day happens to us all, it's not your fault. How you respond to a bad day is your choice. Recognise it, learn from it and know that you are one step closer to a great day. None of us are that good we never have a bad day, and none of us are that bad we only have rubbish days. Our challenge is to reduce the bad days to as few as possible'

So our first step is to take a stock check of where we are in our thinking.

Why are we running a business in the first place?

We all do things for a reason

Nothing ever gets done unless two things happen. The first thing is 'a thought' the second is an 'action'.

One of the most fundamental realisations for me was to learn :-

'the exact place that I am right now is the direct result of all the decisions and actions that I have taken in my life'

Once we have gotten over this hurdle, we accept that we forge our own destiny and that the decisions we make provide us with the consequences or results that we receive.

Every action we take is initiated by a thought behind which, is a reason. Go to visit my parents, that's the action. The reason, care?, Concern?, Love?, Duty? Or combinations thereof.

If someone asks me to do something for them there is a reason. A reason why I was asked, not someone else, the reason why they don't do it themselves, there could be many reasons. But there is always a reason, and sometimes it's not in our best interest either!

There has to be a reason behind why we run our own business, I'm sure in the list below you will find your primary reason(s) :-

- Be your own Boss
- Control your own destiny
- Earn what you're worth not what the jobs worth
- More time to spend with the family or what you want to do with your life
- Work with people you want to work with
- Work at your pace
- Work when and where you want to work
- Redundancy
- An opportunity came your way and you took it
- By accident

Whatever the reason(s) were for starting the business, it was this that lead to the path of running a business. Now we are there, what is it that keeps you steadfast at the wheel, why do you persist? What is the motive?

What's your motive?

For a large majority of business owners the primary objectives for running a business are control over your own life and more money. Few business owners for example start their business with the motive to, employ 20 people and fund those peoples lifestyles and mortgages, but this might be what happens!

Everything we do in life has a beginning, middle, and an end, businesses are no different. Most of us will either be in the beginning or middle cycles of our endeavours, but what is the plan for the end part? Do we have a plan for the end of our direct involvement with the business?

Commonly called an exit strategy, again many of us have a vision that we will be able to do one of two things :-

- Create a business that we are not required to manage day in day out and thus have more time to do what we want to do, which may be to start another venture.

- Create a business which is a valuable Asset that can be sold for a large cash amount. The proceeds of which may be used for a lifestyle of your choice used in some other way perhaps to help others.

I am sure there are other flavours of the end game above and beyond the two I've listed, but these are the main ones I hear from the many business owners to whom I ask this question.

Interestingly enough in both of the cases I have listed the business no longer has your direct involvement on a day-to-day basis. In order for this to happen, you must either find another you, or ensure that everything you do can be learned and performed by others. The simpler this is, the more people you have to choose from and the greater the chances of success.

There may well be other goals in your life apart from those that relate to your business, spanning family, spiritual, sport or other leisure activities. Many of these are interwoven and to achieve a balance in our lives we must bring these into our thinking. Perhaps the motivation to go to work is driven by the need to provide the lifestyle you want for your family, it all boils down to the same thing in the end, money to provide the freedom to spend our time how we choose.

It is TIME not money which is our greatest goal I would suggest. TIME, we can never get back, TIME, is in short supply and we never know how much TIME we have left.

'if you asked a dying person what they would like most of all, they would answer, one more day! How sad it is that most of us squander so many days without a thought'

If we put ourselves in the position of the dying person, and had just one more day, how much would we cram into the next 24 hours, and more interesting than that, what, and with whom would we spend it? Perhaps here we will find the things that are the most important in our lives?

When do you want it?

As all self development books will teach, there is no point in attempting anything unless there is a goal. You cannot be fuzzy with the brain. If you give your brain a direct order the chances are that it will obey you, anything else just won't do. So it is with goals, clear, unambiguous messages, within your capabilities and relying on no one else. In other words it's up to you!

Reminds me of a story that I once heard, about the best archer that ever lived, he could kill a charging rhino with a single arrow, kill a white shark under the water with a bow and arrow and split a first arrow with a second at 30 metres... and yet I could teach you in one hour, to score more direct hits than him... providing you had an able body and mind!

You might ask, how on earth could you do that, it's ridiculous?

Not ridiculous, if I blindfolded the archer first, then spun him round six times, so that he had no idea in which direction the target was!

You might then say, 'of course... how can you hit a target that you can't even see?'

Here's a better one, 'how can you hit a target that you don't even have?'

It is not the purpose of this book to go through goal setting exercises, however there is one important point to make here. Unless you set goals, write them down and put dates against them, then it won't happen the way you want nor in the timeframe that you want either.

If the target is to build your business so that it is a valuable asset that another company might like to acquire, then state this in your goals. If you want this to happen within 5 years and to sell for $5m then write this down.

Do you have a plan?

It is amazing that once you have written your goals, thought about what it is that you want somehow it is a big weight off.

It is a sad fact that most people spend more time planning a 2 week summer vacation than they do planning their entire lives and then wonder why they never achieved the kind of results for themselves that they would've liked.

There is a famous saying which is very true :-

'If you fail to plan, you plan to fail'

Having set out your plans however ambitious the next step is to break these down into smaller tasks all of which contribute towards the end goal. It may be that there are a number of sub-goals each with smaller goals, it really doesn't matter, remember it is your plan you can do with it what you want. This exercise again might take a weekend to complete, but the effort is well worth it.

Earlier on we spoke about the topic of bad days, it is on these days that the goals can be brought out and looked at again. It is these goals that keep us fixed on the task in hand, that make us endure and persist with our project. Some people use visual aids like a picture of the car that they want to buy or a holiday destination for the family and put it in a place where it is seen throughout the working day as a kind of subliminal affirmation of why you are doing what you are doing.

A superb book 'Think and Grow Rich' by Napoleon Hill (if you haven't read it, then please do) will help with this section.

Attitudes and belief

Success and failure are packaged in the same box and it is our attitude that will determine our altitude.

Life always presents us with two choices on how we respond to any given situation. Is the glass 'half empty' or 'half full'? a decision between the positive and the negative way of looking at something.

We can all pinpoint someone in our lives who we can smile about because they are always positive and see the bright side of everything. These people may not be successful according to your measurement criteria but they certainly seem to be enjoying life.

To be positive requires no more energy than to be negative, so the question is, am I likely to be better off with a positive attitude rather than a negative one?

Positive people are fun to be around, their energy and enthusiasm is contagious. Positive people attract not only others to them but opportunities as well. If we think about this for a minute, if you had a good idea would you take it to a negative person or a positive, energy enthused individual?

The second question is, do successful people work any harder than regular folk in normal jobs?

The answer to this question is of course no. I know many teachers who work very long hours at their school and then go home to mark exam papers or review homework from pupils. I also know some successful business people who regularly spend the day playing golf and appear not to work very hard at all !

We need teachers of course and an academic life is the calling for a great many people, but the point here is about being effective not just busy.

There is another great book called 'The Four Hour Work Week' by Timothy Ferris which will revolutionise your thinking about effectiveness, please read this book also.

'Perfection is not when there is no more to add but when there is no more to take away' – Antoine De Saint-Exupery

The second part of this section concerns belief. An unshakeable belief in whatever we do is paramount for our success. The path which we are on is beset on all sides by the 'dream stealers' and sometimes these are disguised as friends, work colleagues, family and even our partners.

I have worked in a number of situations in the past with companies where a new computer system was to be implemented. Only on the occasions where there was an unwavering belief from the top down in the decision and the project did the full set of benefits get realised.

Throughout my working life I have been told many times, 'why don't you get a proper job', 'what you're doing will never work', 'if you haven't made it by now you're never going to'… and these were from the closest people around me!

It's not that they were attempting to dispirit me or make me unhappy, no, far from it, these people want the best for you they don't want to see you hurt. They ask questions about what you are doing, often don't really grasp the whole concept but feel for you during the low points, hence the comments.

If you are sure about your business, products and services and the size of the market for what you do then the only variable in the whole project is yourself. Unshakeable faith and belief is a vital ingredient and leads to enthusiasm and energy when communicating your message, both highly infectious and attractive to customers.

Decisions, Action and Focus

Making decisions is something we do every day. Some people make far more decisions than others. When running a business decision making is critical. Without making a positive decision we have effectively taken a decision by default to do nothing and this is exactly the same as in life. If we don't take control we will be controlled by others who make decisions.

For some making a decision is fraught with danger. What if I make the wrong decision? What if? Decision making is a habit, the more we do of it the less each decision affects us. Make 2 decisions a day and get 1 wrong could be serious, making 100 decisions and getting 50 right is less of a problem.

The crucial element in all of this is that without making a decision and obtaining a result we have no feedback on which to improve our decision making in the future. I know all my decisions will not be correct but I have enough confidence and belief to be sure that I can take further decisions later on with increased knowledge to get back on track.

'Success is on the far side of failure'

'Successful people have just failed more than others'

'Those who have never made mistakes, have never done anything'

There are two sides to any decision. For those who are experienced in selling this is quite easy to spot. The first is the intent, this is the desire to take the decision to do something. The second is the emotional attachment to the result of the decision.

This can be explained by a simple invitation of a friend to a party. The friend can easily say 'yes', and we go away with another attendee, or do we? How many times have we heard a yes but thought, 'they won't come'. Why does someone say 'yes' but mean 'no'?

If we can picture ourselves at the party, emotionalise how good it will be catching up with past friends then we are hooked, we've sold ourselves on the party. If we cannot emotionalise the result then the 'yes' is a fob just to not disappoint you or to prevent further discussion on the topic. This second part is crucial for the next topic 'Action'.

Having made a decision this is swiftly followed by Action. Without Action nothing changes. Even if we are doing the wrong thing, we will experience results different from those we sought and be able to retrieve the situation.

Let's be clear about Action. Action means following through on what you have said you would do. One of the most important rules that I set up for myself in business was to :-

'Do what I said I was going to do, and expect the same from others'

This is a very simple rule, but it ties me to my commitment 100%. If I say I will do something then it will happen. By applying the simple principle into the ethos behind the business, trust and integrity can be established.

'Reputations cannot be built on what you are going to do'

The only thing that counts is what Action was taken, not what you might do or could do, only what you did do.

Accompanying Action must be Focus. If we are very busy working on 100 projects simultaneously we will achieve nothing. The term 'Jack of all trades master of none' springs to mind here. Each Action must be accompanied by a target completion date and resourced accordingly.

'Action without focus is just motion'

We have already discussed the issue of TIME and the lack of it, care must be exercised here to ensure that projects come off the list and this can only be achieved by Focus. Writing this book is a great example of where nothing happened until I set a deadline for completing it. Although the deadline was missed it was by a relatively small and acceptable margin. More importantly it was written and the task removed from the list.

Personal coaching and Wealth guidance

Earlier in this book I mentioned the emergence of a whole industry geared up to teach positive thinking, NLP, and other personal development techniques.

Whether you need to appoint someone to ensure you stay positive, keep focussed and to monitor the goals with you is a personal choice. For many people the additional pressure of having to 'report in' is necessary to ensure certain tasks are completed.

Coaching can be delivered in a variety of ways now from email correspondence right through to video / teleconferencing and in some cases actual physical meetings as well.

Whether you embark on a program of self tutoring or gain professional assistance the key is, you develop a positive mindset. The brain is like a parachute it only works when it is open. By being open minded and positive we are likely to discover avenues that were closed to us before.

Closely aligned to Personal coaching is the topic of Wealth coaching. Wealth coaches have often added to their original skills as Personal development coaches so as to add further value.

Wealth coaching is targeted at assessing how you as an individual are participating in the main wealth creation channels Business, Internet, Property and Stocks / Shares.

As business owners we are already working hard in the Business area, however few have tied this in closely with the Internet which is a natural extension. Step 4 covers this topic in much greater detail.

Becoming a member of a group such as the respected Money Gym very often opens up opportunities to diversify (as and when appropriate) and use money to generate further wealth creation activities.

For help in this area why not visit 'The Money Gym' website or at the very least pick up a copy of 'Rich Dad Poor Dad' which is an excellent read and quite an eye opener!

Results and Rewards

There is little more rewarding than setting goals and then meeting or even beating them!

How do we know if we have met a goal? Sometimes this will self evident, other times we may need to record figures and then monitor against our goals to see whether it has been reached.

We all need positive input, praise can brighten the dullest of days. By carefully setting goals and ensuring that there are regular small achievable steps that can be knocked off along the journey are invaluable to keep up momentum and affirm our progress.

As small business owners we are very often accountable only to ourselves. Although for many this was the main reason for going into business in the first place it does mean that we have to decide to measure ourselves as no one else is going to!

Results are the consequences of our Actions. Analysis of these results helps us to improve and hone what we do, the formula for success is :-

'Adopt – Adapt – Improve'

Results are what they are, if they are not what you expected then something needs to change. Results are not right or wrong nor are the actions that created them. By carefully analysing what has happened changes can be made that provide the results that you are looking for. What you have done is successfully devise a way of creating the results that you have experienced, now we need to adapt this to get the desired results!

Business Owners and Entrepreneurs often do not blow their own trumpet or rejoice when a milestone is reached. An achievement is worthy of a celebration. A small not necessarily expensive 'Treat' is your reward for achieving an interim goal. We reward children in this way, sadly as adults we seem to have forgotten how to rejoice at a triumph however small.

The reward needn't be huge, a trip to the cinema, a night out, a special bottle of wine, just something to help balance the work / life equation.

How have we run Businesses up until now?

How have we ended up running businesses the way we do? It is an interesting question. Who decided we would do things this way or that?

In some cases we have little or no choice. For example we must file accounts if we are a limited company and there are rules for this depending on the turnover of the business.

In other areas such as Business Processes, how we actually process the paperwork through the various people or departments is largely up to us. Today, almost all businesses have computer systems of one type or another, handling different aspects of the process.

What systems we use to manage our business can be determined by a number of factors :-

- Previous experience in another business

- Advice of a trusted business associate or friend

- Guidance from an independent consulting firm or group

- Internet research / forums and open information

- Solutions providers

I am sure there are others we could add to this list, but these are the main ones and most of these people will be offering similar or the same business software.

Having run Small and Medium sized businesses for many years in my opinion the software that we are offered, given a blank sheet of paper does not represent what businesses would really like… more on this at the end of this section.

To fully understand why we manage our businesses the way we do, and perhaps take a peek at the vision of the future we must first understand how our processes and systems have been formed from the past. Below we can see the evolution of Business systems over recent history.

Ledgers and Paper

Initially transactions were recorded as they happened in physical books or Ledgers with a quill and later a pen.

These were simply a written entry on a line, in a book for each transaction that took place. Completely manual these were laborious days with rooms full of clerks recording, checking and summarising hand written ledgers.

Double Entry Bookkeeping

The first evolution was the standardisation of how bookkeeping should be performed and the emergence of Double Entry Accounting. Now the transactions had to be recorded not once, but twice! A simplified example of this for a sales transaction is shown below :-

We sell $1000 of goods to a customer and in our example we have sold $1000 of 'Business Consultancy services'.

The $1000 is added to the Customer account, they now owe us this money and we need the visibility to see this. In addition two other transactions take place

The $1000 is added to the Debtors control because we have made a sale. This is a running total of what is owed to you

The $1000 is also added into our 'Business Consultancy Services' account. This is a running total of how much 'Business Consultancy' as a company we have sold. Different services can be put into different buckets, allowing us to see easily the sales of our key lines.

Because we have 'double entry' the two sides must always balance. This was a vast improvement in bookkeeping providing an automatic internal self checking mechanism. Anomalies are easier to find and it makes sure the job is completed properly.

As you can imagine this ballooned the amount of clerks required to manage the increased work.

The first computers

We may well laugh about it now but the first computers filled three rooms, weighed a few tons and were only capable of adding up a few numbers. Nothing more than glorified calculators and not very clever at that!

These early computers consisted of valves and mechanical elements and were a far cry from the digital computers that we know today.

The Main Frame

The next major advancement was the introduction of the 'Main Frame' computer. These were enormous powerful computers located in specialised facilities. These were available to educational and government establishments initially, but as technology improved big businesses began to adopt the technology for their operations.

The topology of these systems was a star network. The Computer was located remotely and communication was provided via direct (and expensive) modem connections to it. So like a star, lots of points (remote connections) all feeding back into a central powerhouse.

The Mini Computer

The emergence of the Minicomputer in the late 1970's made a huge impact on businesses. The affordability of Mini computers (still vastly more expensive than today's systems) enabled many more companies to introduce computers into their business.

A 1mb upgrade for a mini computer was around $5000 and a cabinet container with 3 disks (each 456mb) was $150,000.

A keyboard at this time was $200 and just a screen for viewing information was $1100.

Packaged software solutions emerged to fulfil the growing demand as organisations rushed to computerise. Companies were eager to obtain the promised cost savings and improvements in efficiency not to mention the reductions in time it took to process information.

The minicomputer did however radically change the topology of computing. Now the powerhouse was brought into the Business. The basement was often converted into a computer room with air conditioning and raised flooring.

The minicomputer brought computerisation into a company but it was not like today. Not everyone had a computer screen and what you could do was very limited. Only key people inputting information like Invoices onto a system or perhaps the stock controller recording movements in and out of stores would have access. There was little or no email in these days and no need for many staff to use the computers.

The Micro Computer

The early 1980's saw the emergence of the Micro Computer, the Personal Computer (PC). Who could not remember the IBM XT and AT computers? Now anyone could own a computer!

For less than $3000 you could buy an IBM PC running MSDOS, twin 360K floppy drives (these were removable soft disks to store your data on) with 32k or 64k of RAM (memory).

The size and power of these computers seems both pathetic and amusing today, but this was the start of an irreversible revolution.

The emergence of the early version of Windows enabled ordinary people to manage the files stored on their computer. The introduction of a point and click mouse replacing the need to know gobble-de-gook computer commands.

A raft of stand-alone business applications started to appear that enabled individuals to learn and use computers as never before. These really were exciting times!

Server / Client networks

From the development of the PC came the joining together of PC's onto a network. This concept spelt the doom of the mini computer. No longer was one computer at the centre doing all the work, everyone had their own engine under their desk.

This transformed the workplace and opened up business computing to much smaller companies than ever before. Low cost equipment and Business Software meant anyone could now computerise their business.

At the heart of these networks was the Server. A bigger higher spec PC than the others this computer provided access to shared applications and files and often was the gateway to email and access to the emerging Internet.

The topology of computing had changed once again. Now computer power was in the hands of the individual on the desktop and not buried in the basement of the building.

A huge new industry suddenly appeared at this time, the IT Support and Service business. Small companies do not have the finance to hire a specialised IT person and couldn't keep them fully occupied even if they did. IT Support companies provided access to the skills required but at low rates. As networks became more complex, do-it-yourself IT Support was no longer an option and engaging an IT Support company became an essential component of IT strategy.

The Internet Age

And now the Internet Age is upon us. In terms of topology the Internet will bring about the most revolutionary change in computing so far.

The Internet means that the four walls of a traditional business can be completely removed. Every computer (and therefore every business) can be connected to every other on the Planet!!

What has effectively happened is that the networks we got used to over the past 20 years inside our businesses have been relocated outside our companies so that we are part of a globally connected massive network.

No longer is our server required to be inside our business it can be in a secure data centre server farm anywhere in the world. Using the Internet all of our staff whether they are in the office or anywhere else can access all the company data. Not only this, any business partners, associates, outsource workers can be provided with access to shared information as required.

The ramifications of this are so huge it is sometimes difficult to comprehend, but let me summarise some of the real tangible issues that the Internet Age solves :-

- **Cost Effective** because businesses no longer have to buy and install a server for their company, they can either share a server with other companies or rent one.

- **More Secure** all the information is stored amongst thousands of servers in a 24/7 guarded, secure facility

- **Environmentally Friendly** no software distribution costs, less travelling to support IT on-site, staff can work from home as easily as at the office.

- **Better Quality Software and Support** as everything can be upgraded and supported remotely. No installations, no disruption on site, faster quicker fixes. Everyone is on the latest release solving version issues.

- **Pay-As-You-Go** means improved customer care and healthier longer business relationships with software companies. Now the risk is shared more fairly and long relationships means everyone wins.

- **Removal of Business Walls** means that you can now engage more effectively with customers, suppliers, associates, outsource resources even your accountant by providing controlled access to your business information. All they need is an internet connection!

- **Family Friendly** to your staff as you can enable them to work more flexible hours even 1 or 2 days a week from home as their circumstances require it.

If this was all it was then it would already be fantastic news to almost every business but the reality is that there is even more!

Up until now software developers have been creating business tools to solve specific problems. Accounting systems to do the bookkeeping, email systems to manage our electronic mail, Contact Management systems to help with Customer relationships and servers to share documents.

All of the systems were designed to work inside our business on our internal networks prior to the Internet Age. They have also been produced by different companies with different technologies at the heart. Joining up these systems passing information between them has never been easy. Synchronisation is sometimes available but often doesn't work and other options can be expensive.

The Internet Age has finally created an environment where software companies can create Web based Business Platforms that integrate the main systems we need to run our companies. There are some enormous benefits of having a single Web Based Business System and I've listed a few below :-

- **One Number** to call to resolve any Business system issues

- **No Software to install** in your business. All you need is a web browser which comes with Windows anyway

- **No Duplication of data.** I have to admit this has always been a bug bear for me. Why do I have to put the same information into more than one system? With a business platform data is entered once and once only!

- **More effective and Manageable Email.** Email has become a huge burden to us as well as the most useful business tool. Improved email designed for the Internet means 7 years of history can easily be stored as well as being far more efficient.

- **Simplified Learning** because all the applications are designed by the same people, so they look and feel the same whichever part of the system is being used.

- **Built for the Internet** these systems allow you business to take advantage of all the benefits of being web side.

- **Internal / External** issues removed as everything is on the internet, online catalogues or other web service can talk directly to your Business Systems.

- **Automated, Reliable Backups** are performed without your knowledge and without any involvement of your staff. Even all the incoming and outgoing emails are backed up! Backup worries are a thing of the past.

The impact of the Information age and pace of life?

Some time ago I watched a version of Pride and Prejudice. As I watched the events of a bygone era unfold it is easy to see how far we have come and perhaps some things we have lost.

Of course much of what we have today would be unimaginable for them, but although there have been vast improvements there have also been some important things lost.

Go back 100 years

A car was a pretty unique thing, movies, TV, even the telephone were all very embryonic. No computers.

Communication in the main was Newspapers and Letters delivered via the email service? A journey of 100 miles was a huge adventure and people pretty much stayed within a few miles of where they were born. Life was much simpler then.

Perhaps in this era though, deeper stronger relationships were forged. Decisions were pondered over with much more deliberation and haste was a nasty word.

Go back just 20 years

This was the era of media advertising, TV, movies, music. The computer age promised much and the arrival of the personal computer as mentioned before promised intelligent games and devices which continue to develop.

Sources of information now extended to TV, but even 20 years ago if you wanted to research something it was a trip to the library or encyclopaedia.

Telephone technology was vastly improved and at this time was the most important business tool in conjunction with the regular post.

Email

The arrival of email to the masses really started in the 1990's. Until this time few people had email and of course the majority of people were still using Dial up services.

Email however was destined to be the most important business tool, even surpassing the telephone over the next 15 years.

Email has brought unparalleled improvements in communications. The whole world is connected and documents can be sent and received instantly across the globe.

Email success has been accompanied however by a similar increase in the success of Spam where approximately 70-80% of all email is actually garbage. In addition computer virus's designed to damage our computers and networks are propagated through such emails, culminating in huge amounts of wasted time and effort to resolve.

The more sinister and yet undisclosed by product of email is how little thought is applied to both the reading of emails and replying. Email has undoubtedly turbo charged communications, but I often find myself in a conversation discussing a topic that I have answered in a recent email which was not completely read. I have now said on many occasions, 'did you not read my email' only to hear on the other end of the phone, 'hang on, got it open now, oh yes, I must have missed that bit'.

Email is quick and convenient but it is responsible for reducing the depth of understanding in the communication itself. If we received one letter per week, we would study each word, ask questions like, why is this word used not another? Or what were they thinking when they wrote that sentence?

The speed of today's communications means we have less and less time to actually understand the meaning behind an email and we fire off quick responses with scant regard of the potential effect on the intended recipient. I question whether this is a step forward. Progress is made through understanding and we are perilously close to losing this skill.

The Web

The World Wide Web as we know it today started life back in the very early 1990's. Few recognised in those early days how this would revolutionise our lives.

Websites began to emerge most of them poor and by the late 1990's a website had become a 'must have' for any kind of business. The end of the 1990's saw the dot com bubble burst. Companies making no money at all had consumed vast sums of funding only to disappear without trace. The industry was still trying to work out how to make money from the Internet.

After all the hype of the dot com bubble the Internet industry regrouped and went about establishing ways to monetise the web. Companies such as Google established adwords and adsense as ways of advertising and referring other people's products. At last the Internet had established a solid base on which to build.

Today the internet is almost unrecognisable from those early days. What on earth did we do for information before the Internet? Today powerful search engines enable us to find out anything we want, from cooking recipes and TV Shows through to the specification of medicines we are prescribed by the doctor.

From a consumers perspective we can now buy online or research new products and services to improve our understanding before using this knowledge to negotiate better deals on the high street.

But the Internet has yet much more to offer. New software solutions and applications are being continuously added online, providing convenience and speed to us all. We can file our tax returns online, pay bills, run our bank accounts and even manage the affairs of our entire business from anywhere in the world via the Internet.

The arrival of Social Networking sites also means that we can now find people anywhere in the world, re-establish contact with distant friends and relatives and communicate as never before.

Blogging platforms have arrived that enables business owners, companies and in fact anyone at all to become a publisher, offering readers a diversity of information unparalleled in history.

The now economy

The pace of life and availability of information has without doubt contributed to the Now Economy. Somewhere over the past 15 years the ability to wait and relish the excitement of a something new has been lost in favour of, I want it so I'll have it now!

This style of thinking of course has lead to problems as individuals and companies create more indebtedness than they can financially support. Fundamentally though the desire to save-up and own something has been replaced by the age of rental and the pay-as-you-go philosophy which now through the Internet developments applies to software and business solutions as well.

Time, no one has any of it!

There is a famous quote :-

If you want something done ask a busy person!

This still holds true as busy people generally make things happen. There is a difference however between busy and effective! The goal is to be extremely effective in the time we work and therefore spend less time working.

With the world seemingly turbo-charged and the pace of life getting quicker all the time, it is inevitable that time the one thing we don't have any control over becomes more precious to us.

There is a point where the extra money is not worth the sacrifice of the 'free' time. A point where the value put on Leisure and how that time is spent has higher value than the payment for working in that time.

In order to bring some balance and sanity into the 'Time' problem, in the developed world there is a trend towards more flexible and family friendly methods of working. Those working for themselves have always had the opportunity to choose their hours of work and for most this has actually meant longer hours! For those in employment it has been more difficult with little or no flexibility to adjust work and leisure time with the fixed office / factory hours.

As nations become more developed so 'Time' becomes more precious. This can be observed in the USA, and in Western Europe where a good quality of lifestyle exists with surplus money to spend on Leisure pursuits. Other developing countries produce more at lower cost. The desire to earn money and improve their quality of life far outweighs free time to spend in relative poverty. And so the cycle repeats itself over many 10's and even 100's of years, with shifts in wealth and prosperity around the globe. The richer countries rest in their wealth and comfort whilst the developing country's hunger drives them forward relentlessly.

Family values and quality time?

Ironically the drive for a better quality of living can push us in the opposite direction. Under significant pressure to provide more and more for the family, we often witness couples both working initially to get the family home set up and then secondly to keep everything afloat.

Many would argue that the family unit has suffered at the hands of the capitalistic society and a return to a different form of work / life balance is now inevitable.

I want my time back to use how I want

I think most people would agree we are better judges of how best to spend our money than the government. Roughly translated that would mean a smaller state influence in our daily lives that would cost less with fewer civil servants and more money in our pockets to spend on products and services that we choose.

In the same way most people are of the opinion that so long as our work gets done then how and when it is done broadly speaking ought to be left to us. Of course there are many instances where this model just does not apply, but there are a great many where it could.

The pressures on businesses

As a business owner myself I have often quarrelled with myself about what I do with my time. When in employment life is much simpler. Go to work, do the hours and when the time has come leave the work behind and now you're in your time.

In today's world it is not quite as simple as described above. More demands are placed on staff to work flexible hours than ever before as competition from a global economy grows.

Business owners need the mentality 'to do what it takes' and putting in hours at the weekend and evenings is commonplace. As we move through the 7 Steps in this book, we will see how being a business owner with the correct decisions and processes in place can actually give time back, and enable different choices about how the time is used.

In the meantime we are under pressure from the Governments and from the working population to offer much more flexible working options. With traditional systems and thinking it is difficult at best to enable people to be equally effective remotely as they are in the office environment.

Herein is the headache for business owners, how can we run and manage our businesses and keep pace with the changing world and pressures being put upon us?

Without doubt the rules of the game are changing. The successful businesses of the future will be able to adapt to these pressures and embrace flexible working. These businesses will attract and retain the best people.

The perceived cost of flexibility

To transform a business from a more traditional model to one of more flexible working for staff and ourselves alike will be expensive right? Not necessarily, it depends entirely to what level we want to take it to.

One of the reasons behind the reluctance to accept change is fear of what will happen once the change is implemented, what will be the outcome? The other is simply lack of understanding or being unaware of the possibilities.

Traditional company systems that are installed at the office on servers can be accessed remotely over the internet today. These generally require some technical setup and perhaps additional software but it is nowhere near as complex as before.

Remote working or providing access for Business Partners can be achieved in a variety of ways today. The cost of setting up someone to work on the system remotely with modern web based systems can be zero if the person is already configured as a user at the office.

To provide the ultimate in flexibility where Suppliers, Customers, Remote workers, business associates, in fact anyone who is working with the business can gain access to your business network we need to think a little outside the box, but the technical challenge has now been removed and it is no longer cost prohibitive either!

The working from home conundrum

Working from home is seen by different people in different ways and also presents a new set of challenges for the workplace.

First we must analyse the different types of working from home :-

- Member of staff working from home 1 or 2 times per week

- Sales team member predominantly working remotely

- Micro businesses where some or all staff are working from home

- Virtual Assistant working from home for other remote businesses

- Team participants / Clubs where there is no office environment

- Collaborative groups contributing to a central project or objective, e.g. www.willmeon.com a project to support and raise finance for a British London 2012 Olympic hopeful.

Of course there will be other categories but most remote workers will fit into one or another of those listed above.

I have seen half day presentations detailing issues for companies that introducing remote working brings and listed a few below :-

- Remote working staff health and safety considerations

- Availability of the tools to do the tasks as if staff were at the office

- Backup and security of information created and stored remotely

- Management and Measurement of remote staff

- Social office environment missing

- Implications of Staff home lives and imposition on the family

For most small companies the advantages to staff of being able to work from home far outweigh any negatives and can engender employees to greater levels of achievement. Some of the benefits are below :-

- Flexibility on start and finish times

- Working at a time when you are most productive

- Fitting in working time around family commitments

- Savings on travel costs

- More production, fewer wasted hours in traffic jams

- Positive attitude to the employer and the company

- Loyalty through increased trust and responsibility

For businesses the benefits of remote working introduce equally attractive direct benefits but also open up other opportunities :-

- Better working conditions for staff retaining the best

- Attracting the best people through flexible working arrangements

- Increased Trust and Loyalty from staff

- Higher productivity with reduced travelling

- Reductions in office space requirements with less people in the office at any given time

- Access to lower labour cost remote markets, such as India, China or the Old eastern block

- Ability to outsource some or all of tasks to a growing Outsourcing population

The 'Modern Marketplace'

As we begin to understand the possibilities in the Internet Age the market place will be changed. The stigma associated with home working is now fast disappearing. A new breed of Individuals wishing to escape the rate-race of the corporate world but with extensive skills and knowledge are emerging in the 'modern marketplace'. These professional and highly skilled individuals are positioning themselves for the Internet Age, exchanging highly stressful jobs for a better quality of life.

Traditional career paths have been established for years. Move up the corporate ladder, increase income, increase responsibility and increase stress. Although suitable for many people who enjoy the power and the money, for many the sacrifice of personal time and the impact on their private lives is such that there is a constant work / life battle. There is some evidence to support that this is responsible for many of the issues in our community today. As we strive for improved lifestyles and personal growth there are more relationship breakdowns, fewer hours devoted to our children and the inevitable breakdown in the functioning of the family unit.

The 'Modern Marketplace' provides us with more choices, and for many, an end to the traditional workplace model. Working as an independent (remote), integrated (via the internet), intelligent (aware), and knowledgeable (experience), individuals can offer their services by the hour to a global marketplace. The advantages to those seeking a more flexible approach to work are clear to see :-

- Work as much or as little as is appropriate for you income and the amount of time you wish to work

- Work with the people you wish to work with

- Undertake the projects / work that you enjoy the most

- Live where you want, the internet knows no boundaries

- Balance work, family life and leisure time as you wish

The growth of the 'Modern Marketplace' will be fuelled not just by the desire for individuals to escape the corporate world but because it offers the Small and Medium sized businesses some significant advantages. In our own business Internet Power Systems, a small business we have enjoyed the benefits of working with individuals with experience and knowledge that would have been unavailable to us in the past.

A great example is that of Claire Raikes – BusinessBlogAngel. Claire has developed into a personal friend as well as a business associate. Claire lives some 200 miles away and we have met only once. Claire's background was owner/manager of a Marketing company in London. With years of experience Claire offers unparalleled marketing knowledge coupled with a vast experience of Internet Marketing, Social and media technologies. Claire has helped us move our business forward on a consultative basis at commercial rates acceptable to Claire and enabled us to tap into skills that would otherwise have been far beyond our reach. Rather than invest in a whole person to build our Digital Marketing platform, Claire's contribution has taken us forward at a fraction of the cost on a very part time basis. This is a classic Win / Win.

As the Business world progresses and adopts web based technologies, so the business map will change. Historical locations perhaps remote or inaccessible for traditional business, offer quiet and peaceful locations in which to live… and now work.

All of the above relies to some extent on staff or participants being able to connect to a central resource and be as effective as if back at the office. In fact Internet developments and new technology has created a world of collaboration opportunities which will transform the way we work forever.

Environmental Issues

Few can now doubt that the human race is contributing to a global environmental problem. We are probably faced with our greatest challenge in attempting to reconcile what we have done, what we are still doing and what the effects of this will be in the future. There is little doubt that whatever steps we take will appear miniscule in comparison to the task at hand and that whatever we do will take decades to have any real effect. We have caused a problem for the next generation that will take two generations to put on a corrective course.

Of course with problems and huge challenges also come opportunities. A huge industry has emerged which is Green centric. Suddenly it is fashionable to be Green to get a competitive advantage and offer a more environmentally friendly product or service.

Going green mad

Whether the business is directly in the environmental industry such as recycling services, energy conservation, or reducing carbon emissions or whether we as individuals are just looking to improve the way we work and play to 'do our bit for the environment' it seems that the whole Planet has gone Green Mad.

The Green lobby would have us all fully embrace the movement to a Greener lifestyle and their urgency to do this does have some merit. The biggest change (which is still work-in-progress) initiated by the concern over the environment however, is one of Mindset.

We are now being presented with Choices, a choice to remain where we are or a choice to adopt ways of doing things which are more environmentally conscious. Once there is general consensus that Green is good and that following a non-green lifestyle (in whatever we do) is socially unacceptable then we will have made a significant shift. Similarities in smaller areas such as Drink Driving and Smoking habits have resulted in huge behavioural changes that have had a major impact on businesses too.

The cost of not going green

It is an interesting question, what will happen if we do not 'go green'. The answer is no one really knows. What we do know is that our use of fossil fuels does have a huge impact on the amount of Carbon in the atmosphere which does affect the temperature and weather of our planet. The weather and ecosystems are finely balanced closed loop systems of which we are a part.

The question then is not one of should we 'go-green'? But why not embrace ways of living and working that does less harm than we have been up to now? The facts are that we now have more information and knowledge about what we are doing than at any time in history and more reason to do this than before.

It is a difficult case to answer when the developed Western nations of the world preach to developing nations that they have to introduce 'greener' approaches to doing things when we have been (and still are) polluting the planet for decades.

The answer must be clear and we have to vote with our wallets. If we are prepared to pay a little more for products and services provided in an environmentally conscious manner then we will encourage all businesses wherever they are to adopt better practices.

Those that continue to operate outside the 'Green is good' movement will find over time that their opportunities and marketplace is diminishing.

How can a business go green?

It sounds like a simple question, and of course there are many ways to cut down our use of energy, recycle a little more or use companies offering 'greener' products and services.

Half the battle is being aware of things that are available which can reduce our 'carbon footprint', conserve resources or recycle more of what we consume.

The other half is to perhaps look at changing the way we do things. If we started to ask more searching questions such as :-

- Do all my people need to be at the office every day?

- Could we operate from a smaller office if less people come every day?

- Could we cut fuel consumption with less driving / office space?

- Could we use technology better to reduce travelling and the need for physical meetings?

- More production with the same resources, by increasing efficiency and reducing wasted time, e.g. stuck in traffic jams?

By looking at the problem from a different angle many more

opportunities present themselves for how we can not only become more environmentally friendly but at the same time improve efficiency too!

Don't fight it, embrace it

I don't think any Business Owner or entrepreneur likes being told what to do. The 'Green Lobby' making demands of us to spend more on more bureaucracy on environmental issues when it is tough enough running a business already could seem like a bit of a lost cause.

If we were to look at Green issues specifically from a point of compliance then it will take a long while for us all to get to the place where we need to be on the 'green road'.

To gain momentum there has to be reason for people to change. Businesses will far more readily move to adopt change if they can see a direct benefit not just additional cost.

If we take a more practical approach and look at ways to save money, produce less waste, become more efficient, thereby generally improving our businesses, whilst at the same time we introduce Greener technologies then we have a real chance of achieving the 'Green Objectives'.

Competitor Pressure

Running a Business is a complex process, made even more difficult with red tape and bureaucracy thrown at us with legislation from governments. We also have to compete in a free market with the inevitable competition from other vendors offering similar products or services to ourselves.

In the 21st century our marketplace is as big as the planet and the Internet now provides us with access to a much larger market if this is applicable to our particular businesses.

The internet helps us in two massive areas :-

- To develop an abundance mentality

- Provide information for us on our market and our competitors

We will develop the concept of the Abundance Mentality later in the book, but the key is that our competitors are actually our friends not our foes. They are developing the marketplace for our products and services as well as we are and not everyone will buy from the same place.

The Internet is awash with ideas about how we can leverage off our competitors and share in their success without compromising ourselves.

The Importance of Knowing

Many of us are so wrapped up with our own businesses that we fast lose touch with what is actually happening in the marketplace.

The Internet is a vast knowledge base available to us that can assist us in a multitude of ways. Since the mid 1990's it has been an information resource that we can tap into to find out almost anything about our business sectors and our competitors. The Internet is also a social networking haven. Open Forums, Business Groups, Networking sites all combine to provide a rich resource for collecting other people's opinions on products, trends and the marketplace in general.

Once we tap into this 'online' world we can quickly realise how large the market is. The key here is to harness the Internet, use it to get the information we need to ensure that we stay ahead of the competition. Use it as a marketing tool to build awareness, confidence and trust in our own products and services.

Action is required here... Our competitors will make the leap (if they have not already) to use the Internet to further their businesses even if we don't.

Be the best, kick the fear habit

What if our competitors are gaining a competitive advantage from the way they run and manage their Businesses?

What if our competitors have reduced their costs and are now offering similar products and services at more competitive rates?

What if my competitors are developing something new which will strengthen their position in the Market?

These and others are very valid questions. It is very important to 'know what is going on' in the market, but fear of what others are doing is brought about by a mindset problem.

If we believe we have a great product, if we believe there is a market for our product and we open our minds to ensuring that we have the tools and technology to take advantage of that market then we are empowered to be the best in the market.

It has been said many times that it is not always the best product that becomes the Market Leader. It is not essential to have the very best product, but it is essential to have an Action Centric Attitude and knowledge breeds enthusiasm breeds success.

Part of our Mindset is not to fear the Internet and technology, this would lead to no action. Embrace it, understand what it can do for you and build this into the overall strategy for the rebirth of your business.

Doing the right things – Deciding to Lead

Leadership is about 'Doing the Right things', Management is about 'Doing things right'.

A great analogy of this is a company that is producing timber for a special purpose has the most successful tree cutting period in their history, only to find later on, that they were in the wrong forest cutting the wrong trees!

What is the point of climbing the corporate ladder only to find that you are in an industry that you don't really like, wrong ladder !!

Leadership for any business is the visionary element, the direction the business is taking. Leadership can only be provided by those who know the full picture of your business.

I have often seen decisions taken by business owners based upon comments or opinions of employees who do not really see the 'Big Picture'. Of course we do not want to make staff unhappy, nevertheless everyone has their own agenda, experience, grievances and ideas about what they want, what we must do is make sure that the Agenda we are following is our own.

It has often been said if you find yourself amongst the majority then you are probably in the wrong place!

The Effect of Staying still

Let us be crystal clear about this. To not make a decision is actually a decision to do nothing. This course of action may appear to be a 'safe' option, but what it actually means is, stagnation, languishing in the comfort zone, learning nothing new, developing nothing, changing nothing!

No one likes change and the old cliché of 'the only thing that doesn't change is that change is inevitable' holds true as it always has.

Anita Roddick once said 'learn to nest in the gale' roughly translated, start to get comfortable with change. Acceptance that things do and will change is half the battle. Embracing change in a positive and creative way opens up new opportunities and growth.

In fact it is only by pushing our boundaries, getting outside our comfort zone can we grow. This is the only place where we learn. It is a difficult place because it can expose our vulnerabilities and puts our inexperience into the open. On the far side of this short lived period of discomfort however is a much longer period of success and enjoyment.

Communication is the key

To take a Business in a new direction means going through changes. This is not always the easiest path available and requires careful management whilst the changes are implemented.

There is a whole industry given over to this 'Change Management'. New systems or processes are easy to develop it is people who present the greatest stumbling block to any new initiative being introduced.

Communication is fundamental to ensuring that the people in the organisation are supportive not disruptive in any change in direction.

Small companies or business units remain far more flexible when it comes to adopting new ideas or strategies. Mainly this can be put down to a single decision maker with a clear vision and purpose but there are other reasons.

Smaller business units have less layers of communication. Everyone by default is much more involved in the company's overall performance and everyone sees the value in what they do and recognition for their contribution. Correctly explained at a simple staff meeting, ideas can be quickly communicated and adopted. Everyone knows that the future of the business and their salary relies on everyone 'doing their bit' and everyone 'going in the same direction'.

Larger companies have many more layers of management and communication channels. Very often the message or underlying objective can be mutated in the communication to fit in with 'Staff members private Agendas'. Getting up the corporate ladder and gaining political advantage somehow become more important than the goals and objectives of the business which seem very far away possibly decided in a different country.

The difficulty for large companies is trying to communicate that everyone is important, every cog in the wheel is as important as all the others and that everyone's contribution is recognised and valued.

Recent successful large business groups have often consisted of many smaller independently managed, highly incentivised operating units rather than amalgamating into one large corporate entity. This has all the advantages of being a smaller business but with the backup and support of a very large corporation.

In this section we have discussed many areas relating to the MINDSET. Re-Assessing what we want out of life and our business going into the future, I hope you agree is pretty important. This is not something we want to leave in the lap of the gods or worse still in someone else's hands.

If you set yourself up with a clear purpose from now on everything you do should align with this mission. If it contributes and supports the overall strategy, it's in, if not then it has no part in your plan. This applies to staff, business opportunities, distractions and many other things. Each needs to be assessed against your target, weighed up and acted upon. With new found direction believe me things cease to be grey, they are either black or white, period!

Clarity of purpose brings increased drive, energy, enthusiasm and a positive attitude which flows into your personal life, leisure, sport and spiritual worlds. Now and only now are you ready to meet the challenges of steps 2 through 7.

Step 2
Business Analytics – 'Doing Things Right'

The last chapter was about taking stock. What do you want in your life? We should be looking at the changing environment of 'doing business' and starting to build a new game plan to create the kind of future that you want.

This chapter moves away from getting our mind 'prepared for change' and now we turn our attention to what we want to do with our Businesses. Utilising our Leadership qualities we now know in which direction we want to take our business forward, the changes we must implement, new innovations we must adopt. The next step then is the 'How to' which involves analysing our business and creating the strategy for change.

Why analyse your business ?

Default Business processes

Most of us starting a business (unless we're serial entrepreneurs) have no experience of running a business. We are probably doing this for the first time ourselves. So basically we have a good idea, we are enthusiastic and energetic, but we are novices at running and managing a business.

Most people are under the illusion that their business is unique and that they are different to other businesses and so their... awkward method of management is perhaps justifiable. Fortunately this is an illusion, there are different types of businesses but in the main we all need the basics in place and these are :-

- Business systems e.g. Accounting, Stock management, Order Processing

- Emails and other Office tools

- Contact Management system

- Document filing and sharing

Apart from these there maybe associated industry specific tools such as Timesheet recording, Specialist Quoting systems, Manufacturing or Contract Management systems.

Most entrepreneurs suffer from the 'Not invented here' syndrome and others believe they can always build something better. It takes a bit of effort to realise that Systems take years to perfect and what is really required is a set of business tools that do 80-90% of the job well, so that you can get on with your specialist endeavour, whatever it is.

Once this decision is out of the way, learn the tools and how to use them effectively and then concentrate on being the best you can be in your business sector.

Key influencers

Apart from ourselves what else shapes the way we do things? The most obvious contributors to how things happen in our Workplace are our staff or colleagues. Staff are often hired because of their experiences and knowledge in addition to the direct skills they will be bringing. A good example of this could be someone who has helped a previous company achieve ISO9000 quality accreditation, something your business might be aspiring to.

Of course their contribution is invaluable and on many occasions I have heard stories of how a staff suggestion box has rewarded the contributor but saved the company concerned many thousands of dollars.

But it is not always positive or helpful suggestions either that we have to face. Change and the fear of it, is one of the biggest factors influencing how staff react to 'new things'. Another is personal position and power, 'what's in it for me' or Wii-FM for short.

Often staff and colleagues will evaluate what the changes mean to them and their position, will they be one of the winners or the losers in the upcoming shake up. You can depend on it that losers will be negative about the change and may in fact actively try and derail the project!

Comments and Improvements suggested by staff & colleagues need to be evaluated and weighted based on the circumstances under which they are made. Of course every comment should be listened to and considered, this is all part of the 'buy-in' process'. Staff however rarely have the 'big picture' view of the entire project or the business implications, so it is essential that strong Leadership and a clear focus on the objectives is adhered to. Deviation away from your new course must be taken only after due consideration.

The historic factors

Many of us entrepreneurs start our businesses in a small way, a back bedroom, garage conversion, or a small dingy office somewhere. We also have 100% control over what goes on! There are no meetings (unless partners are involved), you can work all the hours you wish at a time that suits you. The processes and procedures you implement work the way your mind works and everything is very straightforward.

Then, the inevitable, staff or colleagues join us. Suddenly there are more PC's, shared files, many places to store (or lose) documents, and people working and thinking differently to us.

Now we start to need systems to cope with how we do things. These systems very often become amended versions of the ones we first set up in the first place and they morph into fairly unwieldy blunt instruments. No one says anything because you are the boss and you designed the systems and are familiar with them so the systems remain.

As tasks evolve so do the systems and we can often find people who are doing similar tasks working in very different ways. Quite often little or no instruction is provided to staff, the job that is required may be explained but the 'how to' very often left to the individual with simple guidance such as 'you can use a spreadsheet to do that' or why not do it this way or that way?

The result is a collection of disjointed systems developed by individuals (like mini islands) serving their own needs and job functions with little or no regard to other areas of the business. This results in duplication, repetition and a great deal of wasted effort.

Accountants or financial managers often implement controls to assist with data collection for business reporting purposes. These are typically regarded as additional work and a necessary evil as the information required doesn't easily fallout from the processes themselves.

Sadly business process reviews do not regularly feature in company staff meetings. Time spent looking at what we do, how we do it and seeking more efficient methods is considered a waste of time and a pure overhead. We're all just far too busy producing 'Output', too busy cutting down trees with a blunt instrument to take time out to sharpen the saw!

It takes a staff absence or a valuable team member to leave to finally get around to asking the questions 'How do we replace this person?', 'who have we got that can do this job?', 'what do they do and how do they do it?' These are all valid questions that should be asked of any individual when they are performing the role, documented and reviewed regularly to seek improvements, but who has the time do this ?

The 'How to?' in recovering your time

In this section we start to develop the process of recovering your time. Time not money is the most precious commodity we have. Ask anyone who has limited time to live what they would most want? More time to spend with the family, more time to repair some broken relationships, more time to do some things never done... time is something that presents a finite boundary for all of us.

Funerals I find always a very humbling experience, they somehow bring us right back down to earth. It's at moments like this that we reflect on what is important in our own lives. Business and money pale into insignificance compared with being healthy and relationships with loved ones, heightened even more with the 'not knowing' when our own time will come. We really get the meaning of 'make the most of every minute', a minute wasted is a minute lost forever!

So with such a precious resource the ability to control our own time and choose how and what we do with it should be pretty high up on everybody's agenda.

Where do you want to be?

The first process in extracting some of our time from the business is to first of all picture the ideal day. What would the day consist of what would you be doing?

It might well be that the ideal day is extremely busy, maybe even full of work, but there is a huge difference between 'having' to work and 'wanting' to work. It might be that you are happy to be busy but doing more enjoyable things than you do right now.

One of the most important things is to 'get rid' of jobs you don't want and do more of what you 'do want'.

Let's say you are busy running a successful business but you are completely tied to the business. If you stopped turning up for work each day then the business would flounder and fail. How do you get from that position to one where the business stands on its own and doesn't depend on you? If your business can survive without you being there then you have a business, if not, quite simply you have a Job with no one telling you what to do each day!

I have had countless conversations with business owners who love their businesses but want their businesses to be more independent.

The business is like a child in many respects, not grown up enough to look after itself and requiring your full time attention. Business owners don't want to abandon their business or even abdicate just get to a point where it can continue down the path laid out (and reviewed regularly) without constant supervision.

What would enable that to happen?

I regularly hear entrepreneurs complaining on the subjects of staff quality, responsibility and empowerment. How many times I have heard from Business Owners... you just can't get good staff these days! Or I'd like to delegate more but I just can't trust people to do what I would do and Staff just don't seem to care and take no responsibility for their actions.

All of these statements, and there are countless others point to key problems in the business :-

- Unclear set of behavioural, codes of practice, i.e. Policy and Procedures Manual

- No job specifications with targets and agreed review periods

- Undocumented Business processes

As a result of not attending to these points, we are effectively leaving our fields fallow and letting weeds take over. Then we complain that we haven't harvested a good crop!

Staff need order, direction, clear rules / guidelines and to be advised how and what tools to use in order to do their jobs. They need to know what is expected of them (their job specification), what is considered good, acceptable and not acceptable and how often they will be reviewed against these measures.

Everyone in a company needs to understand their part in the Business Process and how it integrates with all the other processes going on around them. This amplifies the feeling of being part of a well oiled machine with every function just as important as any other to ensure the effectiveness of the business. It is proven that in the workplace recognition is just as important if not more important than the money.

Planning the change

One thing for sure if you recognise any of the symptoms described above in your business then you will need to implement changes.

People in general have an aversion to change therefore this has to be pitched right to get people on board. Positive, creative people will have no problem, negative and analytical people may be more of a challenge.

Asking management to meet with their own staff and jointly prepare Job specifications, targets and goals and even canvass for ideas on how things might be done better is a great way to involve everyone and create an outcome that everyone agrees with.

The management team in turn can then prepare their own analysis for discussion with their Director or business owner. Having worked through their staff they will know exactly how to develop their own Job Specifications and set out realistic targets and goals for themselves.

This exercise creates a real team spirit and involves the whole organisation on a quest to deliver excellence. This then has the makings of a company 'Mission Statement' which everyone has bought into.

Mapping the business

Every business has a series of processes that are performed to deliver their services or products.

One of the simplest business models as an example might be the sale of an electronic product using a web based Sales Page. The Business processes for this business once the product has been set up and the sales and download pages created is very simple.

The customer Pays and downloads the electronic product, they are automatically inserted into the Auto Responder database and thanked for their purchase. This requires no participation in making the sale from the company making the sale, as this has been automated almost entirely.

So what does the company selling the online electronic products have to do? Well pretty much the whole of the activity is related to marketing via the Internet. This will include :-

Analysing visits to the website and calculating conversion ratios from visits to sales. Identifying links and lead sources that are working and those that are not

Writing and submitting articles to bring traffic to the web sites

Blogging to develop a relationship with the audience and

to develop expert status

Downloading monies paid and accounting

Each of the above tasks can be turned into a process. This means documenting what is done and how each step is performed. This can then produce a report for review or result in a list of actions based upon all the potential outcomes.

Let's take the first step above, analysing the website. This step could be defined to just produce a report which is then fed into the management team to decide what should be done next. The alternative is that based on the results a statement of actions could be defined e.g. if a link is performing well leave it alone, if average then look at ways to improve it, if badly then change it or look at another approach completely to improve sales performance.

In this way each of the business processes can be broken down into its components and all outcomes documented along with what do to in each eventuality.

Now... this sounds like a lot of work! Why would we bother to do this? Well this is true it is probably the first time that most businesses will have looked at what they are doing and tried to document it. What you will have at the end of it though is a document containing how your business operates, or possibly would like to operate... the bible for operating the business!

Having documented this, or even during the process, potential issues may be highlighted or improvements identified to streamline what goes on.

The significance of doing this cannot be underestimated and in my opinion one of the key reasons why some businesses go on to become very successful whilst others fall by the wayside.

When a business has been mapped onto a series of processes what has happened is that the operation of the company has been documented into a series of teachable, easy to follow steps. This means that the knowledge has been removed from people's heads and can be taught to others easily. This has very clear benefits to business owners :-

- Removes indispensability, strengthening the business resilience against sudden loss of personnel

- Increases the available workforce, people just need to learn what each task / process is and follow it

- Improves staff performance with clear guidelines on each process and job specifications

- Develops and enhances the business processes

- Enables people to learn other roles and become substitutable

Of course the most important two reasons for laying down the business processes for the Business owner are :-

Enable the Business owner to reduce direct involvement with the business and have more choices over how their time is used

The Business stands on its own as a living / breathing business which is an attractive proposition (if profitable) to other businesses who might wish to acquire it

At last the Business owner has a business not a JOB in their own business!

Building flexibility with processes

Processes are therefore the key to automating our businesses and releasing that much sought after commodity time, but they deliver much more than this. Correctly thought through and developed good business processes will provide the business with a much higher degree of flexibility. This leads to faster and better decision making and the increased agility so necessary in today's fast moving commercial world.

Delegation

Delegation and substitutability are very important in any business. When companies need to make staff redundant part of the process is evaluating 'how useful' staff are. This means, how many roles can they fulfil, how adaptable are they? The more flexible an individual is the more valuable to the business.

Good business processes enables staff to be more flexible and quickly pick up new skills within the business. Documented and easy to follow processes means it is easy to delegate tasks.

Sourcing staff

Finding staff that can just slot into an organisation and become effective almost straight away is a difficult task. Even if an individual has been performing a similar role elsewhere, methods of working and differences in the organisations often means it can take quite a while to get someone new 'up to speed'.

For most of us who have hired staff before the introduction of a new person into the organisation engenders mixed feelings. On the one hand it will be good as the business is growing and another pair of hands will help with the workload. But it also, in the short term at least generates more work as inducting new people takes time. They ask lots of questions and reduce the effectivity of the existing people for a while.

Well defined processes help with recruitment in many ways :-

De-Skill

When processes are introduced, the task of working out how to perform a function is removed from the Job Specification. What Management should be doing is deciding 'How to do the job right', what the person performing the role should be doing is following instructions.

By removing the 'How to' from the Job Specification we have a much larger number of people who can do the job and because it is now much less skilled we can hire lower cost people.

Cross Training

Good business processes enables us to enrich the variety of individuals within the organisation. So long as an individual can follow instructions we can 'add value' to people growing their capabilities and developing new skills. We are no longer tied down to hiring from a specific sector of the population.

Win Win

Taking on new staff ought to be a win, win situation, a win for the new employee and a win for the business. The organisation wins if the employee can slot into a job and perform the function required. The Employee wins if in addition to earning a salary they can also develop their portfolio of skills not just get 'used'. A person who delivers constantly but who in themselves is not growing will become bored, jaded and unchallenged and consequently leave the business.

Good business processes enable us to bring people into the organisation that can use their existing skills but easily pick up new ones. An organisation who offers the opportunity for staff to develop themselves will be more successful in retaining staff and recruiting new ones.

Outsourcing functions

As we begin to turn our business into a collection of processes, this reveals to us a clarity of thinking relating to what are core business activities and which are not. With compartmentalised processes we can also start to look at how to best to tackle these processes e.g. is this best performed as part of the business or outsourced to an external supplier.

The business world is changing as and as we saw in the previous chapter 'micro businesses' are springing up everywhere today offering tailored services covering every aspect of running a business.

Processes give us the flexibility to provide a 'parcel' of work to an external service provider. This introduces a huge new dimension to our business, now we don't have to hire staff necessarily, we can try things out via an external resource and then, if successful bring it back in house if desirable later on.

Working with a recent client the capability to Outsource has meant delaying recruitment while the business was reorganised. Once the reorganisation has settled down it will be much easier to determine what staff and skills are required and then hire accordingly. This has saved a considerable sum of money, whilst sacrificing nothing in terms of business performance.

Growth and sustainability

Business processes take experience and knowledge from peoples' minds and delivers it instead in a documented form.

In order to achieve growth, people must develop, take on new roles and the organisation must mutate constantly. Lack of proper business processes hampers growth. Staff are left to 'do the job' in the way they see fit, retraining staff takes too long, hiring mistakes are made and people put into roles they cannot perform. All of these are cleared away with well documented, managed Business Processes and the price? To do the thinking and write the business processes.

Business Processes should be stored centrally, accessible by anyone and amendable (in a controlled manner). Processes should be regularly reviewed, optimised and updated.

Having introduced Business Processes into your organisation probably for the first time the business is sustainable, i.e. the business and the people in the business could survive without the Owner or entrepreneur.

Getting rid of indispensable people

We all have them in any business. Those people who without which the business would be seriously impacted. The trouble is very often these are the people who founded the business in the first place or the business owners themselves… but not always.

The problem with indispensability is very clear to see, the business is over reliant on a single point of failure. One or maybe even more than one person are over important in the business which is dangerous. If this person leaves the business, develops a long term illness or just plain falls out with someone else then the business is left vulnerable.

Indispensability can also be a restriction on growth. In effect it is a bottleneck through which no more work and no more growth can take place. Some people like to develop their indispensability, this gives them a sense of security, their importance level is very high and they earn respect because they do what it takes 'for the good of the business'.

Indispensability is negative on all sides, for the individual, the business, for growth and for flexibility and it must be removed from the business as fast as possible. In a very small or young company this has to be one of the goals, it is often not achievable until the business achieves a certain size or profitability, but it needs to be on the Agenda and a goal.

Business Processes help to eliminate indispensability by documenting all the tasks of a business, the tasks can then be more easily divided up and shared amongst the staff restoring the balance in the business.

Mirror the structure of a limited company

A limited business is a business which stands on its own two feet. The directors manage the business but the company is a legal entity of its own.

Business processes need to work in the same way. Employees and Directors are operators of the processes that enable the business to function and grow. They interact with the business through the processes and these processes if executed correctly should determine its success or failure. Keeping an eye on the roles of individuals and ensuring that changes are effected when necessary in the processes themselves rather than offline human knowledge will ensure that the business stays on track.

Keeps costs low

By adopting the above practice and taking personalities out of the equation, the whole business can operate from a lower skills base. Easier to recruit, easier to retrain, reduction in indispensability all works for increasing efficiency whilst at the same time reducing costs.

Increasing the Business Value

One of the key business drivers for any business owner or entrepreneur is to create a company which has real net worth.

Now let us picture a scenario where an interested party was looking at two businesses in the same field in order to make an acquisition.

One of the businesses had good well documented processes, are operating in a controlled and efficient manner with high levels of substitutability and low levels of Indispensability. The Owner of this business regularly reviews key business measurement criteria to ensure that the business is on track but is not necessary for the day-to-day operation of the business.

The second business is profitable but there are a couple of really gifted individuals who run and manage everything. These two owner / entrepreneurs are indispensable to the business, without either the business would be likely to fail. No documented Business Processes exist in this company, everyone is too busy to create these and most of the knowledge is stored inside the heads of the key players.

Which of the above two companies would be most attractive to an acquiring company. They both provide an opportunity to participate in the same market, but they are clearly not the same proposition. The first will enable a clean break from the existing management team and the business will continue to operate under new ownership whilst the transition to the new owners takes place.

The second company would be a real nightmare for the new owners. There is no way either of the two owners could be dispensed with and therefore a good working relationship will need to be formed with them. The challenges of trying to integrate this new business and keep the old owners positive whilst change is being deployed is a volatile situation and fraught with difficulties. This presents a much high risk and therefore much lower value proposition.

In conclusion the owner(s) of the first business are in a much stronger negotiating position. They have a business which stands on its own, operating with good solid processes effectively on tick over. This type of business is very desirable and much easier to turn into real wealth.

In Conclusion

Ironically having written this chapter I see many way of improving our own business. The simple act of documenting and re-iterating the importance of processes has made me re-evaluate where we are and set new goals to ensure we get ourselves out of the indispensable arena as fast as possible.

So in summary businesses really consist of four main elements :-

The Business itself, the legal entity

The Board of Directors who decide if we're cutting down trees in the right forest, or whether we should be cutting down trees at all, or doing something else, i.e. setting strategy or 'doing the right things'

The Management team, deciding how best we should organise ourselves to get the job done. Defining and redefining the Business Processes, 'doing things right'

Staff, these are the team players, who follow the scripts and act out our Business Processes. These people carry out the daily functions and tasks that operate the business.

Element number two above is unique in that this is the only component that requires considerable amounts of flair, vision and ideas and a thorough understanding of the market and the business environment.

Elements 3 and 4 can be almost entirely turned into Business Processes that enable the company to carry out the strategy agreed by the board of Directors. A business operating well defined processes has the capability to 'plug & play' people into different roles, bring in outsourced services as required and retain flexibility without sacrificing efficiency.

In the next chapter we see how involving new internet technology and Web based Business Platforms can further enhance a business.

Step 3

Running a Business Online

The previous two chapters have helped us to re-evaluate whether our business is actually working for us or whether we are just working for the business. Chapter two has shown us that to really get time back into our lives then we must introduce solid processes which help our business to mature and run themselves.

This chapter provides us with the tools for our business. We now know the importance of business processes, now we need some 'systems' to 'enable' our organisation and manage the business.

The Internet and the Web is bringing a completely new way to operate businesses. In this section we go through why it is happening, what is possible, the benefits and some real examples of companies that are already working in the 'New Way', Running a Business Online!

What do we mean by 'Running a Business online' ?

In simple terms 'Running a Business Online' means that all the Computer Business Systems used by your company are accessed via the Internet through a Web Browser. When I say 'Business Systems' this refers to systems such as Contact Management, Email, Accounts, Document filing, diaries, in fact all the programs that are used day to day to control the business.

In order to connect to your business systems you would use a web browser and all the people in your organisation do the same. There is no extra software installed on your computers, no server in your offices and really very little in the way of technology to buy or install at your end.

If you think about it for a minute what this means is that it doesn't matter where you are. As long as you have an internet connection and a browser then you have access to your company business systems. Taken to another dimension if you have an intelligent mobile device and wireless connectivity you can have access to all your business information anywhere, anytime!

'Running a Business online' is now considered to be the way software will be used in the future. It has some new fancy names too, like 'Cloud Computing' and 'Software as a Service' or 'SaaS', there is even 'PaaS' now - 'Platform as a Service' where complete business solutions for the entire company are provided through one website or business system.

Why is this happening now?

It is an interesting question, for things to change there has to be a very good reason. For years we have been using networked PCs and Servers at our offices, why fix it if it's not broken ?

Well some major technological advances have taken place. Yes you've guessed it, the main one is the Internet. This has gone from a simple place to expose your company, with a kind of Web Brochure, to a completely new dimension. Now it is possible to run Business applications on the Internet which can replace many of those that we used to run on our PCs and internal servers.

> **Question** : But so what? Why would I want to replace a program that's working perfectly OK on my PC or server and move it into hyperspace ?

> **Answer** : Good question, and if that is all it was then my advice would be don't do it! There are going to be applications like spreadsheets and wordprocessors that we will want to keep local to us. You can even get them online now as well, but if you already have made the investment why change? and quite right too!

No, the real reason why businesses initially adopt an 'Online' application is because it does something that can't be done easily using your internal systems. A good example of this is an 'Online Sales Catalogue'. This has to be online because that is its nature. If you want to take orders over the Internet it has to be 'Web side'.

Another good example of 'Online' easy to use tools quickly adopted by SME's was the Newsletter or ezine email. These enabled companies to manage a list of email addresses of people to email weekly or monthly and then prepare a nice looking newsletter to keep your customers or prospects up to date with new developments.

But some of the reasons why companies are re-looking at what they do is not just down to technology improvements! There are many other influencing factors on todays businesses one of which is the much hyped, but important one of 'Environmental concerns'. Another is that we must offer more and more flexible work arrangements to employees (whether we like it or not really), all of which adds to the headaches of trying to run a business.

Online Applications give businesses the opportunity to offer staff the option to work a couple of days a week from home with no additional costs to the business and provide a more 'family friendly' environment. This makes a positive environmental impact (less fuel / pollution), saves money (fuel and possibly less office space) and, makes staff happier, that'll be a 'win, win, win' then!

......so what's the problem, we have programs on my PC/Server and some 'new style' ones on the Internet what is wrong with that?

Islands of Information

Most Small / Medium companies use 4 main applications (apart from wordprocessors and spreadsheets), these are :-

Bookkeeping programs such as Sage Line 50, or Quickbooks

Contact management systems such as 'ACT' or 'GOLDMINE'

Email which is predominantly 'Outlook' using Exchange Server

Document Management - Small Business Server

Now... if you add to these an Online Catalogue, just one additional application, this as we already agreed has to be on the Internet, we now have a new problem.

All the regular systems are Internal, the Web Catalogue is external. How do we get information from outside our company's systems into our internal systems? The most common method is simple, email. An Order is taken online and we receive an email with all the details. Nothing wrong with that, certainly no worse than a Faxed order.

But what if you wanted the Order to go straight into your Order book without human involvement? Well that's not so easy, it can be done but is often expensive and can go wrong as things change e.g. a new version of your software comes along.

Question : That's OK if you need an Online Catalogue, our business is a service business we don't need one of those.

Answer : Well, please read on a bit, the Catalogue is a catalyst in all of this but there are still issues even with our traditional existing Internal systems.

So what we have here is an Island of Information the online catalogue, but if we look carefully it's not the only one !!!

... if we look again at our traditional 4 main business applications these have always been separate systems that don't talk to each other.

I always remember when first implementing a Contact Management system to control prospects/suspects information and thinking, now which is my main database? Is it Sage or ACT because now I had the same data in both places, certainly for my customer records. Then along came email and inside Outlook I had all the contacts again, with email addresses!!!

Now I had information in three places! As it did with me and I suspect with many others we just don't keep things up to date in the end, 3 systems, it's too much like hard work! Slowly the systems fall into disuse, this is probably the single most familiar reason why Contact Management implementations fail.

Question : *OK, I can see that having all these separate systems is a pain, but how can we get around this problem then? Not only do we have Islands of information internally but we're getting them externally as well now?*

Answer : *The answer is surprisingly simple, we move them all External, and now the Internet has evolved it's not difficult either! There are now Business Platforms available that provide all 4 Main Business Applications in one system so there are no islands of information and..... if you need online catalogues these can be integrated as well !*

But that is not the end of it... by moving our systems external onto the Internet, you can start to get some other real benefits as well.

Question : *OK, like what ?*

Answer : *Let's just take a look at a couple.... You won't need an Internal server anymore, this will reduce IT support costs immediately, and in the future.*

Backups.... these are now all handled by the company providing you with the Business Systems normally as part of the rental price! This is a major worry for small business owners and to be rid of this is a huge weight off.

This reminds me of a story I heard of a Business Owner who had organised for a member of staff to religiously each night take out last nights Backup Tape and insert the next days. Well eventually there was a Server failure and the backups were required, only to find that nothing was ever being written to the Tapes. No one had ever checked to see whether what was supposed to be on the tape was on the tape. The company survived, just, but what a nightmare.

So we have seen above with a simple introduction to 'Running a Business Online' that something is going on. Below I begin to explain in greater detail why 'Running a Business Online' is set to become the greatest revolution in Small & Medium sized computing we have EVER SEEN!

A Blueprint for your business

As discussed earlier for many people who run their own enterprise they are often doing so for the first time. I've been there before too although a goal I set myself at the tender age of 15 was to learn what I needed to know to be able to run and manage my own company.

I was lucky I guess I joined a company where I was the 17th employee and finally left when there were over 200 people. I was able to change roles every 2 years within the same company moving from technical through to Sales / Business Management. I saw how to get things done, and of course how not to. We sold business systems and so I was able to study my customer's business processes as well, seeing a wide variety of business types first hand.

For many of us the Business Systems and processes for running our businesses are stumbled into not planned. This was described in more detail in Step 2. But where can we go to learn about this? The answer is… other successful people, consultants or friends that run their own businesses.

The fact is that most of us are NOVICES with regard to how do we go about defining Business Processes and then how to turn that into 'Systems' that enable us to carry out our jobs.

Most of the time we are at the mercy of sales people who promise that what they have will do everything under the sun for us, and we are not really qualified to contest the point. As described in the 'Islands of Information' section above, software companies have their own interests at heart. Historically it's been about unit sales whether you use the application you have purchased or not, no one really cares, you've paid your money and that's that.

With Web based business platforms for the first time there is a 'joined up' suite of business tools that deliver a complete set of Process Flows, designed by experts especially for Small & Medium sized businesses.

'Best Business Practices' underpin these products coupled with the latest web based technologies can provide 80-90% of everything you need to become efficient, streamlined and positioned to take advantage of the whole Internet revolution. These solutions provide a 'Blueprint for running a business' and with the correct guidance these products can be configured to closely mirror your business type.

The Evolution of Web Based Solutions for Business

When Online Business Applications started to emerge, the software industry targeted big businesses, why not that is where the money is! These big corporations have very deep pockets and were able to pay the large sums demanded by software developers in this emerging market. The SME (small and medium sized business) was unable to participate in this arena primarily on cost but also because of lack of knowledge and awareness.

The uptake of Broadband and the acceptance of Web based services such as Facebook, Google mail and other online services has meant that almost all computer users are familiar with using software delivered to us in a web browser. The low cost of the web model but the potential high volume has now created an emerging market for Business Systems aimed specifically at SME's.

SME's are quite a demanding bunch though! They require highly functional systems that are easy to operate and low cost. They want a single system to manage their entire business with data just being entered once. They also want remote support, high availability and reliability and to be able to connect from anywhere using anything from mobile devices to desktops. Oh yes, and they also want backups included at no additional cost.

What is not on the shopping list but in my opinion is one of the important elements to any Business Process software is support and guidance on the implementation. Now lets take a look at why this might be. There are two main types of services on the web.

<u>Mass Market – Simple Applications</u>

This is the marketplace of millions upon millions of individual consumers, personal users in the main. Typical products that fit into this arena are email, social networking sites, tools and utilities such as google analytics, Blogging platforms etc.

They solve specific problems, do not generally integrate with back-end systems and can easily replace something you may have used before on your own PC.

These systems require very little in the way of support, you get what you are given and are usually non-critical to your business. The providers of these services make their money from advertising on the sites and this is how the services can be provided pretty much free of charge.

Very often these products are lite or cut down versions that are missing some of the really useful functions. Upgrading for a relatively small monthly fee normally provides some support and much better functionality.

<u>Large Market – Complex Business Applications</u>

Services and Solutions that fit into this category are very different from their cousins described above. The fundamental difference with these products is that they are mission critical to your business.

Products that fit into this space are Business Process applications and Business Platforms that enable you to run and manage your entire business using nothing more than a web browser.

Typically these systems will include, Contact Management, Email, Sales Order Processing, Invoicing, Purchasing, Payments, Stock control, Document filing, Quotations, Online Catalogues and collaboration tools such as diaries, alerts and messaging. All of this is delivered via one integrated system.

As you can imagine implementing a system such as this has the potential to affect every facet of your business. The rewards are extremely high as we will see when we look at some live examples, and the benefits so overwhelming that this genre of applications is set to revolutionise business computing in the future.

However as mentioned before these applications cover a

wide range of business processes and are tightly integrated. Implementing these solutions requires guidance, consultation and a good knowledge of business processes.

Whatever Web based business platform is chosen the importance of support cannot be over stressed. Your business will rely on the system being available for a very high percentage of time and to have people at the end of the telephone to answer your queries is essential.

Support and service can never be free in a commercial model. Most business people do not want their application plastered with adverts either, so the reality of Web based business platforms is that they will cost money. But the cost of these solutions is miniscule compared to the savings that can be gained. There are very many free Business tools out there, but free software does not mean savings. Implemented solutions which deliver real benefits for your business is the goal, for this you will need help from the experts. The chances of doing it alone are slim, and you would not work for nothing, so don't expect that others should either. 'Fairness' is the essence of business and 'value for money' is part of that equation.

The Reluctance to Change

Information Technology is a complex industry that is constantly changing, and at a rapid pace, so quickly in fact that even those in the computer business itself often get left behind.

Everything goes in cycles and what is happening in the Computer Industry today in this Internet transition period is that very many IT companies are left with the skills and knowledge which belongs to how it was, not how it is going to be.

This happened with companies like IBM and Digital Equipment when the micro computer and then networked computers emerged. Computing was changed forever and these companies had to change or die, in the case of DEC (Digital Equipment Corporation) it died.

We are again at a crossroads for the IT Industry. Companies either have to adapt to the Internet Age or they will fall by the wayside.

Unfortunately for Small and Medium sized businesses while the IT Industry drags itself into the 21st century, it still wants to sell products and services that have been developed over the past 20 years. This means often the advice and guidance we are receiving is more about what people want to sell, not what is best for our businesses. Education and training products must also change to extol the virtues of modern computing and all of this introduces a latency that slows up the process of change.

Major 'by-products' of Running a Business Online

We've already covered some interesting ground with regard to 'Running a Business Online' and if this was all there was it would already be sufficient justification for embracing these solutions.

However, there are other very important 'spin-off' benefits that are worth of mention detailed below which will further convince you that it is just a matter of 'when, not if' these solutions will proliferate across the business community.

Pay-as-you go

Since the 1960's software has been developed, packaged, shrink wrapped and sold to us. We have paid our money and obtained a licence to use the software in perpetuity forever.

The vendors however knew that we would want to upgrade (at a modest upgrade fee) or to buy an alternative at some point in the future (no doubt with increased functions – most of which won't be used by us anyway) which renders the 'in perpetuity' as null and void. Also we could find our support arrangement terminated should we choose to not upgrade to a later version which means if something goes wrong we're on our own.

Another interesting point is that I have witnessed and been involved in many system implementations that stopped after the initial momentum waned. These were not considered failures far from it, but the impetus ground to a halt. The software was paid for or written off, sufficient benefits were obtained to declare value for money, but the real payback probably hadn't been fully realised.

Pay-as-you-go has two obvious attractions, one there is no huge upfront investment tying up your cash in the business and secondly if you stop using the system then you stop paying for it, simple as that... or is it?

When we make business strategy choices with regard to how we intend to run and manage our businesses these are never taken lightly. A choice to base your business on the Microsoft Platform would have been a conscious and very important decision which had implications long into the future irrespective of today's investment.

The same applies to IBM, Digital or Mini / PC architectures going back into the late 80's and 90's and so it is with 'Running a Business Online'.

Of course stopping the payment of a modest monthly sum is possible, but this is insignificant in terms if the retraining and re-engineering of the business processes that will need to take place when moving from one way of doing things to another.

And so it is with 'Running a Business Online', undoubtedly the future for the way we will run our businesses, but a fundamental decision nevertheless and one which will shape the way you do business long after the decision is made.

The Jewel in the Crown

There is another benefit to 'Running a Business Online' which has largely gone unnoticed. Up until now, in my opinion (and fairly out of character for the computer industry in general) smaller businesses have had a rough deal from their IT companies.

Many of us have purchased business applications in the past which have either never been installed i.e. are still sitting on the shelf, or have installed them only to never really use the application.

If for a moment we analyse what has happened in the situations described above.

- The software vendor has written an application

- We have been sold on the concept

- We have paid for the application up front

- We have derived no benefit

The software vendor in this case is always a winner. Whether the software is used or not, they have been paid up front, the entire risk is borne by the customer.

With SaaS (Software as a Service) and 'Cloud Computing' the risks are much more evenly distributed providing a much 'fairer' deal for the customer.

The software Vendor no longer receives a cash lump sum up front but is rewarded through a much longer and interactive relationship with the customer. If everything works well in all its facets, software performance, upgrades, support and responsiveness then it will be a long term mutually beneficial relationship.

I believe this is the first time in the history of computing where finally the balance of power is more evenly distributed between the Customer and Supplier which has to be a good thing.

In the future we will see a much stronger link between solutions providers and their customers with both in the boat rowing together to a common goal. This in turn should lead to a much greater level of successful software implementations with more customers achieving the benefits that were set out at the start of the project.

Better implementations should lead to cost reductions, improved efficiencies, greater flexibility in the working arrangements for staff, and more agile 'Greener' businesses going forward.

Minding your own Business

We have already seen that by reaffirming our goals and ambitions for the Business, establishing processes that define the way our business works we can now effectively run our business from anywhere in the world. Now your business can be connected to by your staff, remote workers, business associates and partners across the world. The opportunities that this presents for collaboration, new products and services and managing the business using external service providers cannot be underestimated.

Computing has come a long way since the 1980's. At this time a computer user really was considered a 'specialist'. Today nearly everyone uses a computer, whether it is to play music, store Digital photos, email or just browse the internet for information.

Here's a good question then... with all the developments and improvements that we are told about in computing, why is it that things keep going wrong with the computers at the office? Why is it that as a business owner IT often gets in the way of us doing business and is still a way too high, unpredictable cost to us?

Actually as a small business owner for many years, my experience is that IT is so important that you either have to become a part time IT person yourself or hire someone who is, or just pay, pay, pay for the experts to keep the whole thing running.

None of the options above is ideal, so how does 'Running a Business Online' help alleviate these issues?

Simplify Computing

The reason why business computing goes wrong is not really to do with the computers themselves which of course do have problems from time to time, but more to do with the network.

Once a network with multiple PC's is introduced into the business, the complexity increases significantly. Access to printers, shared files and folders, servers, internet access, email, security, virus protection and business applications all combine to make your installation totally unique.

Once you introduce different versions of operating systems and download patches and plug-ins for browsers or install MSN, Skype and other communication applications things are complicated still further. Each workstation becomes unique and the support and maintenance costs go through the roof.

The answer lies in 'KISS', keep it simple stupid. The more complex your systems, the more to go wrong, 'Running a Business Online' can have the effect of removing your internal network. Each PC becomes just a workstation connected to the Internet through a browser. This is very simple indeed and it is the Collaborative Business Platform at the centre which joins everyone together.

By adopting this approach, three levels of PC could be specified for the business, Occasional / Low level user – minimum configuration with some word processing software and a Browser, Medium user – additional software such as presentation creation, image manipulation and spreadsheets and then finally the Power User – with perhaps more specialised applications. This strategy keeps support and maintenance to an absolute minimum and by having a spare machine of each type, if a machine fails the user can be back up and running very quickly.

By adopting a 'Running a Business Online' strategy all important business files can be stored on the hosted application. This removes the importance of the local PC's and turns them into a simple window onto the company's information systems. Local PC's become in effect like a hot desking environment where anyone can work from any PC in the company.

'Running a Business Online' opens up the possibilities of simplifying your entire network and centralising all the Business Applications such as Contact Management (CRM), Accounts (Bookkeeping) and email into one integrated system.

But the most amazing part of this transition is not that your office computer solution is vastly simplified although this is fantastic in itself, no, what has happened when you do this is that your company network is now the Internet. This means that any computer anywhere in the world, with the appropriate login / security credentials connected to the Internet can now be used as a workstation for your business!! Think multiple office connectivity, working from home, Outsourcing, improved communications with Suppliers and Customers there are so many advantages it is overwhelming.

This fact and this fact alone provides your business not only with enormous flexibility for the future but at a much lower cost as well!

Less to go wrong

By simplifying your business network internally and adopting the Internet as the backbone for your business, there is already far less to go wrong.

Network Architecture is only one component however, and we have already discussed above that the software we install on each workstation can rapidly make each PC unique which in turn quickly racks up the costs when things go wrong.

A third area where we can soon find ourselves with problems and additional costs are software upgrades. Software vendors look out for their own applications. They test their applications in a huge array of different circumstances and conditions... but not yours necessarily and not with the different applications that might be installed on your network.

The basic fact is they can't, it would be far too difficult and there are just too many combinations and options. The result is we often install an upgrade only to find that certain functions and features now cease to operate as before. Not only is this frustrating but we have often paid to have the upgrade installed and now find ourselves having to pay to get the new problem fixed as well. Couple this with the disruption and the downtime it is no wonder that IT people are viewed as a necessary evil.

So how can 'Running a Business Online' help in this area? Well 'Online Business Platforms' offer a single complete Business Application that cover all aspects of running a business. These are often referred to as ERP (Enterprise Resource Platforms) and join together all the business processes necessary to run and manage the entire business.

What this means is that all the different systems we use, CRM (Contact Resource Management), Email, Accounting & Bookkeeping, File sharing and even collaborative tools such as Diaries, Workspaces, Tasks are all brought together under one business system... all accessed via a simple web browser.

As these systems have been designed and built by one software company we no longer suffer from incompatibilities between systems and even more exciting is that we don't need any IT people to visit us either! Very often the upgrades are included in the monthly rental contract. Upgrades are also deployed 'out of hours' and so there is practically no downtime at all.

Focus on your business

The routes into running our own businesses are many and varied, however one thing is clear we got into our business because we are good at what we do and with dedication and persistence we believe we can make a success of it.

Very few of us started in business wanting to be IT Specialists (unless we're in the IT industry itself), we use IT to 'get the job done', it is a tool like any other and that is how it needs to be. The trouble with IT is that too often it is not like this, we get drawn into sorting out problems. If staff can't do their job, it costs us money, if we can't get invoices out, this costs us money... IT has to work it is as simple as that!

'Running a Business Online' helps to simplify IT, it removes many of the issues which makes IT unreliable for us. Today with the Internet it is possible to host our Server, Business Systems and all our information and locate everything securely in a professional data centre environment. This is all managed and maintained for us remotely by technical IT specialists who never have to set foot on our premises.

What this means for Business Owners across the world is that we can now truly start to use Information Technology as a utility. No Server to worry about, backups taken care of automatically, advanced joined up business applications, less downtime, improved service and performance levels and all for a lot less money!! Now, finally we can get on and Focus on our own Businesses.

Staff Recruiting and Retention

'I just can't get good staff these days'

'Staff just don't seem to care like we did in the old days'

'No one takes any pride in their work anymore'

'Taking responsibility seems to have gone out of fashion'

I've heard these quotes and many more like them from disgruntled Business Owners over the years. Human Resources and staff motivation is not part of the scope of this book, however, it is worth considering the impact that 'Running a Business Online' can have on staff members.

Get the right attitude to staff

Win / Win mentality

Most of us at some time in our lives have been employees. We can therefore cast our minds back to those times and remember what it was that made us feel good about working for the business (or not) as the case maybe.

My recollections of working in a good business were varied, but one was the desire to impress and be recognised as having made a valuable contribution. Another was to be respected amongst my peers and be one of the team. A bit like being part of a family all of us working together.

A key component in this was a high regard for the business owner. This company wasn't large, he was a real person, he was sat in the same office as us, he somehow commanded loyalty and respect and because he was human, knew our names, showed an interest and was fair, we liked him and wanted to do our best for him and his company.

I don't ever remember since this time working in a company where there were so many gifted individuals certainly in the early days... many of whom have gone on to be very successful in their own right.

Now I think we would all like our staff to have the outlook described about, so what was the magic that held these very good people together?

Looking back it was the desire to always create a Win / Win with the staff. This was an IT company that was growing, new technologies, new markets, new ideas were emerging constantly. The company was able to offer the employees the opportunity to develop their talents, expand their skills and improve themselves. The company on the other hand had a very adaptive, flexible set of staff who could pretty much adapt to any shift in direction that the business might need to take.

This was a real Win / Win and certainly, if this being part of a small team where everyone pulls together, is flexible and positive can be retained even when the company expands then it can become one of those exceptional businesses.

Later on we shall see how today not only do businesses themselves need to retain flexibility but that the whole concept of what and how a business operates is undergoing a metamorphosis. How we adapt to these huge changes in the workplace will determine our future success.

Our Businesses consist of People

Without Staff our businesses are nothing!! Who can argue with this statement? Except for the very small Micro business where the owner is also the staff, businesses rely on their employees to turn up for work or the business stops.

So the most important asset of any business is its employees… or is it? This point raised by this question will not be answered here but covered in detail in a later chapter. While considering staff in relation to a business they are indeed the cogs which keep the whole business moving.

Let us ponder for a minute in our business and in dealings with staff, do we treat our customers in a manner differently to our staff? If we do why is that? Are our customers more important to us that the capability to service them?

In fact they are both people without which the business would suffer. The point being made here is that keeping staff happy, motivated, recognised, trusted, empowered and rewarded is as important if not more so than the customers we service.

As the Business World grinds through the changes being brought about by the Internet Age, the whole topology of Running and Managing a business will shift, this means the very foundation of how we view what a 'Business' is defined as, where staff work and how they perform their jobs will require us to be much more flexible if we are to keep the best people working with us.

Everyone is important

A business is a complex system of highly integrated functions... similar to a car engine... if something stops performing correctly then the car might run for a while but in the end the symptoms will cause other failures and in the end it stops.

So it is with Business, in my companies I have always had the view that the person who does the smallest perhaps simplest tasks is undertaking a job that needs doing. An analogy is the washer bottle in a car... not the most necessary thing, and certainly not critical, but on rainy, horrible days the ability to clean the screen is vital to our safety and the vehicles operation... on a summers day the washer bottle is not required at all.

The chairman of a company performs a series of tasks important to his or her role, the person who sorts out incoming mail performs a task without which the Chairman could not perform his/hers. Both are vital. A business is a collection of people each with an assigned set of responsibilities.

I heard a story which crystallises this point, an exam at a junior school where the teacher asked a number of maths questions except for the last which was 'what is the name of the cleaner who cleans this classroom'. One of the pupils asked is this a joke, do we need to answer this question? On later analysis the simple truth of this question is that everyone knew who this lady was but that no one had taken the time to chat with her or even ask her name. She was vital to the school and to the welfare of the children, and yet somehow went unrecognised. The lesson was absorbed by those that understood the import of the question.

Retaining the Best staff

The Business world is changing as the Internet unfolds and as more of us are 'Running our business Online' then the impact on how we see our businesses physically and spatially is changing also.

Smaller businesses are beginning to see the attraction of distributing their workforce. Staff working from home travel less which saves time and possibly results in higher productivity. Less people in the office concurrently reduces office space requirements so they can be downsized saving on Business overheads.

Most importantly change in the Business world however is the flexibility of working arrangements that can now be offered to staff. Gone are the confines of the 9-5 operation in a fixed location. Now we are truly able to accommodate staff who need to fit 'work' around the calls on their time from 'family'. It doesn't matter very often when or where people work as long as the tasks assigned are completed in the time frame allocated. In many administrative roles how and where the tasks are undertaken is becoming less and less of an issue.

Two great examples of the increased flexibility that can be offered are demonstrated in the two situations below :-

Important Member of staff moves abroad

In this situation both the Company and the Member of staff were able to negotiate a period of continued involvement, as the duties could be performed equally well overseas as from the Office.

This actual example was a Stock reordering function. The complex buying knowledge could be retained by the business even though thousands of miles now separated the staff member and the business. Good for the individual and the company.

Snow causes devastation on the roads

But using a Web based business platform, staff can perform at almost 100% effectiveness from Home. Keeping staff safe and preventing unnecessary travel in difficult driving conditions.

'Running a Business Online' opens up the Business and empowers the owners to be able to offer a much more flexible set of working methods not based on time spent at the office but based on tasks and actions.

The best people by their nature want to manage their lives effectively, maximise their work / life balance and work when they are perhaps at their most creative or when the children are tucked up in bed. By empowering staff in this way we will encourage them to higher levels of achievement and retain their services far longer.

Making sure the best people join us

Good staff are spoilt for choice about which company they ultimately might join. Of course the overall package and benefits will be an important consideration, but ultimately in a win/win environment an employee is looking beyond the simple salary package.

Even today the best people will be looking for remote working capability, the higher the position in the organisation the more important this will be to them. Generally Management will already be on performance or task related goals and so late hours at the office of yesteryears have now been replaced with the capability to continue work 'as if at the office' but from home.

When evaluating a company to join the extent to which the business owners have adopted and implemented good modern technology platforms such as 'Running a business online' will have an impact over their eventual decision.

Flexibility, work / life balance, reduction in wasted hours travelling and maximising effectiveness is what key people will be looking for… adopting a modern Web based business platform will give all the right signals that your business is adapting to the 21st century and the irreversible changes in the modern workplace.

The Green component

No one is going to revolutionise their business because of an overwhelming desire to be 'Green'. But, if while overhauling your business and setting the wheels in motion to implement 21st Century Business Technology you could for no additional effort include a whole set of 'Green' initiatives as well that wouldn't be a problem would it?

'Running a Business Online' really does enable your business to publicise that you are making a significant contribution by adopting the latest 'Green' business platforms. The list below are some of the main 'Green' benefits of using web based Business Platforms and 'Running a Business Online'

No packaging or Shipping (software products)

Web based systems delivered through the Internet have no Packaging materials, shipping or distribution costs. Not only this but upgrades are performed online, saving further shipping and production as improvements of fixes are rolled out.

No driving to site for support or upgrades

Online systems remove the need for engineers to come out on site. This saves not only costs for the business for the Engineers time but also on Petrol, Road Usage, not to mention the downtime and productivity costs that are also entailed.

Savings in staff travelling working a few days from home

Online Business Platforms spread the availability of your company data outside the walls of the business. Now staff can have access with their logins from anywhere with a simple Internet connection and browser.

With staff being equally effective working from home as they are in the office, new work schedules can be constructed with agreed 'out of office days'. The company can easily publish journeys saved and the subsequent CO_2 reductions.

Reduce office space requirements

With staff schedules being redrafted to include a percentage of home working and as we will see in step 5 an increase in outsourced job functions the demand of office space will reduce.

Reduced office requirements means smaller premises, which in turn reduces the carbon footprint of the business. Eventually as larger corporate businesses recognise the topology of the working population is changing the need for such elaborate and largely wasted resources ploughed into corporate offices will diminish. This money can be poured into building new environmentally friendly offices that are self sustainable and perhaps other more useful projects.

There is no question that the Internet and Online Web services will drastically reduce the way we look at office space and its role in running a business. This won't be lead by the 'Green' charge but its contribution to reducing carbon emissions will play an important part.

Increased usage of web based services less travel

In the next chapter we will discover a whole host of tools and techniques to develop an online presence for an offline business. Inside this chapter contains products such as Skype a communications platform that enables collaboration through voice, video and screen sharing.

Technology now exists (bandwidth availability dependent) to have good quality face to face meetings across the internet and at very low cost... often free.

Blog sites, Video recordings, Podcasts and even streaming TV are all available enabling us to communicate with our customers, staff and business partners without ever leaving the office (wherever that is).

e-learning and online training can now be delivered easily and effectively in small digestible chunks at the time and convenience of the consumer all via web services.

The net effect of these technology advances once embedded within your business culture is the downward pressure on the need to travel so frequently and culminating in a huge 'Green' contribution.

It has been stated that with just a small percentage of the working population working a day or so a week at home would result in a massive reduction in traffic congestion... dramatically improving journey times for those that do have to travel, reducing carbon emissions and giving business productivity a massive boost to boot!!

The important question that needs to be asked is not 'How can we reduce journey times?' but 'How can we use technology to reduce the need to travel?'

Savings in paper usage, envelopes, printer cartridges

We have seen since the late 1990's the huge rise in the use of email as a means to communicate between businesses. This has got to the point where this is now viewed by many as the most business critical application.

This has been the first step on the road to moving away from business practices that have been dominated by paper and printing. There is still a long way to go, however as web based business platforms are adopted then many of the traditional documents such as Invoices, Statements and Purchase Orders will become electronic.

The savings in this area can be very significant, with postal charges continually rising, the concerns over paper wastage and consumption from the 'Green' lobby and the expense over printer cartridges, it is just a matter of time before electronic documents become normal practice. In purely financial savings this move can be easily justified, with 100's of documents sent electronically costing almost nothing compared to the pain of Paper, Envelopes, Printer cartridges, processing, posting and then all the resources involved in the ongoing final delivery.

Data Protection, Disaster Recovery and Virus Management

For those of us who are old enough to remember when microwaves first came into the marketplace they were viewed with a lot of scepticism. Indeed I remember neighbours and friends stating they were dangerous and we were more likely to end up cooking ourselves with this new technology rather than the food.

Today it would be unthinkable to imagine a kitchen without the flexibility of warming something up or defrosting using a microwave, it is easy, convenient, and simply not dangerous.

As with microwaves the pioneers of 'Running a Business Online' technology have got a lot of arrows in their backs. The reluctance to change and scepticism is brought about by lack of knowledge and understanding of this emerging technology and by an industry trying to halt the speed of change and hang onto their business model as customers begin to move away from the old Client Server model.

One of the Myths which holds people back from changing to 'Cloud Computing', 'Software as a Service' or 'Running a Business Online' is one of Data Protection, where is our data? Is it safe? Can't anyone just hack in a steal it? What if the people looking after it lose it? How am I protected from Virus's?

These are indeed valid questions and concerns and should not be brushed aside as nonsense but looked in detail and compared with where we are today to see how the 'new technology' compares with what we have accepted as the norm.

Data Protection

We say it, we mean it, and yet for many of us they are hollow words. Protecting our data especially in small businesses does not have a good reputation. Many of us make a mental note to get a proper process in place and for whatever reason in the hustle and bustle of business we never get around to it.

We are walking the tightrope. Technology is much better than before, more reliable more robust, but it still does fail.

For me and I know I am not alone, being creative needs some work too in whatever capacity be it programming, writing an article, writing a review is enough, without having to write it all over again because it got lost or deleted or worse still not backed up. I cannot think of anything more irritating than having to do something all over again that took hours or maybe days because I simply did not take enough care to backup what I had done.

Let us analyse the two main approaches to Data protection for both Micro and SME's.

The Micro Business

When we are running a very small business, maybe just one PC, we can easily back up our data. Maybe we have an external backup device such as a USB disk drive, or even a USB memory stick for very important items.

The prevalence of working from home and the uses to which we put the spaces in our homes has driven more people to use laptops rather than dedicated workstations. The flexibility to take our computers with us and working in different locations is now how many of us choose to do things. The proliferation of Flat Screen TV's has helped drive prices down so that Laptops have become very cost effective.

The portability of computers however brings its own threats too. Theft, poor handling, temperature fluctuations are new problems brought about by computers on the move.

Whatever the preferred way of working, whether it's a dedicated fixed workstation or a mobile computer the issues are the same, it makes sense to keep a copy of the data elsewhere.

The Traditional Model

So let us take a look at the thought processes behind how we have been working. The computer is our hub. The software that we use is normally installed on our computer, the documents and files we create are also stored in the same place.

So to back up our information we copy the information from this computer onto some external media, this could be another computer, a portable disk, CD, DVD or USB memory stick. Some people still use backup tapes but these are now largely redundant.

The key here is that we must take action otherwise we are vulnerable. We back up our data. If we are too busy, forget, procrastinate and don't do it, then we risk everything.

A Different Approach

Suppose the computer you use was not the Hub? Suppose that we took a paradigm shift and took on board that our important data and even systems (software) that we used were located somewhere else. Let's further suppose that this was backed up and stored in multiple locations so that we were totally protected and let us suppose that we had a contract with this company that ensured they took responsible care of our data and protected access to it to us alone.

Now our computer becomes a tool to access the software and data, not the hub at all. If we lose our computer for whatever reason, it is an inconvenience because we have to buy another, configure it and set things up again, but it is a far cry from the disaster it might have been.

The Small and Medium sized business

The dynamics of computing once we introduce multiple workstations into an organisation are very different from a single user environment.

The Traditional Model

We have to start to consider our whole data strategy for how the software will be accessed, where will it be located, how are our folders and documents to be stored and who will have access to what.

With a jumble of older and new computers and a variety of operating system versions all trying to work together it is no surprise that a whole industry to ensure that we can keep working has emerged!

So what about Data Protection? Once a company gets to a certain size there is an inevitability about commissioning a server on the network. It makes complete sense. A central resource, everyone shares the workspace and everything can be backed up easily. This almost achieves the same ideals as mentioned in the previous section, storing everything elsewhere and reducing the importance of each PC to that of a simple plug and play workstation.

Sounds ideal but there are a couple of things to consider. Not everything might be stored centrally, for example email is often delivered to the actual workstation itself. This is rarely included in server backups and with energy conservation these machines are turned off at nights when backups are normally taken. In some companies the email system contains the majority of live actions and correspondence relating to what is going on right now in the business and is critical to the operation.

The second consideration is the complexity of the solution now in the business. The cost of the maintenance and support to ensure that these systems are available constantly is high, and, disproportionately large compared to the size and turnover of smaller companies.

The third consideration is that the entire company's Information systems are located in the office. Often under a desk, in the middle of a busy office or kept in a warm tiny room, there is a sense of security that, if we want to, we can go and see the computer where everything is stored.

We do not understand the server though, we know why it is there, but we are at the mercy of our external computer specialists to ensure everything is OK.

Do we actually know how and when our IT Support people can connect to our server remotely? They have access to everything, they have to have absolute control as they have set the server up in the first place. Do we know whether they have implemented all the necessary controls to prevent others from 'getting in'? What if a disenchanted employee leaves their company who has access to your data? Would we even know if anyone had accessed our systems?

Far from a safe, protected and secure environment, actually we have been vulnerable all along we just didn't know it.

A Different Approach

If we haven't been protected all along how does 'Running a Business Online', Cloud computing fare any better?

Again lets take a huge paradigm shift. We wouldn't think of having our own electricity generator in our office, so why do we think we should have our own mini computer centre in our office either. Imagine if we took the whole server issue, signed a contract with a specialist computer company who would manage the entire thing 'lock stock and barrel'. Power, Connectivity, Security, Hosting, Clean environment, Hardware, Software, Upgrades and Backups, all for a low monthly fixed cost... that sounds painless!

Let's take this step by step issue by issue as if we were a business that had it's own dedicated server.

Firstly with Cloud computing the server is hosted in a dedicated purpose built computer server building. This means dust free, clean air environment with uninterrupted power and all the internet connectivity we could wish for, plus 24/7 security year round. This is far superior to the environment we can provide for our own onsite server.

Secondly the hosting service provider will only set up connection to the server for specific nominated locations and dedicated people, reducing the threat of unauthorised access. The remainder of the regular users connect through a web browser with their own login credentials to access the systems.

With Online Business Platforms the entire business data is held centrally including email which means that nothing need be stored on your in-house computers. When backups are performed ALL the data is backed up, not just bits of it, better still no one in the business has to worry, it's done automatically every day.

By addressing the issue of data protection with a mindset shift and setting the business up to be managed by the experts, we have also increased the flexibility of the business as well as reducing the IT Costs significantly.

Disaster Recovery

The trouble with Disaster recovery from an IT perspective is that it both rarely never happens (the good part) but that it is often catastrophic (the bad part) when it does.

The cost implications of complete Disaster recovery, i.e. that no one noticed that a disaster happened at all, is very costly, but lets first take a look at what constitutes a disaster and how we might deal with this from both a traditional perspective and also the 'Running a Business Online', Cloud Computing model.

Disaster – Traditional Onsite Main PC or Server failure

In this example we are using a Disk failure as the most severe because it is unlikely that the data can be recovered. In the Traditional non-cloud based business, there are really four levels of severity

1. No Backups

    Not a good place to be. If this is the position that you find yourself in, then your supporting paper filing system and external media is all that you have.

    It might take weeks or months to recover from this position and your business will be set back for a considerable time. There is no reason why this cannot be avoided with some scheduled backups and today service providers offer online backup services via the internet that will copy the contents of your system onto their servers at pre-defined time(s) each day.

    All your business software will need to be re-installed, the data will need to be re-input. Your business has stopped. It's survival will depend on how quickly you can get back to where you were. This is an unthinkable situation and if your business is currently exposed at this level, please take one thing from this book and sort this out.

2. Data Backups (only)

    A few days downtime as all the Business Applications are reloaded and then the data is imported from backups into the systems.

Not all of your information may well have been backed up, it is only when restoring from a disaster that we find out what is missing. It is good practice to try recovering from backups when you haven't even had a disaster to see if the strategy holds up!

3. Data and program backups

   This would normally be a complete Disk copy where the entire contents of the system are extracted onto external media, this might be another computer or a high capacity external disk drive.

   Recovery can be hours once the main computer / server is replaced. No data is lost, however reconfiguring systems can take many hours depending on the complexity.

4. Mirrored System

   This is only likely to be the situation where a server exists in the business and is designed specifically for disaster situations such as this. The downtime is likely to be minutes rather than hours and barely noticeable within the organisation.

   It is almost the optimum solution but quite expensive, effectively a completely redundant machine is ready and configured on standby in case of such as disaster.

Even though the Mirrored system above is almost the optimum solution there is one more which is necessary if Business Continuance is to be taken to the highest level. In this case a secondary alternative switchable system would be needed in a completely different location. This is only realistically found in highly critical situations such as military, governmental, health, aviation and energy type installations.

Disaster – Cloud Computing online business

In the **Cloud Computing – Running a Business** online situation disaster recovery is more simple, it's about which level of service you wish to pay for. Typically a much greater level of redundancy will be built into Cloud Computing servers to minimise the risk of downtime.

1. No Backups

   This is not really an option, data backups are normally provided as part of the service. Options 2 would apply here.

2. Data Backups (only)

The service provider will commission a new machine, re-install the software and then the data can be reloaded.

The system would typically be up and running within 1 day.

3. Data and program backups

The cloud computing model passes the responsibility for the service provision i.e. the software to the Hosting / Solution vendor. If the service stops working or is unavailable then you can legitimately complain and if unresolved then a different vendor for similar services can be subscribed to.

The more applications that can be used via the 'Cloud' the simpler the business computing model will be. Each provider is responsible for their own systems availability so there is little or no software / programs to install at the customer side.

The use of different vendors for Marketing, Business systems and even Wordprocessing and Spreadsheets shares the risk and increases the likelihood of systems availability

4. Mirrored System

For mission critical applications delivered via 'The Cloud' using a dedicated server such as a complete Business Management system, you might elect to utilise a Mirrored system approach. This is far simpler to provide in 'The Cloud' server environment and multiple clients can be earmarked to use a single central disaster recovery resource, resulting in a much more cost effective solution to any one individual business.

Data is simultaneously replicated into different servers, shortening disaster recovery down to minutes or sometimes removing it entirely. Once disaster strikes, the mirrored machine is switched into live mode and processing continues uninterrupted.

5. Co-Located Mirroring

If disaster really strikes and the whole data centre where the systems are located is wiped out, then it is possible with some providers to operate mirrored solutions that span spatial distances.

With super high speed networks, data updates in one location can be replicated simultaneously in a completely different building often in another town entirely.

Co-Location mirroring represents the ultimate in Disaster recovery and now affordable to much smaller companies than ever before.

Virus Management

'Running a Business Online' and the Cloud Computing model, does change the dynamics of what has become a very serious issue, that of controlling and reducing our exposure to the threat of computer Virus's. We are all well aware of the havoc caused by malicious code present in email attachments and Spyware.

Cloud Computing as a model does not in itself remove the need for us to protect our Computers but it does change the nature of the problem. With a 'Non Cloud based' local network based operation, all our computers are much more tightly connected inside the office, when and if a virus finds it's way in, it can easily locate other resources on the network and replicate itself, quickly spreading onto all computers causing widespread disruption and even bringing the network down.

With Cloud Computing, the connectivity between computers does not need to be nearly so tight. Documents and Files can be shared via the Cloud (web application), stored remotely and downloaded as necessary onto individual workstations. When the document has been worked on, the file can be returned. The central storage on the Cloud will have anti-virus protection and won't allow infected files to be re-uploaded. In this way so long as the individual computers are protected then virus's can be contained and with less communication directly between individual workstation computers the spread of virus's can be far more easily controlled.

In conclusion, Data Protection and Disaster recovery rather than being objections to prevent the migration to 'Cloud Computing' or 'Running a Business Online' are in fact arguments for it !!

In all honesty to put your data and systems into the hands of qualified, experienced computer specialists who manage whole legions of servers for large and small companies alike seems to make perfect sense. The Internet has enabled this transition to take place, which means businesses can stop worrying about technology and concentrate on driving their companies forward.

Upgrades and Support

Patches, Bugs, Fixes and Upgrades are terms that we have come to recognize when dealing with software to run our business. These terms apply equally to operating systems that control the operation of our computers right through to the Business Applications we use such as the Email, Contact Management and Bookkeeping systems.

We have all been there... attempting to implement a recent patch knowing they are necessary but reluctant at the same time because if something goes wrong then the system probably won't work, will we be able to restore back to where we were? Are we technical enough to answer some of the questions we might be asked during the process? Will what we are doing affect some other program we use or the linkage we have built to export information to another system?

With thousands of users and an almost limitless number of different configurations and operating environments that customers have on site, the Software companies are in a very difficult position. The preparation of a patch, upgrade or bug fixing release is a complex, time consuming, costly and difficult task. If they get it wrong, then armies of angry customers will inform the marketplace and we all know how quickly bad news travels. If they get it right then no thanks will be given, just comments like... well you should've written the system properly in the first place without bugs. It is indeed a thankless task, but very necessary as new issues come to light over time, especially with hackers and malicious programs such as Virus's seeking ever more sophisticated ways to infiltrate our computers.

The move to 'Cloud Computing' and 'Running a Business Online' has a significant number of advantages compared to the 'in-house' systems approach. The simplification of computing in the business leads to a reduction in the number of different systems that will need patching or upgrading locally, leading to fewer occasions this task needs doing and less problems as a result. Many of the operating systems nowadays will download their patches automatically anyway if so desired and so this task has become less painful for the customer.

Below we investigate how 'Cloud Computing' takes us away many of the problems associated with both Upgrades and Patches and ongoing general support for the products and services we subscribe too online.

Upgrades

In the Cloud computing environment as we know the software and data is stored on the Hosting / Service provider's server farm in data centres. The hosting / service provider will have direct access to the Production Servers on which your copy of the system will be running and all other customers of the same services.

To Upgrade the systems the provider needs to connect to the servers in turn and upgrade each application. This can be achieved using an automated process which requires no travelling, no packaging, no distribution and in relative terms much less cost. This is a much more effective method of supporting the client base than the old way.

Very often the Upgrades to the systems will be performed in a backwards compatible mode. This means that new functions and features are controlled via new configuration options. The system will normally perform in exactly the way it used to unless the client switches the new functionality on.

The final icing on the cake for all subscribers to Web Based business solutions is that the upgrades are being performed by the experts themselves, the people who are providing the software and services. That's one more technical computer related task we the users don't have to worry about. Not only this it is done outside of regular work hours and therefore does not interrupt or effect the normal working day. This results in little or zero downtime for subscribers to the service.

Support

The Cloud Computing model enables the Hosting / Service Provider to manage and control the applications far more easily than ever before. All the clients can be kept on the latest release, this improves the reliability of the application and improves the support to the end users.

With a single version of the application in use amongst the clients, support queries are much simpler to diagnose and remedy.

One huge benefit to customers of any Web Based application is that whenever a problem is revealed this problem is resolved not just for that customer who reported the issue but for every customer. This removes much of the support traffic which is multiple reports of the same issues. Once reported and fixed this problem has in effect gone for every subscriber to the service.

Cloud Computing not only provides the Subscriber with a better quality of service but it is a much more efficient and cost effective method of providing software solutions. It is very rare that such a large number of compelling arguments come together at a moment in time which represent a win / win, both for the client and also for the supplier of the products and services. Cloud Computing and 'Running a Business Online' is one such situation.

What's in it for me (Wii FM) : Real Case Study examples

To provide examples of how Cloud Computing and 'Running a Business Online' can transform regular everyday businesses below are some real live Case Studies of organisations already operating in this way. To gain further insight into some of the examples we have recorded interview with the Business Owners which can be listened to or viewed by clicking the links provided.

University of Westminster – Access Centre

As early as 2001 the Access Centre part of the University of Westminster had uncovered a problem best resolved using Web based cloud computing technology... even though the term would not be invented for another few years yet!

The Access Centre at Westminster University is one of many around the country responsible for evaluating individuals with learning difficulties due to conditions such as Dyslexia or Dyspraxia. Students are evaluated and then a report is produced with a series of recommendations for computers, related equipment and supporting software to enable the student to achieve higher education qualifications.

The Access centres have come a long way since those early days with now the need to produce alternate quotations for as many as 8 or 9 technology vendors rather than just the 1 or 2 when the project first began.

The problem that existed for the Access Centre was that the assessors needed to produce reports that contained technical cost summaries for equipment which formed part of an overall recommendation proposal for the student. There were 35 assessors all working odd hours and who were not based at the central office either. Product amendments and prices were issued via email to the Consultants who in turn used this information to compile their reports.

Problem Number 1 : Not all assessors used the latest copy of the price list and so often the reports were incorrect.

Problem Number 2 : Some of the items are VAT free if ordered along with other major components, although not complicated this area resulted in many errors and omissions.

Problem Number 3 : Maintenance of the Price list was both laborious and time consuming.

Problem Number 4 : Two staff at the office were in place to check the proposals to make sure that they were correct before being submitted.

Problem Number 5 : Reporting and analysis was both tedious and slow as all information was stored on paper.

Quite clearly the Word document managed centrally and circulated to the assessors was well past its sell by date and a new solution needed.

The i-Tr@der business platform was implemented as a technology platform to underpin the Access centres needs. This provided all the necessary security, login and system management functions.

Added to this was a custom database that housed all the specific data needs for the assessor's technology application.

So how does the Cloud Computing Web based solution compare now to the old circulated Word Document from the past?

In order to compile a new Technology report for a student the assessors now login to a web based application with their own login credentials. Once logged in the Assessor can look at previously completed reports, create new ones from the beginning or copy an old similar report and amend it as necessary.

All the Product Data is held centrally along with the rules that govern when VAT is not charged. Supplier partners are able to login to the system and amend their product descriptions and pricing directly. Suppliers without completed pricing are excluded from the final quotation list so they are incentivised to ensure their prices are kept up to date or risk losing business.

By implementing a Cloud Computing solution the Access centre has achieved some amazing benefits.

- The assessors can produce a report from any location as long as they have an internet connection

- There is no longer any need to check the student technology report at the centre because the data used is always accurate and the VAT calculations correct, the two staff members being redeployed for more productive tasks

- The Access Centre no longer needs to manage the Product pricing this has been outsourced back to the Suppliers themselves each of them updating a bit of the database rather than one person managing it all

- Statutory reports required by the education authorities can now be produced at a touch of a button, rather than weeks of tedious paperwork

So successful has the project been that there are plans afoot to roll the system out nationwide and include other Access centres around the UK. The scalability of the system will enable the benefits achieved to reach a much larger number of assessors and standardise the approach for this sector.

Healthcare Products Distributor

Deliver Net Ltd are a Healthcare products distributor based in North Yorkshire. The customers consist of large Care Home groups, smaller groups, independent care homes and also some private individuals.

Goods are brought into the warehouse where they are then broken down into smaller orders and then delivered using their own drivers on a milk round basis, nationwide. Deliver Net regularly process 300-400 orders on a daily basis.

Back in 2005, further to an initiative to introduce online ordering for a large care home group, i-Tr@der was selected as the platform to roll out a simple forms ordering system. Historically orders had been faxed to the office for processing, 6 customer care staff were responsible for entering orders onto the system.

The initiative was instigated in an effort to streamline the operation by reducing the data entry task as well as removing the inevitable errors both from incomplete or duplicate faxes and keying errors when entering orders onto the system. Orders collected electronically would then be automatically imported into the main system and processed in the normal manner.

3 months after the original discussions the system went live, with over

200 remote care homes ordering through online forms. Apart from the regular minor teething problems and training issues the migration to the online ordering was highly successful. Two months after this project was completed the Online Catalogue also went live to provide smaller independent care homes and private individuals the ability to order directly anything from the extensive range of 1400 Medical, Janitorial and Chemical products.

18 months after the original introduction of the Online Forms ordering facilities, the second phase of the original project was kicked off. This second phase was to see the migration of the entire Business Systems to the i-Tr@der Web Based Business platform.

The project which would take over one year to fully implement would include the following areas, Contact Management, Email, Stock control, Sales Order entry and Sales Order processing (picking lists, delivery notes), Purchase Ordering, Goods Receiving, Sales Invoicing, Cash Collection and allocation, Purchase Invoice processing, Purchase Payments, the General Ledger and Management reporting.

So what have been the major highlights and benefits from introducing the i-Tr@der Business Platform at Deliver Net :-

- Close to 1,000 remote homes / locations now ordering directly without the need for Customer care to handle the orders at all

- 98% of orders are now serviced from stock and handled only once. The correct products are being stocked and double handling of orders has been reduced significantly

- Fewer errors or queries on Deliveries

- 80% reduction in the time taken to allocate remittances

- Reduction in the number of invoices produced through consolidated invoices rather than an invoice for each shipment to larger groups

- Invoices and Statements sent electronically saving Paper, Envelopes, printing and stamp costs

Deliver Net are now handling a higher volume of Orders than before but have reduced the administration in the business significantly. Conservatively the cost reductions have been in the region of $75k month on month, leading to better cash flow and increased stocks of the most popular lines.

The future looks good for Deliver Net too. New business being written today is all done through online transactions enabling Deliver Net to provide the best possible prices whilst continuing to provide excellent service. Latest software improvements on the Online ordering has enabled Deliver Net to extend Budget and Cost management controls through the online system to customers and provide comprehensive reporting tools so that the clients can login and access what they have been buying, who's bought it and in what quantities.

The flexibility of Cloud Computing for Deliver Net has also meant that the Suppliers can be provided with Logins and their own reporting capabilities. Suppliers are able to see which locations are ordering their products and in what quantities. This kind of information is invaluable to the Supplier and enables Deliver Net to work with the Client and the Supplier to provide a much greater level of satisfaction.

What Deliver Net has experienced is that the migration to Cloud Computing technology has enabled sales to increase at a rate much higher than the administration costs thus increasing the profitability. At the same time a much closer working relationship has developed between Deliver Net, their customers and the Suppliers which strengthens and enhances the business going forward.

Garment Manufacturer

Blue Autumn is a garment manufacturer servicing the Healthcare, Beauticians and Cleaning market sectors. Blue Autumn is based in Northern Ireland with the manufacturing taking place in Lasi in Romania. Historically the two business locations were managed with independent systems, the owner spending a considerable amount of time massaging spreadsheets and establishing production plans.

The vision for Blue Autumn was to significantly streamline the operation and remove as many of the Administrative elements as possible leading to a series of well defined business processes that would effectively run the business. Ultimately James (the owner) needed to spend more time developing the business rather than tied up in the day-to-day running of the business.

Within a single year from the commencement of the 'Cloud Computing' project deployment the following major actions had been completed :-

- The two trading locations had been integrated into a single copy of the i-Tr@der Business Platform

- Staff in Romania had taken over the main administrative tasks of the system, including stock checking and production scheduling, Invoicing and statements, Order processing, picking and delivery management

- Administration costs reduced significantly with lower cost base in Romania

- Complete end to end order processing from Order Entry (online) through to Order Processing, despatching and Invoicing. All handled via the i-Tr@der business platform

We can never predict the future and the sudden loss of a major client meant that the Blue Autumn turnover was slashed significantly. It is highly probable that at that time had Blue Autumn not migrated already to the i-Tr@der platform and lowered the operating costs that the business would not have survived.

The future looks bright for Blue Autumn now. The business is completely scalable and with good business processes in place James is able to manage the business in just two hours per day enabling him to spend the majority of his time on the business. Blue Autumn are now seeking to continue growth through the appointment of Business Partners in the UK, while servicing the Irish market directly.

Blue Autumn are well into step 4 of the 7 Steps programme, working hard on increasing their online presence to assist with the appointment of Distributors for their product range in mainland UK. Blue Autumn now feature on the front page of Google for one of their key products and are seeing enquiries directly as a result of the Digital Marketing strategies put in place in 2008.

Largest building company in England

Towards the end of 2008, Select Plant Hire Ltd a division of Laing O'Rourke one of the largest construction companies in the world approached us about a potential involvement of i-Tr@der in a high profile building project in central London.

The One-Hyde-Park project is the construction of four extremely high class pavilions between Knightsbridge and Hyde Park itself. The location is just a few minutes walk from Harrods.

The main issue with the project is the lack of space on site for the storage of any products or materials, neither is there the possibility of access by large trucks as would be the norm on building projects of this type.

The 'Fit-out' of the pavilions was to be serviced on a Just-In-Time basis from a consolidation warehouse location based in Wembley. Small trucks would provide up to 9 deliveries per day down to site delivering materials called off directly by the Sub-Contractors performing the various works on-site.

The system specification needed to allow for the following elements if it was to be effective :-

- Controlled Access by the Sub-Contractors from On-Site, from the consolidation centre and from their offices to their own data only

- Sub contractors to be able to book orders for delivery into the consolidation centre

- Sub contractors able to place call off orders for product delivery to site

- Sub-Contractors to have reporting visibility of their Deliveries into the warehouse, stock position, stock movements history, Goods Received Notes, Call off orders to site and signed delivery notes.

- Consolidation staff (Select Plant Hire) personnel to have access to the entire system for management and control

The underlying consideration for the project was the need for the application to be delivered in 'the Cloud'. There are around 12 or so sub-contractors on the fit-out project and some 50+ users, but they work from many locations, so the solution had to be web based.

The second consideration for the project was the support and hosted nature of the solution. The technical staff within Select Plant Hire and Laing O'Rourke were tied up with their own internal IT projects and support with no time to learn a different platform. It was crucial for this project that the software worked, was durable and was well supported.

The project went live in early March 2009, with on-site training provided to each Sub-Contractor individually. Each Sub-Contractor interacts slightly differently with the LMS (Logistics Management System) dependent on the nature of their role within the fit-out process. Kitchens and Bathrooms require different modes of operation for Stone work or dry lining and as such a fairly detailed knowledge of the peculiarities of each trade was required to ensure the smooth implementation of the web based Business Platform.

This is an excellent example of how a 'Cloud Computing' solution, in this case a subset of the i-Tr@der Business Platform can be used in specific situations for larger corporate clients. The ability for a Web Based solution to be quickly set-up, configured and put into operation without diverting internal resources is a huge advantage in situations such as this.

Table Tennis club

Urban Progress TTPro is a Table Tennis Club based in South West Herts. The club is hoping to build in the long term a national network of clubs built on the same premise as the first one currently in operation.

The Club itself is a virtual business with coaches working from home and delivering sessions weekly into both Junior and Secondary schools.

Being a virtual business and with the need to take in contributions from spatially distributed individuals at the heart of the business needed to be a central resource which could link all the people together. i-Tr@der provides the underlying business infrastructure for this disparate business. The club utilises the whole range of modules from Contacts, Emails and Bookkeeping right through to a specially developed Membership database that contains more detailed information regarding their status.

i-Tr@der has provided this start up company with the ability to get all the necessary business controls in place without the need to invest in any hardware or software. The simple pay-as-you-go approach fits well with the monthly membership subscription model the club has in place and helps keep the cash flow synchronised.

The second important criteria for the Table Tennis Club was the ability to easily replicate the business and to spawn new Franchise units. The simplicity of the i-Tr@der business application, it's low cost and the ability to help others use it effectively with online training makes it an ideal business tool for this type of club.

i-Tr@der has brought together a spatially distributed team of people together under one system. All correspondence from the business is maintained under a common look and feel which adds to the professional nature of the club. i-Tr@der acts for Urban Progress as the central office, the glue between all the separate cogs.

Urban Progress TTPro has now embarked on step 4 of the 7 steps and started its own Blog site to promote and advertise the Club using Digital Marketing Strategies. The club is now well on its way to achieving the second year targets and on track for the much longer term goal of turning an amateur sport into a professional one in the UK.

Supplier of ATM machines to West Africa

Hysen International is a business based in the Channel Islands that does the majority of its business in North West Africa. Hysen International has country licences to supply and install the second most popular ATM's in the world (those manufactured by Wincor-Nixdorf). These countries are currently, Ghana, Gambia and Sierra Leone.

The head office is based in London in the UK and the directors of the group business were looking for a Cloud Based Business platform that could be rolled out inexpensively across all the countries in which they operate. Key to the thinking was the uniformity of the data collection and reporting which would ensure that the consolidation into group accounts would be as painless as possible.

Other key criteria for Hysen was the ability to manage and control each of the applications for the satellite countries in West Africa. Skills on the ground in these countries are rare and expensive so the ability to manage these from the London head office proved to be invaluable during the configuration and set up stages. By implementing a 'Cloud' based system the only requirement locally within the country is a Browser and a connection to the Internet, this keeps things simple and removes unnecessary IT costs.

Apart from a known requirement to handle an obscure accounting requirement in one of the West African Countries and to implement a set of reporting layouts with no VAT column, the implementation progressed smoothly. Hysen elected to learn the configuration and system management functions for themselves. With potentially 6 separate companies using the system undertaking the necessary training to manage the system internally made perfect sense.

Cloud computing has presented an opportunity to Hysen International not available at this level in the market before. To implement systems in subsidiary companies overseas but all centrally controlled and managed from the Head Office. They have been able to standardise their systems across all the operating units, manage and control the business effectively and keep costs down to a minimum.

Bookkeeping Bureau service

KD Accounting is like many other small bookkeeping bureaus around the country. A small business that takes on the bookkeeping function for small and micro businesses who either do not need or want to learn how to manage their own accounts or who have elected to Outsource the task as there is not enough work for a full time or part time person.

Small and Micro businesses are not really too worried about which software application is being used to generate their financial results so long as the accountant can make sense of it, give financial advice as appropriate and file the returns to ensure that they comply with all the necessary legislation.

KD Accounting has been a specialist Sage Line 50 bookkeeping service and reseller for many years. The recession however has taken its toll on a number of accounts, some going out of business whilst others have been reigning in the costs and undertaking the work themselves.

KD Accounting were approached during 2009 to undertake the Bookkeeping services of a new client, however on this occasion the client requested rather than using a copy of the more traditional software such as Sage or Quickbooks would they be prepared to learn a different system which was already being used.

The software being used was the i-Tr@der Business Platform and a new user was set up to enable the people at KD Accounting to login to the system and undertake the bookkeeping work remotely though a simple Web Browser. Having undertaken some basic training and being show where to find all the common bookkeeping functions KD Accounting were soon handling the new client's Purchase Ledger and then soon after the Sales Ledger.

Looking at the above it would seem that nothing exceptional had happened at KD Accounting. It all seems fairly innocuous, they had taken on a new client using a new system which happens to be web based, nothing extraordinary about that. But let us take a closer look at the implications of this development, not just for KD Accounting but for the '000's of other Bookkeeping / accounting service providers around the UK :-

- They were provided with a Username & Password and with existing software on their computer they were able to login and work on their clients system

- Their client and them are looking at the same information in real time, there is no need to exchange data back and forth

- KD Accounting could easily work on many different clients i-Tr@der systems without moving from their offices

- KD Accounting could start to access other revenue streams by offering additional modules of i-Tr@der above and beyond simple ledger bookkeeping to these customers, e.g. Contact Data Cleansing, Email management, diary management, Email Marketing, Debt collection and even document filing

- KD Accounting could benefit from re-selling online training and other 3rd party products to help their customers get the most from the i-Tr@der business platform

- KD Accounting can now recommend the system to other clients and receive a royalty each month for referring the client to i-Tr@der

Cloud computing Business solutions reduce the IT element to setting up and managing a business. Once on the 'Cloud' with a suitable business application like i-Tr@der businesses like KD Accounting can offer a much broader range of services not just bookkeeping to smaller businesses. This strengthens the relationship and instils good business processes into these companies right at the start; so that once they begin to grow they have the right scalable systems to take them forward.

KD Accounting and companies like this are now in a position to grow out of just providing a bookkeeping function into being more like an outsourced virtual office. This enables the Micro and Small businesses to get on with their business rather than worrying about how to organise themselves, this can be left to the experts.

In this chapter we have covered a great deal of ground regarding the why's and wherefore's of 'Running a Business Online' or Cloud computing as we now know it. The attractions and benefits of this technology are irrefutable. This methodology for delivering business solutions will gather pace over the next 10 years until we have a 40% penetration or more in the market of Business Platforms such as i-Tr@der.

Consider that today we are at the worse point in time as far as 'Cloud Computing' is concerned. From now on in the Internet will get faster, the solutions will become ever more sophisticated and integrated and the costs are likely to reduce. The era of the traditional Server Client model is slowly coming to a close!

Step 4

Increasing Sales – Digital Marketing

In general the greater the Turnover and Profit in a business the greater the value of that business. The previous chapters have put in place all the necessary processes and products to automate a business, but just as important as automation we have built in scale-ability.

By building our processes for the volumes we would like to be doing in the future and by introducing a cloud computing web based business platform which can service a much larger organisation than what it is today, we negate the need for moving to different systems later on. This saves money for sure, but removes the biggest hidden cost to the business which is the investment in knowledge, procedures and processes, and the change management of having to move to a different operating platform.

This chapter now addresses how we can leverage off the biggest change in business since the industrial revolution and of course I am referring to the Internet. As the Industrial revolution forced company owner's way back then to re-look at their businesses, so today, the Internet asks us to do the same.

The Internet is no longer just a website delivery mechanism, a way of sending and receiving emails, or buying a few products cheaply here and there, no, it will start to pervade every aspect of our businesses. From running and managing our business information as we have seen in chapter 3, right through to finding external resources to compliment our own company staff (chapter 5) and probably the most important factor of all, to Sell and Market ourselves, our Brands, Products and Services in the Global Economy (if appropriate to your business).

In the following sections this book will unveil a whole industry – Digital Marketing, which has sprung up since early in this century and which will force every company (and its key staff) to adapt new techniques and practices to ensure survival. I hasten to add… this is not just, 'a few new things have emerged which we need to get up to speed on', this is a radical shift in how businesses and their brands, products and services will be discovered in the future. This is the 'Digital Revolution' and will hit the business world like a Tsunami. Some will not survive the challenge, but ALL will need to re-evaluate their strategy going forward.

The Internet is growing up… it is constantly morphing and changing as new ideas and technologies become available, it will get faster, better and more powerful. It is here to stay, and '**Digital Marketing**' – which is the way you, your business and your future customers will find each other are inextricably linked.

Digital Marketing in all its facets will decide the winners and losers in business in the future. The 'Digital Age' will become a multi Billion dollar industry as businesses wake up to the massive potential for growth and develop strategies to maximise their advantage from the Internet. Those that ignore the information in this chapter may survive... for a while...

The Need for Leads

There is not a small business that I have dealt with that would not be grateful for more leads. The amount of business that we do is in direct proportion to the number of leads that we process. More leads in, more business out... simple as that.

By definition however entrepreneurs and small business owners are very often technical or designer types. This group of people are innovators or creators and perhaps not in their comfort zone when it comes to selling in the traditional sense.

In the UK unlike in other parts of the world 'Sales and Selling' are not thought of as true professions... rather a necessary evil filled with egotistical people fond of their own voices, driving flash cars and using the latest gizmo's.

I have often heard it said... *'I could never be a sales person I think I am basically too honest'*. In actual fact Sales People... good ones just learn the customer's requirements (by using their ears) and then help the customer to find the most appropriate solution for their needs.

Marketing itself is often thought of by Small Business Owners as a much more preferred method of selling... No cold calling, no difficult sales approaches... customers who like the message will come to us! Marketing comes in two main flavours, awareness / brand building which rarely generates volume direct leads but does subliminally get the brands and products into the marketplace, and secondly direct marketing targeted to a particular audience with the intent to generate leads.

For many Small Businesses the costs associated with Brand building and potentially the size of the response (which might be too large to handle with the company's existing capacity) is not often viable, so direct marketing / lead generation is the most widely practiced.

The traditional marketing methods

Traditional marketing approaches have included the following :-

- Mail shots

- Cold Calling

- Direct Marketing (companies running telephone campaigns for us)

- Business Directories (e.g. Yellow Pages)

- Advertising (local / national newspapers, or industry magazines)

- Chamber of Commerce or Institute of Directors

- Through Industry groups e.g. British Merchandising Association (BMA)

- Leaflet drops

- PR Announcements

- Editorials in Business Journals

- TV Advertising

More recently this list has been extended with :-

- Web site promotions

- Email marketing

- Banner advertising on customer of supplier websites

If we look at the lists above almost all our marketing efforts must start with a targeted list. This could be either a list purchased with certain demographics or honed for our target market, or it might be a list which we have painstakingly built over time or hand crafted from business directories.

Once we have a list the regular normal process might be as follows :-

Telephone validation of the Database with correct contact / addressing details

Artwork for whatever we are sending / mailing

Labels for the envelopes

Introductory letter – Sales Letter

Envelope stuffing and mail-out

Campaign Management Spreadsheet creation

Follow up telephone calls (and resending of literature that never reached the intended recipient)

Transfer of interested contacts onto the Prospect list

Work with new prospects

Depending on what type of marketing is being undertaken some or all of the above might be necessary.

What is very apparent about Traditional Marketing is the amount of effort and cost that goes into a campaign such as the one detailed above. Artwork and postage is an actual cost but the time it takes to organise, send and then follow up is the real cost.

So there is a lot of hard work and the bad news is that there is no guarantee that it will generate any business either! Very often a small business campaign might cost $2k - $3k, a significant investment indeed and with no idea whether it is going to work!

Take a look at direct mail leaflet drops as another prime example. How many of us actually look at them anymore? I just pick them up and throw them in the bin I do not even give them a cursory glance... perhaps with the exception of the local Pizza, Chinese, Indian, and Kebab takeaway menus! Here's the question, if we're throwing these away... what would your customers be doing? Or do you think you are the only one thinking this way?

The other killer is that if you want to run the campaign again… marketing rarely works on a one-off hit… the costs are pretty much all repeated perhaps with the exception of the artwork.

We know that we must market ourselves but you must sympathise with business owners who know that the majority of the money is just being thrown away …

As Henry Ford quoted very succinctly :-

'I know half of my marketing budget is wasted, the trouble is I don't know which half'

So… business owners are in a quandary, they don't like sales, they certainly don't like wasting money and yet marketing is expensive and only yields variable and unpredictable results ranging from 1-3% success rates… and is very time consuming too.

The rise and rise of Business Networks

In recent times the lead generation conundrum has spawned a plethora of Business Network groups. The intention of these groups is clear, provide a forum for business owners to meet, network and perhaps pass leads or enquiries to each other.

The concept of networking in business is easy to understand. If 20-30 people are familiar with your business, products and services and know that you are professional and have good referrals from happy customers then… if they discover a requirement which fits the profile of what your business offers, then they pass the lead to you. In effect you have 20-30 unpaid salespeople advocating your business in a passive manner.

Each business networking group have variations on the theme, but in essence they target the same problem. The success of these groups is predominantly down to the Small and Medium sized business owner who, faced with the alternative marketing approaches, is likely to favour a good breakfast in the company of other business owners facing similar challenges.

More on Networking is covered in Step 7, where this topic is covered far more comprehensively.

What is Digital Marketing?

The Internet has opened up another opportunity for Business owners to market themselves using a completely new medium which has taken quite a while to rationalise and get sorted out. Internet Marketing is simply a collection of Tools, Services and Internet Based products that can be used to promote anything to do with your business, or applied to your online content to market You, your Brands, Products and Services. There are many facets to Internet Marketing, from putting together a simple video introducing your business and using it online to encourage people to visit your website, right through to using Social Media sites such as Facebook and Twitter to build up your database of contacts.

We will be looking at all the components of Internet Marketing later on in this chapter, but first of all let's look through the early stages of

Internet Marketing to see how it has evolved to where we are now :-

The Early Years

In the beginning... during the early to mid 1990's the Internet was nothing more than an information resource and a means to communicate using Email.

Most connections were dial up, so access to the Internet was intermittent and slow, Emails were downloaded hourly or most likely daily and the number of people using email although growing was still relatively few especially amongst Small and Medium sized businesses.

It was not uncommon for instance for an email to be sent and then a follow up conversation via telephone a few days later only to be notified that oh... we get so few emails we only check them once in a while... So as a means of reliable communication it still had some way to go.

As we moved through the 1990's so the access speeds grew faster, more and more information started to pour onto the Internet. Businesses were starting to use the Internet not only as an online Brochure but additionally to sell products and services online. I can recall enormous excitement and huge expectation of how the Internet was going to revolutionise business, millions of Dollars would be made... the only problem was no-one had created the mechanisms for this to happen as yet... it was all hype at this stage.

But... something had changed, low cost marketing to millions of people through email had given rise to the first Internet Marketing possibilities... as always the porn industry and scammers were the most creative in devising new ways to ensnare unsuspecting visitors and virus's propagated through email communication. The business world was changing as the promise of the Internet gathered pace, but as we can see it wasn't always a positive experience. Anti-Virus and spyware software became a global business as Businesses and Individuals rushed to protect themselves from cyber-space attacks.

Then... the unthinkable happened. The Dot.com crash. Internet businesses had grown at astronomical speed as Financial Investors threw billions at this burgeoning industry with the promise of massive returns. In effect companies with little or no intrinsic value were valued at 100's of Millions of Dollars. Once business analysts looked at the finances, the investment and the business plan for income generation 99% of the companies had consumed vast sums of money and yet had nothing tangible to show for it.

In short the Bank-rolling stopped and thousands of Internet Companies went out of business just as quickly as they had emerged. Some such as Google, LastMinute.com to name a couple managed to come through, but many did not make it.

A massive setback for the Internet enthusiasts and a huge 'I told you so' moment for the traditionalists who had argued the Internet would never last!

The Wildness of a young new business

In truth the Dot.Com crash helped the Internet Industry. The enthusiasm and excitement which had led to the heady heights prior to the crash had demonstrated how not to 'do the internet'. It took a couple more years for Google to discover the secret and create the platform on which the Internet could be turned into a real money making business.

That platform was delivered through Advertising. Google's first products were, after search, 'Ad-Words' and 'Ad-Sense'. These two products covered the two key fundamentals of making money online. Provide a means for people to pay for advertising their products and services through the Search Engines (Ad-Words) and then provide a means for Content Providers (Businesses and Individuals with websites) to display adverts and earn money when the adverts were clicked on.

These two simple products paved the way for a massive new medium for advertising and selling which was set to overtake TV advertising revenues and start the decline in Newspaper / Magazine adverts.

Something else truly remarkable also took place at the same time which fuelled the above. The infrastructure and availability of the Internet went through a massive metamorphosis. The introduction and adoption of high speed 24/7 Internet through ADSL in the early 2000's, meant the marketplace in terms of just English speaking people was truly global including the USA, UK, Canada, Australia, South Africa and much of mainland Europe.

What this boiled down to was that suddenly individuals could promote other peoples products and services in a global market (soon to be labelled Affiliate Marketing) and make an income online, from just sitting in front of their computer screen at home!

This gave rise to a whole new industry 'Internet Marketing' and the promise of large sums of money, working from home with little or no overheads attracted huge numbers of people to this 'easy money' business.

As a result of the explosion of 'Internet Marketing' a secondary, even larger business opportunity emerged. The initial pioneers of this new business began producing products and services to maximise the potential for both themselves and those entering the market.

The gurus (all marketing specialists) devised Training Packages and easy to follow Toolkits explaining the secrets of Internet Marketing and 'how to' get on board and make millions of dollars with almost little or no effort, a favourite buzzword 'set and forget' outlined the basic principle... find a niche... set up all the online content and sales pages... and sit back and watch the money come in.

Sound too good to be true? Well if it does then it probably is. Of course there are a great many people who have made money from Internet Marketing and by creating products and services to sell into the Internet Marketing industry. No one is forced into Internet Marketing and one can be forgiven for jumping in as it is easy to get carried away with the sales pitch... however, as with any business there is a huge amount of work and effort involved. Many who have trodden the path expecting quick returns for doing almost nothing have left disappointed.

The Internet has not changed the rules of business it has given us a different set of mechanisms and created a very media rich environment to Market and promote whatever it is that we want to offer, but the basics of running and managing a business haven't changed at all.

What is absolutely clear and undeniable is the following :-

- Marketing products via the Internet is here to stay and as we will see in this chapter the only viable approach for the future.

- The Internet Marketing Industry has given rise to a new Profession, Digital Coaches who understand how to maximise the potential of the Internet to sell products and services

- The Infrastructure and tools are now available to deliver a coherent and complete Digital Marketing Platform for almost any business

So Digital Marketing at this time of writing this book is at an interesting stage. Many of the mistakes that could have been made have been made. The people in the industry have years of experience and now we see a maturing business, one with a very exciting future and with huge ramifications for the Business World.

Maturing into a Profession

Without question Internet Marketing has opened up a fabulous lifestyle for a great many people, but it has also dashed dreams for many more. Internet Marketing to date has been predominantly about Individuals making money selling products and services to other Internet Marketers looking to build their own businesses.

The format of large scale audiences gathered together to hear experts confirm their lifestyle and convince us that their programme is the next best thing is now a well worn path. There is always a 'tipping point' where the number of people who no longer believe through their own experience starts the decline... the good news is that this also heralds in the change to a more mature, professional and responsible attitude to the business.

This is where Internet Marketing is now. Until this point at the end of 2009, Internet Marketers have been interested in selling products and services... but with hardly any backup or support for ensuring that those customers derived benefit from their purchase. Ill equipped customers have parted with hard earned cash only to find that to use the product requires knowledge or other services they do not possess. This requires either further purchases or outsourcing to others who have the skills.

With decreasing numbers attending product releases an alternate approach to generating income from Internet Marketing is required. Personally at the time of writing this book, I believe that the biggest and most successful Internet Marketing businesses are just starting or perhaps don't even exist yet, but they will be labelled Digital Marketing not Internet Marketing.

The largest market for Internet Marketing products and services are Businesses. As terms such as Cloud Computing, Software as a Service gain acceptance and the general realisation that just having a website is no longer enough to generate sales, so will businesses look to professional Digital Marketing organisations to deliver a holistic, well thought out strategy for building Internet Marketing departments.

As always large Businesses with deep pockets and large resources will lead the way, and the 'big gun' Internet Experts will look to these large organisations to maximise their income by leveraging on their success and experience over the last 10 years.

But the biggest market is the Small and Medium sized businesses.

Very often with less complicated requirements these companies can experience a huge return on their investment if properly advised and by using the right tools and services. Once the Digital Marketing platform is implemented it can be maintained by external resources or internal staff can be trained to manage and maintain it going forward.

In both the cases detailed above whether it is the large corporate company or the smaller business the emphasis will be on strategy, design, implementation, measurement and adjustment. Digital Marketing is no different to having a traditional Marketing department except that it is technology driven and can reside equally comfortably internally within the company or externalised as an outsourced function.

We are interestingly poised on the precipice of one of the biggest and most exciting revolutions in the history of business. The Internet Marketing apprenticeship has been served, the Internet is improving constantly and Businesses are starting to recognise that in the 21st century the Internet must be harnessed if they are to thrive and survive. Say hello to the 'Digital Revolution'.

Now let us examine why a Digital Marketing strategy represents a better use of our Small Business Marketing budget than conventional marketing and what benefits can we expect to be able to tap into if we decide to go with it.

Why should we be using Digital Marketing in our Business?

In this section we will be examining why for any business Digital Marketing is set to revolutionise how we connect with the market for our products and services. More than that though, Digital Marketing will lead us to reshape our thinking on how we build our brands and the importance attached to our own online social media identity.

How the world has changed?

Since time in memorial people have been marketing their products and services and we continue to do the same to this day. The methods and tools that we employ to market however have gone through huge changes. Let us examine the key milestones during more recent times.

Old style market

Back in the 19th century and early 20th century if you had a product or service to sell the chances are that you would take that product to the town market. People and businesses that had things to sell either had a high street shop or sold their produce from a market stall.

Customers clearly understood where the marketplace was and new that if they needed something that the market or high street was the place where they went to find it.

Newspapers and Mass Media Advertising

Once Mass Media publications hit the streets and later commercial Radio and Television stations began to spring up, there is a complete transformation in the marketing arena.

The customer no longer makes the choice of visiting the market at an agreed time and place and making a decision based on comparisons of similar products located there.

Marketing has moved onto a new model, throw enough information, some will stick and sales will be made. Suddenly commercials / advertisements are bombarding us from every location at any time.

Mass Media advertising takes the product to the consumer, whether you want it or not.

This method of marketing looks a bit like a funnel. So long as the investment we put in at the top is more than compensated by the volume of customers that we collect at the small end of the funnel, then the campaign will have been deemed a success.

Of course most small businesses would not be able to afford TV advertising, but, if you wanted to reach 3 out of 5 people then you might run a TV advert during the Morecambe and Wise show which reached almost half the population at their peak!

Digital Marketing

Once again the wheels turn again with marketing. Now every computer on the planet is connected the dynamics of marketing can never be the same again.

Of course as we subscribe to free online products and service these are paid for by advertisers pushing their products, but this is a small price to pay (seeing adverts) if the consumer is receiving a free service… and of course no one is forced to buy anything.

But the real change is how we the customers find the products and services we want in the modern Internet world… and it is the stress on the word FIND. We are now able to seek out, filter for the products and services we want using powerful search tools. This is a kind of return to the old style market approach before Mass Media advertising.

What it means if you are offering a product or service is that now and even more so in the future if you are not representing yourself properly on the Digital Marketplace then those offering similar services and products may well take more of the business. But it's not just searching as we shall see, referrals and recommendations innocently made or requested in chat rooms, forums and social media sites can very quickly impact the fortunes of businesses today.

The Bottom Line

Let us use TV advertising as a model simply because it is the most extreme and the most impacted by the changes going on in the marketplace. We know from Marketing feedback that more and more of the younger population consume broadcasts through their computers. TV is a one dimensional device, the computer offers the opportunity to multi task whilst consuming TV, it offers more options, more choice and todays user can chat, attend to Facebook updates, twitter and interact with others whilst passively enjoying video / TV.

Let us consider for a minute the impact of viewers consuming live sporting events through Internet Channels rather than the TV. Currently huge sums of money exchange hands for the rights to broadcast live football matches, but what if the audience now wishes to consume these through their computer?

Well this is happening, and there are sites offering these services today, and there will be many more to come. How does this impact the business of live football matches and indeed the advertising opportunity? Well there will be a shift away from paying for sporting channels and therefore smaller viewing figures. This will then broadcast to a smaller audience making the advertising less attractive, so the marketing revenues will decline. If the marketing revenues decline then the amount that can be paid for broadcasting live football will be less… a significant amount of the revenue that enters the game of football comes from TV rights to broadcast.

These events will happen, slowly of course but inevitable... so the model must change. Can you see that the Internet will challenge every business to re-look at how their market operates and is being changed forever. In sport the Marketing model has to move to the Internet, to licence online live sports channels and to seek advertising revenues through this medium, the alternative is to reduce the costs, and in football... the means players' salaries, good luck with that one! Just look at the music industry and how sites like Napster have forced it to rethink the whole strategy with regard to music distribution. The only company who has managed to monetise the music download industry is Apple and still only 5% of all downloaded music is actually paid for!

The Internet is a destructive technology, not of course destructive for the consumer but in terms of business marketing models it essentially wipes the slate clean! Just look at Skype as an example. Skype deliver more international phone calls than anyone else on the planet, how did that happen? Why didn't one of the huge telecommunications companies do it? How could they let a start up company take over such a huge market so quickly?

The answer is simple, if the large telecoms companies had done this they would have destroyed their own business overnight. It required a start up company with no overheads to exploit the Internet model and with no overheads and low operating costs they could solve the consumers' pain... the high cost of international phone calls. A few years down the line Skype now offer other paid for products and services and even with very low percentage take up the company can be hugely profitable.

The same problems are faced by software giant Microsoft, someone went and changed the game to online products but with such an investment in people and infrastructure the challenge for them has been one of protecting what is there already, but at the same time embracing the new Internet model as a complimentary business running alongside their more traditional products.

Amazon, who now sell almost anything, started in a niche market... an online book store, wasn't there other Book retailers out there? Did the other retailers just not see the possibilities the internet would bring? Were they ill advised?

Are we going to be an Amazon, Skype or Google embracing the future? Or one of those companies that let innovative, open minded others take our business away?

Has Customer Loyalty gone forever?

If we take ourselves back a few years our options for products and services were pretty limited, Industry was more regulated and there was one supplier for Gas and Electricity, one butcher in the local vicinity who did a roaring trade on Saturday as most people were off work and this was the mad shopping day.

Actually did we have choice? In reality we had very few options if we compare this to the marketplace today. Today the world has become a super fast, open season with so many choices, how can we 'see the wood for the trees'? We need a way of cutting through all the chaff to find what we are looking for, a filter... a search engine?

The Internet has enabled almost anyone to 'set up shop' and there is no way to know who is who any more. Loyalty to one brand or another has all but disappeared as price wars and special deals dominate the marketplace.

How many readers of this book started with a Nokia phone and have stuck with them through thick and thin? Hardly any of us I would imagine, is Nokia a bad company? Do they not still make good phones? No we are just much more fickle than ever before, and we should expect the same from our customers. This does not mean that we should not give excellent service, but our business model must allow for customers to 'move on' if they choose.

Niche Your Way To Success?

Innovation and sales intelligence is the way forward. No longer is throwing enough mud at the problem and hoping some will stick the answer. The rules have been turned on their head, as has the Marketing funnel concept. Now we can address a vast market potential at the bottom of the inverted funnel from a humble but clever small investment in our marketing at the top.

To broaden our market share we must become Niche in a global market (if global is our potential). Niche enables us to be passionate about a subject... as passionate as our customers are, really feel their problem, and emotionally hook up with them. When customers get emotionally attached to a product or service they buy it... pure and simple.

By getting Niche we do not need to broadcast our message

to millions (at huge cost) we attract those looking, filtering, and searching for our solution. This will attract our clients to us. It will directly affect our online status with Search Engines, improve our online profile and lead to greater sales volume.

The Searching Phenomena

Searching or Browsing for information on the Internet has become a worldwide phenomena. The ease in which we can find answers to almost any question has turned every computer and even mobile device such as a phone into a window onto a global library of information, products and services. Can you imagine having a global information resource in our hands available to us anytime, anywhere? I still do not think those of us who knew times before the internet really appreciate the enormity of this, and those that have grown up with the Internet have no idea what the problem was before without it!

Online retail sales are set to reach 20% of all retail sales in the UK by 2020 reaching $100 Billion USD. The battle for top positions in search engine results is raging now, but will become ever more competitive as Businesses strive for those elusive top ten first page listings.

It has become a kind of standard to measure the effectiveness of one's Digital Marketing strategy by analysing Google Rankings but is this short sighted? Well Google is undoubtedly the leader in search technology today, and is well equipped with a whole range of analysis tools to measure the performance of the Digital Marketing strategy. But there can only be so many top slots, so if the battle appears fruitless, what then?

It is likely that over time direct searches will be replaced by more 'subliminal' advertisements with products and services which 'fit in' with your personal profile and online presence being proffered. Will this then return us back to the Mass Media days of forced viewing of adverts decided for us?

Searching is likely to be far more granular in the future. At present searches can be restricted to within a country, but a local tradesman is unlikely to travel outside his immediate area. Rankings in such cases would be much more relevant in smaller geographical areas rather than nationally. Locally significant searches will provide solutions for both the business people looking to be found and the clients looking to use their products and services.

We can already see the emergence of a much more sophisticated targeting of adverts in online social media sites such as Facebook where the Advertiser can describe to which demographics and even locations they are happy for their offerings to be advertised.

The Google effect

As we saw earlier in this chapter, Google's ability to monetise the Internet on the back of their search engine tools has lead to the emergence of one of the most influential computer companies in the world.

Almost 100 million searches are performed by Google daily and this represents some 35% or so of all searches in any given day. If we cast our minds back 20 years it is almost inconceivable to imagine how we managed to find information back then! I remember ploughing through encyclopaedia's and going down the library... it all seems so time consuming compared to what is available today.

Now we have information on any subject, any product or service, company, organisation or even person right at our fingertips.

We will discuss 'Search Engine Optimisation' later on in this chapter (the way you can improve your chances of coming up top on searches), and we often hear people talk about Google Rankings and there is no denying that it is the preferred search tool for many. But... it is not the only search tool and it is also operating very often in the cold market too! People finding products and services in the cold market are likely to buy on 14% of occasions, but the percentage rises to 60% when the recommendation comes from a close friend or colleague. Think about it, if you want something, who do you go to? Either someone in your network (business club) or... you use search engines to filter for those offering the services you need so that you have a few choices to consider

Other search engines

Although by far and away the market leader, Google is definitely not alone in the search engine space.

One of the most difficult things to grasp when considering search engine optimisation (sometimes referred to as 'Search Engine Optimism') is that none of the search engines use the same algorithms for determining the results set. In other words that which gets a ranking in the top 10 on Google might not achieve the same in Yahoo and vice versa.

This is a little like the age old battle between Coke and Pepsi, they both have the same ingredients but the results are not the same.

Gearing up specifically for one Search engine or another is also a little like putting all your eggs in one basket. There are stories of Internet Marketers in recent times using, considered by many 'on the edge' practices to ensure top ranking positions, only to find overnight the Search Algorithms had been changed resulting in their online businesses being effectively wiped off the Internet!

A business solely reliant on Rankings is therefore highly exposed and at the mercy of the search engine companies. They are at liberty to arbitrarily change things at will (and with no recourse), and these changes can have a significant effect on your rankings. The key to success on the Internet is to build a multi-faceted strategy not too over reliant on any one area or one service provider.

Social Networks

The emergence of Social Network sites such as MySpace, Facebook, Linked-in and more recently Twitter have now begun to make an impact on Businesses.

***** Stop Press *****

Google announce their latest Social Networking and Micro Blogging platform aimed as a major land grab against Facebook and Twitter. The Product BUZZ comes with some interesting features particularly for Mobile users. It is closely integrated with their Gmail product as well as Google Maps. Google are looking to leverage custom from their 17- million Gmail users, but it will be interesting to see whether there is enough here to pull people away from the fiercely independent Facebook and Twitter platforms.

***** end stop press *****

Initially these sites were seen predominantly as places for friends to connect to each other, share pictures, videos and links to interesting items discovered on the internet...

Now however the social profile of those people registering is changing and we see the middle age group and even older coming on board with equally as much information to share with their friends and family. A recent announcement stated that new sign-ups are most prolific amongst women, in the 50-60 age group.

A new age is dawning with Social Media, one where connections are also potential referrers of products and services, business contacts, suppliers or even employees / employers. Business today must start to look at how they are engaging with this audience which offers freely a huge amount of personal information about themselves, their likes and dislikes, and on a huge range of topics.

Linked-in is a social media network aimed at the professional business market. It is reported that as many as 80% of new employees in the USA are initiated or recruited through sites such as Linked-in.

There have been some cautionary tales relating to social networks too. An employee posted on her wall some comments on her job, how bored she is, and how she disliked her creepy boss... only to receive a letter through the post dismissing her from the job. A few days later a reply on Facebook to the original post from her boss explaining that she must have forgotten she'd accepted him as a friend in the distant past, and he had read everything she had written about him and the company.

Now cases like this are extreme, however there are two important points to take on board about social media :-

Personal Branding

Whether we are running a one person business or are the CEO of a large multi-national, people-buy-people first. Social Media sites allow us to connect with hundreds or thousands of people constantly. These sites give us the opportunity to show our 'human' side, our hobbies, friends and business associates.

There is a famous quote :-

If you have not had the time to get to know a person then you can learn a lot by looking at the people around them

WARNING : In the future, the absence of a social media profile will say just as much about someone as having one.

Social Media Marketing

Facebook signed up 400 million members since its launch in 2004. This is one of the fastest acceptance and adoption of a new innovation ever. The ability to access and market to this vast mass of interacting online people is just starting to be explored.

Check out this link for the Facebook Statistics 2010

http://www.in2theclouds.com/Facebook-Statistics-2010.jpg

This is not a fad, social media is going to revolutionise how we connect with people, buy, sell and build our businesses into the future. It should not... no it must not be ignored. The absolute minimum is that we register and start building our social online presence, even if it is to understand what it is and then reject it as a means of doing business.

At the time of going to press Facebook had turned another page in its evolution. The ability to build and insert custom Tabs and Pages into a Business / Fan page profile.

The significance is that essentially a website can be constructed within the Facebook business page... Now you can ask people to 'Like' your business page and additionally take them through a process similar to the one shown below :-

- Tips, tricks, guidance and advice for free

- Likers can be give a password or URL to see further education or videos (only available to fans)

- Free 30 minute Video or webinar provides access to additional information and introduction to other paid for products and services

Those who 'Like' a business page effectively advertise the Page to others via their timeline and the popularity of the business page can grow virally; provided that the content is useful. Another great feature of these pages is the Discussion board which is like a mini forum all wrapped up in the site, making it interactive and by participation by others, increasing its value in a similar way to Guest Blogging.

This of course builds a list (and pretty quickly too), Administrators of such lists can broadcast to those who have 'liked' business pages… how powerful is that? A great example of a page demonstrating this can be found here **Business Coach Social Media** (http://www.facebook.com/businesscoachsocialmedia). This page generated over 400 fans in less than one week. Excellent for providing useful information and content as an expert and bringing other contributors in to help.

By the time this book is launched there will be a facebook page for the SME7 – 7 Steps to getting the Business you really want!

Still not convinced, check out this video on You-Tube below :-

Social Media is it a Fad?
(http://www.youtube.com/watch?v=pkGIBIuiZcl)

18 months ago in the UK, Twitter was almost unknown, today there are some subscribers who have more followers than the whole population of countries like Ireland or Norway!

One 140 character message can reach over 5 million people instantly. Twitter offers a completely new medium for finding a truly global potential market. Some employers have even been known today to stipulate a minimum of 300 followers on twitter as criteria for hiring someone.

If you think the world is not changing then watch this short video : **Human Capital Edition 2009** (http://www.youtube.com/watch?v=kzCQ219bxl8)

These two videos highlight that we have little choice but to engage with technology, but we have to make sure in our businesses that we use it not get abused by it!

Finally, social media is a medium that will follow us where ever we go. People with a strong social media presence with large numbers of connections or followers built up over time will be the master networkers of the future.

The magic of compounding

Let us return for a minute to the conventional marketing techniques. A simple mail shot may cost us $3-$5 thousand dollars from start to finish, a Radio advertisement $8 thousand dollars and a TV advertisement starting at $75 thousand dollars.

In the case of small and medium sized businesses the most widely used would be a mail-shot strategy. Fairly low budget and with a good follow up strategy can produce some results, although as we know nothing is guaranteed.

The problem with this marketing is that once I have spent my money, run the campaign and experienced the results, to repeat the process I must spend again. For a marketing programme to be successful it must be continuous and spread over a reasonable period. Businesses and individuals must be given more than one opportunity to see something. Perhaps the first advert was missed, the second advert the timing was wrong, the third advert... now the timing is good, and we gain a prospect.

A programme such as the one above requires a long term investment and management time to run and control. It is expensive for small businesses and they rarely have the time to commit to such projects. What will often happen is the plan will be put in place, the first prospects and customers filter through, the workload goes through the roof and then the marketing is dropped because of time constraints.

We all know what happens next... a few months down the road, the prospects dry up, and we're back into famine mode. This continual swing between 'Feast and Famine' is a real challenge for small businesses, and one which Digital Marketing helps to alleviate.

So let us now take a look at Digital Marketing and why perhaps for many this could solve some of the issues with Marketing for Small and Medium sized businesses.

The Internet doesn't forget

When material is posted onto the Internet, whether it be on a website, blog, an article, twitter post or even a forum, the information is indexed and filed. As we continue to post material, this is added to what is already out there working for us

Nothing is wasted

Whatever effort is put into producing information promoting our products, services, skills or knowledge is never wasted. Once it is Web side it starts work.

We can also re-use old material and relocate and post again to try different groups of people at no additional cost

Information can be easily joined together

We can join our Marketing information together building links between new material and existing material already on the Internet.

If a business is interested in what we are saying today, they might be even more interested in what was said before but might have missed it at the time.

We can get others to use our material

As our material is on the internet if another business finds what we are producing complimentary to their services they may reproduce our material on their website or blog for their visitors or subscribers. So long as they provide a link back to our main website or blog, they are free to use our content.

This means that if we produce informative and useful material other companies may actually promote us to an entirely new warm market audience on our behalf. This is at absolutely zero cost to our business.

Low costs

Publishing material onto the Internet is relatively low cost. Material which is used in other areas of the business also can be easily adapted for the Internet.

Today Video's and Audio's created specifically for the Web are not prohibitively expensive and really can make a huge difference to the success of Digital Marketing.

Helps to smooth 'Feast and Famine' syndrome

Because Digital Marketing compounds, each new marketing post adds to all the other previous posts (which continue to work for the business), all of the material continues to work all of the time. In our own business we have had material resurface 3 or 4 years after it was originally posted and this is not a rare occurrence either!

This really can help in a small business where traditionally our marketing drops off along with the prospects as we get busy, then we have to ramp everything up again. Digital Marketing keeps our marketing presence going with minimal time and effort until we are ready to give it another boost.

One of the companies that we worked with during the 3rd quarter of 2008, Blue Autumn in 2008 has experienced some interesting results from embarking on an Digital Marketing programme.

The objective was to raise the profile of the company which had almost no rankings on google… the specific goals were to be found in searches for the key product range : Nurses Uniforms, and then use this new popularity to sign up distributors for the product range in Mainland UK.

Having created a strategy (which Digital Marketing products to use) and then a weekly schedule of activity up to 3 months and beyond, the plan was executed.

1 year on there are some 5 distributors in mainland UK, search engine results put them on the top page for the key products and the most amazing thing is that hardly any Digital Marketing has been done in the past 6 months and because all the initial marketing activity is still working hard out there, the results are still happening.

The Global marketplace

As a population we have never been more connected than we are today. With any computer capable of being connected to a truly global network, we can communicate and market to almost anyone wired-in on the planet.

Now of course as we have already seen, if we are offering a locally based service then the Global nature of the Internet is of little consequence with regard to business development.

If however our business is based on a niche product then there are some great examples of where this has worked really well. Dog and Cat Collars, Cookery books for dogs and specialist eating styles such as

Raw Food and Juicing are a few areas where the Internet has enabled entrepreneurs to reach truly global markets.

Each of the above products / services has appeal to a mass audience, there are 100's of millions of pets and a large percentage of the population both men and women are interested in healthy eating styles and losing weight.

The thing that links these products to appeal to a global nature is low value, light weight or the product is deliverable electronically. The electronic products marketplace has exploded over recent years as suddenly anyone with specialist knowledge (and wants to share it) has access to a potential global market of over 1.5 Billion people. Even with the most 'off-the-wall' hobbies and interests it is possible to find many 100's of thousands of potential buyers when considering a global marketplace.

But it is not just new emerging businesses that can indulge this global market. Take an example of a Greeting card producer. This industry is well developed and is big business in the west but much less developed in many of the countries in Europe. By combining Translation skills, cards could easily be offered for sale and delivery in a much wider market encompassing much of Europe (or indeed anywhere else in the world), without setting up huge international operations.

Greeting cards weigh very little and so lend themselves easily to a global business with relatively low International shipping charges. Combining this with cost effective web based sales and marketing, new markets for companies such as this can be opened fairly easily once Digital Marketing technology is embraced and applied to the business.

Joint Ventures

Digital Marketing as a methodology for increasing Sales using the Internet is not only a series of tools that enables us to market effectively it also represents an opportunity to re-evaluate how we think about business development.

The internet has empowered people to create their own businesses offering their diverse range of skills to a wide audience, as kind of freelance service providers. A super example of this is **Claire Raikes** (http://www.claireraikes.com) who offers 15 years of marketing experience in Brand building in London to her internet based clients.

I recently posted a blog entry where I referred to a paper from the

CBI (Confederation of British Industry) which supports the theory that over the coming years the profile of the working population will change and far more people will be operating specialist services via micro businesses (under 5 people) in the same way that Claire does.

So how does this affect a company wishing to embark on a Digital Marketing strategy?

This explosion of skilled independent businesses can provide a diverse range of services and are available to business owners. This provides us with a rich pool of resources and skills that we would never have tapped into before and certainly could not have afforded to hire on a full time basis.

Joint ventures can take different forms. A simple example of how to use a joint venture might be to simply take on an external resource and share the proceeds of the increased business generated with the JV (joint venture) partner.

A more usual example might be the exploitation of a new business idea where two or more people can form a joint venture, pooling their resources and knowledge to form a virtual business management team. Each member of the JV (joint venture) having clearly identified roles and responsibilities working across potentially large spatial distances... indeed it is possible to operate these virtual units across country borders.

Web based business software as we have seen in Step 3 enables these virtual businesses to be operated by the JV Partners from wherever they happen to be which paves the way to accelerate future collaborations of this type.

We may find in the coming years that this type of business collaboration begins to replaces the more traditional business structure. The SME7 Business philosophy is one based on this concept with each of the key participants running and managing their own businesses but working collaboratively on this project to deliver solutions to clients.

Let us look at another type of Joint Venture (JV) collaboration that might take place. A good example is

K.I.S.S. Training

KISS Training (Keep IT Simple Software Training) a company providing Training services but now developing a different set of products which are Online Training.

How… using Joint Ventures could this business expedite sales of their training skills, products and services?

1. Create a product which has huge potential applicability, for example training on 'Getting started with Blogging' and then undertaking Joint Venture deals with Online Marketers who already have large lists of contacts… in other words by working with others opening up access to large numbers of warm contacts of others.

2. Developing training materials for market leading products or working with Software companies to provide online training for their software solutions. As the Software sales increase so will the training revenues. This also provides huge potential for training on new modules and related products.

The above are just two examples where completely independent business entities can start to work together for mutual benefit. In the 1st option above, the marketing partner is providing useful information to their database of contacts about a relevant product or service. The 2nd option provides the software company with a highly valuable business partner who will ensure that customers make the best use of the software and receive the benefits that they set out to obtain at the start.

JV's are about a win / win / win, a win for the Partner offering the JV opportunity, a Win for the new Partner who can earn an income for participating and a Win for the client who receives a value for money product or service.

Affiliates

Digital Marketing provides us with some clever tools that enable us to enlist the help of happy customers or those wishing to earn money by recommending a good product or service.

Modern shopping carts provide subscription tools for those wishing to recommend a product or service to easily register and then place an advert on their website or Blog site. The name given to this is an 'Affiliate'.

Affiliate promotion works best when the advertisement is complimentary to the Web Site or Blog. For example a bookkeeper site might find a receipt management tool - **BillBandit** (http://www.billbandit.co.uk) for their clients a good affiliate product, and the bookkeeper website owner would earn a commission if and when clients purchased via the advertisement.

How can a 'would be affiliate' find your products and services? Good question, but the Internet has a number of Web Site services specifically aimed at businesses looking for Affiliates. These Affiliate sites provide two main functions:-

Provide Businesses with a place to lodge Product(s) and Service(s) that others can sell and make a commission from recommending to others

A place for Individuals and Businesses to browse products and services that may compliment their own and to be able to earn a commission from any sales that take place as a result.

The market leaders in providing such 'Affiliate Product Banks' are web sites like, **Clickbank** (http://www.clickbank.com), **PayDotCom** (http://www.paydotcom.com) and **Commission Junction** (http://www.cj.com).

Sites offering Affiliate products can handle the entire transaction, i.e. deal with Product Sale (if electronic), take the payment, handle the affiliate fees and transaction charges and then deposit the balance in the Seller's account for future transfer.

The above methodology ensures that the Affiliate receives their commissions as the sales revenue is divided up and placed into the appropriate accounts and does not rely on the Seller rebating the affiliate directly.

In some cases to promote a new product or service it is possible for Affiliates to be rewarded with a very high percentage of the sales price as much as 70%. Couple a good percentage commission with a high ticket priced item the more attractive for an Affiliate to recommend the product. In such cases just a few sales a month can provide a useful additional income.

There are a very large number of successful Internet Marketers who combine a Niche, Affiliate products (e-books) and Joint Ventures to produce significant monthly revenue streams. The success of 'Affiliate Product Banks' is testimony to this interesting online business strategy.

What are the mechanics behind Affiliate Marketing?

When someone uses an affiliate link from a website to go through to a product or service that is being advertised the link itself has some additional information. This information has encoded within it an Affiliate ID. To demonstrate how this might look I have provided a couple of examples below

Destination	Actual Link	Displayed Link
In2TheClouds	http://www.in2theclouds.co.uk	In 2 The Clouds
In2TheClouds	http://www.in2theclouds.co.uk?ID=122345	In 2 The Clouds

In the above example the First **Actual Link** is a pure link... there is no affiliate code, so the visitor is passed to the website and if they were to buy the book, then no one is credited with the referral. If on the other hand the **2nd Actual Link** was used. Notice the ID=122345 bit on the end. Well this is the Affiliate ID, and, if the visitor buys the book... then credit is given to the person / business that is making the recommendation.

Notice in the example above that both of the **Displayed Links** look identical... This is because the actual link and what the reader sees can be completely different.

What happens when an Affiliate Link is Followed?

Once a link is followed with an Affiliate ID, the visitor has a small piece of information written to their computer called a 'Cookie'. A cookie is a tiny text file that contains the details of the website and the affiliate ID. This cookie will remain on the computer until cleared at some point in the future.

How does this 'Cookie' work then? Lets say you were to visit the In2TheClouds web site via an affiliate link but did not buy the book, a cookie would be written away to your computer to indicate who referred you to the site. Then 2 months later you return either directly or via another website link and arrive back on the In 2 The Clouds web site and this time purchase the book, what happens? Well the sales process would look for a cookie on your computer and, providing it has not been deleted (this is sometimes the case about 10% of people might actually have deleted their cookies) the original referrer's cookie would be there and therefore credited with the sale.

Only one Cookie for each product can be stored, working on a first come first served basis… so provided that the visitor returns in a reasonable time frame, the original referrer should still be credited with the sale.

Internet Statistics

Digital Marketing so far sounds pretty good doesn't it? Not prohibitively expensive to 'get started' and a vast potential global audience online to 'sell too'. Continuous compounding information about our products and services which can be found through search engines…

We can engage with others either by setting up Joint Ventures and enlist the help of affiliates to propagate interest in our products and services.

So far we have discussed ideas and concepts, now let us take a look at some of the statistics of the Internet, these numbers will put into context the size and scope of the Digital Marketing potential and underpin any sales forecasts that we might make.

How many people are there in the world?

The first statistic we should look at is the population of the world, how this has changed over time and what it is likely to be in the future. The world population has exploded in recent times and this represents the potential size of the audience that could be reached through the Internet.

Below: Historical Trends and the predicted population crisis (Wallace, King)

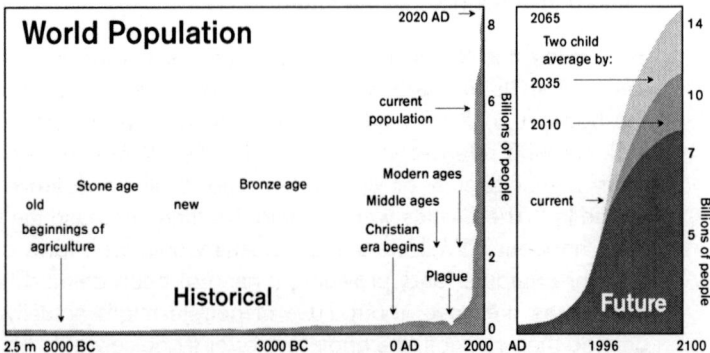

The larger of the two charts above depicts the population of the world from the beginnings of agriculture some 8,000 BC with somewhere in the region of 2.5 million people. For the next 9,000 years the world population managed to grow to around 500 million. Now in the last 200 years the population has grown to 6.75 Billion !!

If we look at the smaller chart to the right we can see that when the chart was created in 1996 the population was almost 6 Billion, and now in 2010 the prediction was for 8 Billion. Well we are now in 2010, and the Population has reached 6.75 Billion, still rapid growth but maybe the growth rate will be less exponential in the coming years.

In reviewing the 'potential' reach of the Internet we can conclude that there is definitely no issue with numbers of possible clients for our products and services.

Even after removing children, those no longer in the working population and those without access to the Internet the numbers are still huge, with an internet audience which stretches into billions rather than millions.

How many People are using the Internet and where?

The first chart below provides us with the raw numbers of Internet users broken down by Geographical Region.

Internet Users in the World
by Geographic Regions - 2009

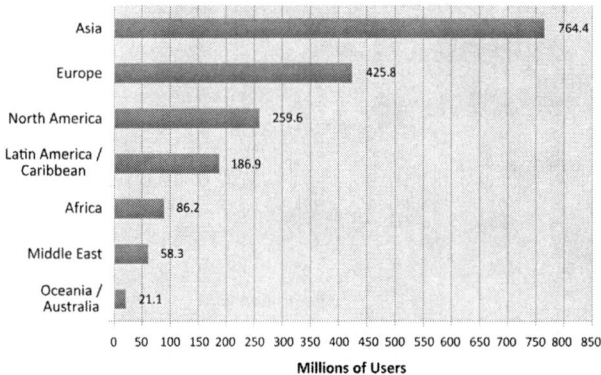

Region	Millions of Users
Asia	764.4
Europe	425.8
North America	259.6
Latin America / Caribbean	186.9
Africa	86.2
Middle East	58.3
Oceania / Australia	21.1

Millions of Users

Source: Internet World Stats - www.internetworldstats.com/stats.htm
Estimated Internet users are 1,802,330,457 for December 31, 2009
Copyright© 2010, Miniwatts Marketing Group

How can we analyse the bar chart above and what is the importance or relevance to our own business?

If your products and services were not tied to a language such as Dog or Cat collars or even as mentioned previously the BillBandit, then the Internet Market is truly global.

If on the other hand the product was an English e-book then the audience might be restricted to English speaking countries and regions, so perhaps parts of Europe, North America, Australia, and areas of Africa.

Most products and services would still even at this stage after applying another level of filtering have a target audience of 10's if not 100's of millions of people.

How many people have still to 'get connected' ?

The Bar chart below shows us what is the percentage of Internet Users compared to the population of the regions.

World Internet Penetration Rates
by Geographic Regions - 2009

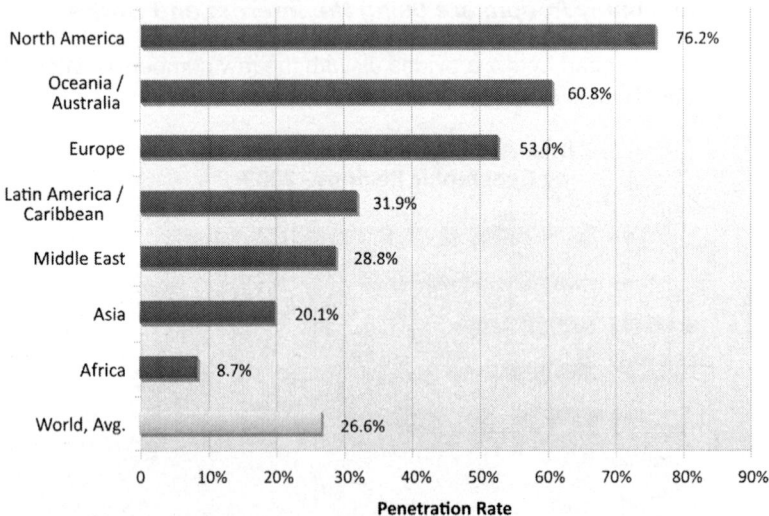

Source: Internet World Stats - www.internetworldststs.com/stats.htm
Penetration Rates are based on a world population of 6,767,805,208 and 1,802,330,457 estimated internet users for December 31, 2010.
Copyright© 2010, Miniwatts Marketing Group

Interestingly, even though in the previous chart the largest number of Internet users was in Asia, this only represents some 20% of the Region's population using the Internet. So this and other developing Regions represent the highest number of future new internet users.

What are the largest Internet User markets ?

Below in the final pie chart we can see the Internet Users broken down as a percentage of the total number of people using the Internet.

World Internet Users Distribution by World Regions - 2009

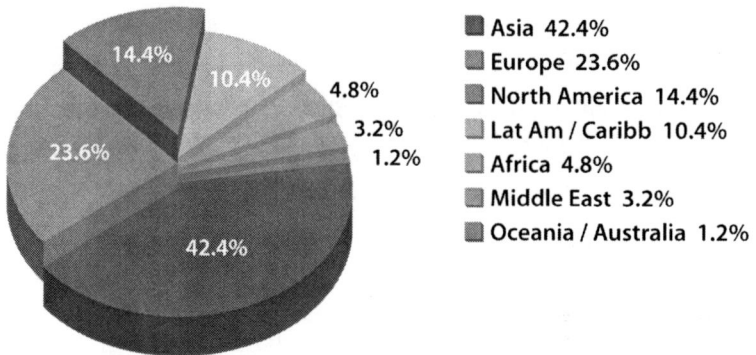

Asia 42.4%
Europe 23.6%
North America 14.4%
Lat Am / Caribb 10.4%
Africa 4.8%
Middle East 3.2%
Oceania / Australia 1.2%

Source: Internetl World Stats - www.internetworldstats.com/stats.htm
1,802,330,457 Internet users for December 31,2009
Copyright 2010, Miniwatts Marketing Group

The sheer size of China and India clearly highlights not only the size of the current market in the Asia Region, but also the phenomenal future potential with only 20% of their population using the Internet currently.

When applying an Digital Marketing strategy to our own businesses, products and services we might reconsider our approach based on some of the statistics shown above.

The International business language is English and to tap into some of the largest economies in the world English is the primary method of business communication on the web. Whether it is Indian or Chinese suppliers looking for new customers in North

America, or UK companies looking for new sources in China, the communication is mostly played out in English.

Consider this interesting statistic… over the coming decade the country with the most English speaking people is predicted to be China !!

So what is it that people are doing on the Internet?

Since the mid 1990's the Internet has existed, but it is a diverse place and can be used for a great many different things. I know people today who will not use the Internet to buy products or services for fear of Credit Card fraud or Identity theft.

As mentioned previously in Step 3 with the Microwave example; some people are early adopters to change and like to be at the forefront of exploration and new technology, whilst it takes quite a bit longer for the 'majority' to be convinced!

Below is a recently produced chart (by Stanford.edu research) breaking down how the Internet is used into a series of common activities.

WHAT USERS DO ON THE INTERNET

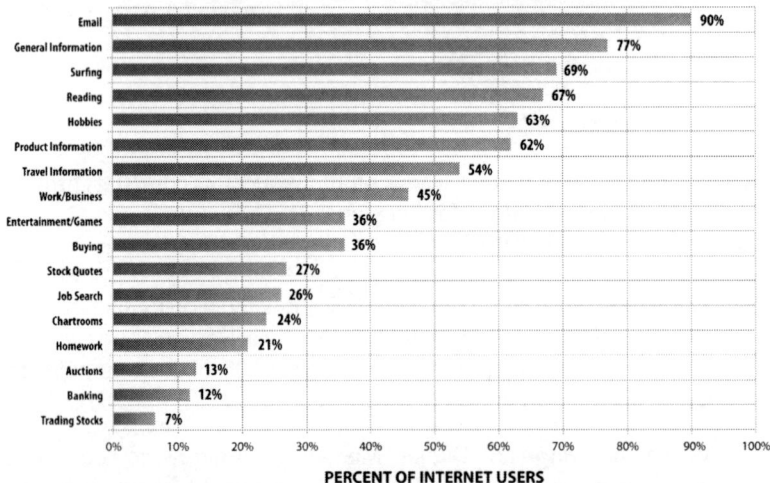

Activity	Percent
Email	90%
General Information	77%
Surfing	69%
Reading	67%
Hobbies	63%
Product Information	62%
Travel Information	54%
Work/Business	45%
Entertainment/Games	36%
Buying	36%
Stock Quotes	27%
Job Search	26%
Chartrooms	24%
Homework	21%
Auctions	13%
Banking	12%
Trading Stocks	7%

PERCENT OF INTERNET USERS

As we might have suspected the highest ranking activities include such things as Email and browsing for information which is where the Internet started back in the mid 1990's. Most people are now comfortable to use the Internet in this way and it has achieved a high level of acceptance.

Must less widely accepted, but still at a fairly respectable 36% we find 'Buying' online. This is the percentage of Internet users that will actually buy something via the Internet. So if our target audience was 150 million Internet users we would still have around 50 million potential customers who might buy our product or service via a website or blog.

Online buying of course will increase over time for a number of reasons :-

1. As the younger population start to enter the main adult population, they will have no qualms about using the Internet for every aspect of daily life.

2. Cost conscious businesses will also drive online trading with reduced Order processing costs improving profitability.

3. Improvements in general Internet security as the industry matures will also build customer confidence and reduce concerns of buying online.

4. Without question the statistics when discussing the Internet involve extremely large numbers. The statistics themselves are irrefutable, and as a basis on which to build a Marketing programme provide us with access to a vast audience.

How we apply this huge resource to our own business and how we maximise the Digital Marketing opportunity is different for every business, but I hope you would agree it shouldn't be ignored.

Viral Marketing

You may have heard this term 'Viral Marketing' so what is it?

In simple terms this is when something catches the imagination of the Reader / Viewer, who then tells (usually via email or through social networking sites such as Facebook or Twitter) other people they know to take a look.

What happens is that 100 people tell 10 each, then that 10 a further 10 and so on…. So in a short period of time 100x10x10x10 is already 100,000 people have been told about an advert, product or service.

The great thing about Viral Marketing is that once kicked off it is virtually unstoppable. Viral Marketing doesn't even have to be necessarily about a product or service either. Susan Boyle of Britain's got talent fame went on to be a world-wide phenomena during 2009 with the publishing on You-Tube of her performance. In one night alone the video was viewed over 20 million times!!

[http://www.youtube.com/watch?v=RxPZh4AnWyk]

Video is a great medium for promoting a product or service, a Furniture company came up with an innovative idea to advertise their products wrapped up in an action video with a really amusing twist at the end...

[http://www.youtube.com/watch?v=X7MVtgXMcll]

Viral marketing can produce amazing results quickly if planned and executed effectively. Large businesses are beginning to wake up the power of using viral marketing to promote services as the first viable alternative to TV. It is now possible to get 100's of thousands of viewers watching a video via YouTube which is equivalent to a Commercial TV advert but for a fraction of the price. We are likely to see a huge shake up in the commercial Television marketplace as advertising strategies begin to include the Internet.

A product or service that will be using Viral marketing techniques during 2010 to increase market penetration is

[http://www.billbandit.co.uk]

A series of Internet YouTube Advertisements are planned and it will be interesting to watch progress as the campaign develops.

SEEDING is a term often used in conjunction with Viral Marketing. Clearly the success of Viral Marketing techniques is the speed with which the project can hit critical mass in terms of numbers.

To help achieve a 'Fast Start' businesses now exist that will push the message into the market consistently over a defined period through all the common channels, e.g. PR Sites, Article Sites, Video Hosting Sites, Social Networks and Twitter. Once a successful initiation has taken place the viral nature of the Internet should sustain a steady stream of readers / viewers with little further investment.

Niche Marketing

There is an age old saying in Marketing which states 'either get big or get niche'. There has never been a better time to 'get niche' than now as the Global Internet Market takes shape.

Consider a Pet Shop in a major town in England. The Pet Shop sells a range of products for Cats, Dogs, Hamsters, Rabbits, Guinea Pigs and Budgies amongst a host of other paraphernalia which is Pet related.

The Pet Shop owner wants to take advantage of the Internet to increase business. Clearly sales of the pets themselves is not viable via the Internet nor are many of the bulky items such as beds and cages. Even consumables such as Feeds don't meet the weight / frequency criteria for a good match with selling online, certainly not internationally.

There are two products which have already proven themselves to work very well on the Internet in this field and that are completely Niche and would work well for our Pet Shop Owner.

Dog and Cat collars – are relatively low cost items, but with a huge variety and light enough to ship internationally. A second option could be cookery books for Cat and Dog owners to prepare good food for their beloved pets. Also light enough and cost effective enough to ship internationally.

Both of the above examples have great marketing attributes :-

1. Huge target audience of Pet Owners... globally

2. Dog and Cat collars are not language dependent

3. Good product margins

4. The product is visual and can be displayed easily via online shopping carts

5. The products are light enough to be cost effective for international shipping

6. There is a 'repeat' opportunity from satisfied customers, collars wear out

7. Expansion ready. Other products which suit the criteria can be added later to make new sales to existing customers

8. Coupled with a Pet Tips and Tricks opportunity to create a large database of Pet Owners to market to through email

9. JV (Joint Venture) with other Pet related Internet Businesses

10. Affiliate potential from other Pet loving Blogs and enthusiasts

Because the Internet contains such a huge community it is possible to become very niche and still work with a big enough potential audience. Products such as Old Steam Train memorabilia for example have a worldwide following and yet in your own area there might be just a small handful of collectors. What might have been quite unviable as a business venture prior to the Internet can now be exploited because of the global opportunities. The internet has given us a methodology to hook up with people who have a similar passion or product need regardless of location.

When applying Digital Marketing to an existing 'offline' business, the key is to make a start. Working with a subset of your product / service range makes it easier to get up and going and provides excellent feedback and experience invaluable for future projects.

The Long Tail

Products have a natural life cycle. There is the beginning when the product first comes out, then the stabilisation as the product achieves maturity and then the end, when the product is superseded, retired or considered 'out of date – no longer current'.

In the UK, Europe and North America the average life cycle of a computer might be just about 3 years, however the actual model that we purchase on any given day might only be available for 6 months before a replacement supersedes it.

The same story can be applied to mobile phones and many other electronic gadgets as the pace of change accelerates.

But… and it is a big but, this is in the west if we look further a field in less developed countries such as Africa, parts of Asia and South America current products are sometimes years behind where we are today in the West.

I remember many years ago visiting Sri Lanka and being bewildered at the cars still in use… most of which disappeared from streets in the UK 20 years previous. The same is true in Cuba and many other countries around the Globe.

The Long Tail is a phrase which signifies the extended marketability of products (and services) long after their regular life end. The Global aspect of the Internet enables these products and services to be offered for sale cost effectively via web sites and at low cost long after they would normally have been discontinued. It could be argued that these products are in fact Niche products now that their normal lifecycle is complete.

Some great examples of products which have developed a long tail include Music in different formats from old Vinyl records and out of production CD's to pre DVD Video's and even comics and magazines from years gone by.

What are the components of Digital Marketing?

So far we have established that Traditional Marketing techniques for small businesses are quite expensive and not as effective as perhaps they at first were. We have also seen how the Internet has given rise to a completely new method of Marketing products and services. In the last section we have seen that Digital Marketing gives us access to vast global marketplace and millions of potential customers right on our own doorstep.

In this section we look at what are the components of Digital Marketing and cover some of the more common terms used by those offering Digital Marketing services.

What are Keywords?

The name would appear to be self explanatory, but there is a bit more to keywords than you might expect. As the name suggests Keywords are words or phrases that might be used to locate the products or services that are being offered. Keywords are important for two main reasons :-

- Searching

- Describing the Product and / or Service

Search engines now consist of highly sophisticated Algorithms and when evaluating a web page, they are not only looking for the presence of the word or phrase being searched, but at the content as well, to see whether it is congruent with the search word.

In other words... if you were looking for a new Collar for your pet dog you might use the search term 'Dog Collars'. Web sites or Blogs with the term 'Dog Collar' on them would have already been indexed. If the content of the pages additionally had, 'Dog Leads', 'Dog Leash', 'Dog Harnesses', 'Pet Products', 'Dog Bowls', 'Dog Beds', 'Dog Supplies'.... Then it would be clear to the search engine that this really is a Web site or Blog that is providing products and services for Dogs and the ranking would be higher than those pages with just the word 'Dog Collars' on them.

So clearly Keywords (or phrases) are very important as are similar words or phrases that mean the same thing or are associated / linked to the main word or phrase. Careful thought needs to be put into your selection of Keywords… one big mistake often committed is not to spend enough time researching and selecting appropriate Keywords for your business.

Keyword Tools

Search companies such as Google and Yahoo continuously collect data as we use their search engines. Each time we search the words we have used in the search are stored. This provides a very useful database of actual search terms that people have used to find things.

Search companies then provide us with tools that give us access to this database to analyse how many times people have used the kind of words or phrases that describe what we do.

So for example I found **Google keyword tool** by typing into the Google search box : google keyword tool

Then by entering the words **Cloud Computing** into the Keyword or Phrase box the following (just a sample of them) were displayed :-

Cloud Computing

The Cloud Computing

Cloud computing services

Cloud computing hosting

Cloud computing blog

Windows cloud computing

Cloud computing uk

Open source cloud computing

Computing in the cloud

Cloud computing security

Cloud computing ready

About cloud computing

Top cloud computing

Secure cloud computing

Cloud computing books

Cloud computing marketing

As you can see they are all variations on my original keyword. Each of these has been searched on before and the Keyword Tool shows how many times the word or phrase has been used in a month, which will indicate how popular that key term is.

The Keyword tools will also look at the word or phrase and make other suggestions about keywords you might like to also consider, below are a few examples of these :-

Cloud services

Cloud Platform

Cloud Engineering

Cloud final fantasy

Cloud conference

Cloud servers

Cloud computing consultancy

Cumulus cloud

Stratus cloud

As you can see, some of the above might be relevant but others about types of cloud formation, Cumulus and Stratus are not.

The main point with Keywords is to try and engineer your content to include as many relevant keywords as possible. So for example I may use a good selection of the above and then combine that with some keywords based around **Web based business systems** or **Working from home** or **Virtual business systems.** By carefully integrating these keywords and phrases into our content we significantly improve our chances of being more highly ranked by the search engines.

Keyword Effectiveness

Continuing with the example above, clearly a word which is very often typed into search engines is **Business Software**, but how useful would this word be on our web or blog site?

This brings us onto the effectiveness of Keywords. A keyword or phrase may be typed into a search engine thousands of times a day, but does this make it a good word to include on our Web site or blog pages?

For us to be able to understand the importance or relevance of a Keyword or Phrase we need to understand not only how many times it is searched for but how many other Blogs or Websites this word is already being used on.

Different Keyword tools may use their own word for this facility, but it is a measure of the competition for the Keyword or Phrase that we are looking for here.

For example we may have a Keyword which in 1 month is used over 200,000 times… we might on the first take think, 'now that is a good keyword', but if this Keyword is already used on 40 million pages, then the chances of our page being indexed highly by the search engines is very remote.

What we are looking for here are Keywords or Phrases with perhaps 1,000 or so searches but where the number of pages is in the low thousands or less.

OK the volume in the above example might not be high, but on those keywords or phrases it shouldn't take that long to start featuring on the first page of Google or Yahoo for those terms, which will result in potential enquiries or prospects.

A great example of where this was performed successfully was a client called Blue Autumn, a manufacturer of Tunics and Uniforms primarily for the Healthcare and related industries, such as Dentists, Beauticians, Chemists and Vets. James spotted that Nurses Uniforms specifically in Northern Ireland was a good Keyword / Phrase that certainly had potential with some of the qualities highlighted above. Within a few months James was featured on the Google front page.

With continued use of the main Digital Marketing strategies and by building this and other similar keywords into his content with a very small amount of ongoing effort James managed to maintain his search ranking position and has subsequently received some excellent leads... and grown the business.

Traffic and visitors is one thing, attracting those who are about to spend money with us is another. Receiving 100's of visitors who do just that, visit... doesn't reward us for our efforts, on the other hand 100 visitors who have done all their research and are just about to buy is another proposition I am sure you would agree?

So how can we separate out the two? Well we can become even more cute with our Keyword analysis. Let us take a look at a few examples of using keywords and how by adding a few extra word qualifiers we can target our audience more accurately. Below are the different search results we receive from the variations:-

Sony netbooks	246,000
Sony Netbook p series	1,000
Cheap Flights	16,600,000
Cheap Flights lastminute	1,000
cheap flights weekend breaks	140
Cloud Computing	673,000
Cloud computing uk	720

By embedding within our Web or Blog site more specific keyword (phrases) we can target those that are 'ready to buy'. The traffic might not be so large on the downside, but on the other hand, the visitors are much more likely to be in a buying frame of mind.

What is a Blog?

I first heard about Blogs back in 2004, however this was sometime after they first started to make an appearance, which was around the turn of the century.

The first simple incarnations of Blogs enabled a user to create a kind of online journal on whatever topic they had chosen. So for example someone might be interested in Fashion and so they started a Blog about this hobby. The Blogger (the person who's blog it is) then can write a new report (blog post) and attach an image of their own, or could make a comment and then refer (using a web link – hyperlink) to other pages elsewhere on the Internet that might contain the information they are discussing in their report.

Of course it wasn't long before professional blogging platforms such as Wordpress, Typepad, Blogspot, Blogger and a whole host of others turned simple blogging into a much more sophisticated business.

Soon simple blogs could be tailored to have a completely different look and feel. Businesses could now set up Blogs with their company colours and artwork and started to look a little bit more like regular websites.

What changed blogging irreversibly was that Blogs began to be indexed and searchable just the same as Websites had previously. Suddenly User Generated content was being looked at in the same way that websites had been in the past, Blogging power had definitely arrived!

As can be imagined, it was now possible for anyone or business to sign up for a Blog (some popular ones even at zero cost), and to start promoting themselves. Effectively the Internet had been put into the hands of ordinary not highly technical people.

Since the early years of Blogging a bewildering range of Blogs now exist ranging from a simple informative Blog such as my own **IPS Blog site** http://www.ips.co.uk right through to sophisticated web site looking blogs such as those on offer at http://www.studiopress.com have now taken their place on the Internet.

Blogging today is a versatile, easy to use platform that anyone can work with and gives us the ability to be our own Information Publishers. Some great uses that a Blog can be put to are shown below :-

1. Daily activity journal

Blogs give us the ability to express ourselves, say whatever we want, tell our story, share information with the whole Internet community.

Friends and family can also get in on the act with Blogs, sharing their own news across spatial distances, even on the other side of the world!

I started my own personal blog in April 2008. This blog (link below) was initially created for my own use to chart what I had been learning with Digital Marketing and record the business progress. It has now turned into a kind of Journal that is religiously kept up to date!

http://www.chrisogle.com

2. Special Interest Information

If you have a passion and enjoy sharing your passion with others then a blog can be a great way to express yourself.

Below is a great example of a Blog that fits exactly in this bracket. It can also serve as a personal advert which could attract business proposals, job offers and a whole range of interesting opportunities.

http://seaofshoes.typepad.com

3. News Reporting

The media were very quick to pick up on the power and speed of blogging. Nowadays information passes around the internet at speeds that make newspapers and TV appear very slow indeed. Blog posts can communicate news and information at lightening speeds.

A great example of a political reporter's Blog, Nick Robinson can be seen on the BBC website.

http://bbc.co.uk/blogs/nickrobinson

4. Local Information Sites

The advent of the Blog has provided local community organisations and social groups the chance to get their information out there and onto the web. Typically this function would have been provided by local newspapers, but with space a premium and costs associated with image / type setting and production there is a limit to how much space can be given to promoting these kinds of services. Local Newspapers have to earn money so there is always a conflict between information / news and advertisements.

Blogs break through this completely and allow the people who are running the organisations or making the news to report directly on what is happening. Collaborative Blogging (where more than one person can contribute to a blog) enables the work load to be shared out amongst a number of people so the burden doesn't fall just on one person. A great example of a community blog is shown below which is the Table Tennis Blog for Watford.

http://www.watford.tabletennisblogs.com

5. Sports Clubs

Blogs really do come into their own in situations such as Sports Clubs. The example below is a Blog for a local Rugby club here in Chesham, Buckinghamshire, England.

With Women's and Men's Teams, Matches every week, a highly active junior section, photo archive, Club Rugby Tours and a lively social scene the club represents a mini community in its own right. Contributions can come from any member of the club and being as there is no office location the ability to update and edit the site from home by multiple people provides a rich, living, breathing resource for everyone to enjoy.

http://www.cheshamrugbyclub.com

6. Charitable causes

Blog sites on the Internet enable us to draw attention to good causes and special needs too. With the ability to publish content easily and to update the information on a regular basis, as things develop it is easy to communicate with the audience / participants.

Many hands make light work and with the ability to collaborate across spatial distances makes the Internet an ideal way to share the workload and reach many people even internationally.

The Internet has also seen some creative concepts for On-line donations and tools to assist with charitable work. This has enabled charities and good causes to reduce their cost base by using the internet as a means to promote and collect donations without large numbers of administrators making more money available for the cause itself.

A good example of a charitable blog and one that I am personally involved in is shown below. William Maybanks is a young talented British Table Tennis player who is seeking donations so that he can reach the 2012 Olympics, and then the site itself which can be re-used for other aspiring athletes.

http://www.willmeon.com

7. Product / Service Sales Blog

Now that it is so simple to publish useful and interesting information about your hobby, specialist subject, or even your own micro business it stands to reason that you could offer products and services through Blogging.

With a global marketplace at your fingertips, people now realise that your knowledge is worth something and that if you offer a product or service which is unique, good quality and value for money then the business of blogging can be turned into an income stream.

There are literally thousands of businesses out there on the Internet being run and managed by regular, non technical people who are turning Blogging into a conduit for both making online sales and generating business for offline products and services.

A couple of examples are shown below :-

http://www.stevewatsononline.com - Internet Marketing

http://www.kisstrainingonline.com - Online Training

8. Business Web Sites

Nowadays when it comes to deciding how you want to represent your business on the Internet it is not as clear cut as perhaps it used to be.

Prior to Blogging if you needed a web presence then it was fairly straight forward, you enlisted the help of a web designer. Today however so many widgets and plug-ins (more on these later) can be added to the basic Blog site that fairly comprehensive and complex sites can be put together quite quickly and at low cost.

By plugging in tried-tested and proven add-ons (and new ones are coming into existence all the time) and by using a Blog Platform that is very Web friendly (that means search engines like them) it is possible to have a site which gives some serious benefits e.g. :-

- Easy to add / change and manage content yourself

- Blog built in to provide constant new reports, information and updates on the business, new customers and staff news (good for search engines)

- Very low cost (good for the budget)

- Internet Friendly – good search results

- Lots of features that can be easily plugged in to extend the functionality of your site

- Many different designs and styles to choose from to make your site stand out from the others

- Easy to integrate with other online applications such as Membership Plug-ins, Social Networking tools, Shopping carts, Databases and many more.

Blogs are starting to evolve into a well developed start position for kicking off a new business and it is no wonder they are exceedingly popular.

A whole 'cottage-industry' has emerged providing 'getting you started' Blog building services to Business Owners. These Blog Specialists have detailed knowledge of Blogging platforms, are constantly informed of the latest widgets and ad-ons that are available and will get you up and running in days not weeks or months.

The great thing about Virtual Blog building specialists is that they can work from anywhere, so now you can use the best resources and it doesn't matter where they are located. Two such examples are shown below :-

http://www.businessblogangel.com

http://www.justaskjean.co.uk

Both of the above are of course Blog sites, businesses and created on a Blog Platform!

Two more examples of sites that have been created by the services of Blog Building specialists are below :-

http://nicolacairncross.com   Wealth coaching

http://www.kisstrainingonline.com   Online Training

9. Membership Sites

One of the key ways to monetise a website is to develop a membership site. The key to a membership site is that the content is constantly updated and that the subscribers will want to keep returning to consume the content.

An example of a Niche product that offers subscription services is the **Financial Times** (http://www.ft.com) newspaper. They do provide free content, but if you want to get into the details of the newspaper as per the printed form then a subscription is required. It works for the Financial Times which sets it apart from other newspapers because of the Niche nature of the news. A more general news content would not work as this is freely available on the web.

On a much smaller scale the **Inner Circle - Judith Morgan** (http://judithmorgan.com/inner-circle) provides membership on a number of levels from a free entry point through to the Pink Inner Circle. This is a business and financial advice club and works within a wordpress blog.

There are a number of dedicated Private Membership platforms a little like private Facebook applications. Two that I am familiar with are :-

Ning Networks (e.g. http://www.sme7.net, Private network for SME7 Clients & Practitioners)

SocialGo (http://www.socialgo.com)

With Wordpress fast becoming an application building platform there are now some interesting plug-ins which turn an ordinary wordpress site into a functional Membership site… Judith's site above uses the first two of the plug-ins listed below…

WishListProducts (http://www.wishlistproducts.com)

– Membership plug in for Wordpress

wpMingle (http://www.wpmingle.com/mingle-wordpress-plugin/) – Social Profile add in for Wordpress

The above two products work together to provide a nice Social Membership site that works seamlessly with your Wordpress Blog.

Another Wordpress plug-in that may be of value to those wishing to work within the Blogging framework is this forum add-on **Simple Press Forum** (http://simplepressforum.com).

10. Corporate Sites

As the transition from traditional Web Sites to Blog based websites gathers pace we can see the emergence of companies specialising on creating a range of diverse templates that can be adapted depending on the type of Blog that is required.

Three great examples of companies making a business out of creating starting templates that can be adapted for Blog / Corporate websites are :-

http://templatic.com

http://www.studiopress.com

http://www.woothemes.com

Studio press have developed a range of templates that are engineered for different types of needs from a corporate feel to a magazine style. Their own site is developed with one of their own themes as is the Wordpress Blog based on their Corporate theme below :-

http://www.billbandit.com

As can be seen these blog sites are now almost indistinguishable from traditional web sites but come built in with such a high level of functions, add-ons and inherent Internet friendly technology that in most cases they are more than adequate for conventional corporate sites.

Let us just take a quick look now at some of the key components of Blogs that make them so attractive as the first step towards Digital Marketing and promoting Products and Services.

Subscribing to a Blog

The concept of a Blog is effectively a website which comes with a set of tools for you to easily add updates (called blog posts) to report on new items that you think will be of interest to your audience.

The big problem with websites however is that people are busy and they either don't remember to come back, can't be bothered, or are just plain too busy to do it. Even if the information that you are providing is really useful to the readers, they may never get to see it.

That's where Subscription to a Blog comes in! Within the Blog it is possible to set up an automatic Feed... so that anyone who subscribes to the blog can be notified when anything changes. Normally this can be done either by email or to a 'Feed Reader' (a piece of software designed to store all your updates from all the blogs that you might have subscribed to).

This really is a huge benefit to blogging and works both ways of course... now we can keep up to date with everything that is going on with the Blog sites that we are interested in... but also others can be automatically notified as we add new content to our own Blog site.

By providing interesting and varied content we can quickly build a large list of subscribers to our Blog site. Remember this list is a warm contact database consisting of people and businesses that may be interested in our Products and Services!

Widgets and Plug-ins

The great attraction to Blogs is that you can quickly turn a basic site into something quite sophisticated. With some standards already implied for column widths in the most common blog platforms a wide range of add on mini programs now exist and can be deployed to give functionality and interest to your site.

Some good examples of this are below :-

A time scheduler and booking application

http://www.web-appointments.com

A Visitors history and where the visit came from plug-in

http://www.feedjit.com

Each of the mini Applications can be tailored by you for colours and style to fit in with your sites colour scheme and there are generally a few options on presentation too.

http://Sharethis.com is a great little widget that allows visitors to easily share your Blog post with their network. This is a nice little tool that helps others to promote your content.

http://friendfeed.com is another add-on that you can locate onto your Blogsite. Friendfeed will collect all your posts from many of the popular web based social networking sites such as Facebook, Twitter, You Tube and present it altogether in one place. You can then locate on your blog a summary of the recent posts, providing content from multiple sources that magically appears on your Blog automatically !!

Wordpress is leading the field for Plug-Ins that can turn a simple Blogging platform into a comprehensive business tool… check out the range of Plug-Ins available via the **Wordpress Plug-in Site** (http://wordpress.org/extend/plugins/).

Monetising a Blog

As we have already seen there are a wide variety of reasons why a Blog might come into being. It could be for a charity, Business, Personal, purely information, community or even support for a group of people.

Ultimately the Blog will receive visits and if very popular a great many visits and possibly global attention. With such an audience of course comes the possibility to turn pure attention into the potential for generating income.

The primary purpose of the site might be to provide help and advice on Diabetes for example, but as with any Journal or Magazine in printed form they might carry some advertisements. So it is with Blogs, a large percentage of the readership on a Diabetes web site would possibly be Diabetics and so interested in products or services that could help control and manage the condition. The next step would be to strike up a relationship with a vendor of products that might be appropriate (a JV – Joint Venture) and agree how any orders are to be transferred, fulfilments costs that need to be considered, shipping costs, reporting on sales and commission percentages.

There are many examples of Blog sites that have become immensely popular, initially created because of an individuals passion and labour of love then going onto become a valuable saleable asset with the potential to generate a large income.

There is now a well established market trading in Blogs themselves. Blogs constructed and that have a large number of subscriptions depending on their market can have a high value for the owners.

Other ways to monetise a blog include offering affiliate products such as e-Products that can be found on Clickbank, PayDotCom or Commission Junction. It is even possible to locate a series of books and create your own personal book store using Amazon and offer a whole range of relevant e-books via a Blog.

Micro-Blogging (Twitter)

This is a term that is now used for products such as **Twitter** http://twitter.com. A service, similar to mobile phone texting which invites users to post 140 characters answering the question : What are you doing right now?

These 140 character status updates are posted onto your page within Twitter, and anyone following you automatically receives your updates. You are also able to follow others and receive their status updates too.

The great thing about Twitter is that you can add to your blog a feed from Twitter that will automatically post your status onto your blog site. So with one simple post updates can go to both Twitter and also onto the blog(s).

Twitter and http://twitpic.com (a photo sharing site which links with Twitter) can be updated via Mobile phone applications as well as through sending a text and or email.

The power of Micro Blogging is that even on the move and from anywhere with a mobile connection it is now possible to post instant updates to blogs and social media platforms maintaining communication with those that are interested.

To find out more about Twitter, listen to this Online Radio show: **Why Twitter Works - by Mark Shaw** (http://www.blogtalkradio. com/louisebj/2009/08/03/flr-28-why-twitter-works).

Micro-Blogging (latest developments)

Just to prove how fast the Internet is moving, as I am writing this book so I became aware of a micro blogging platform that essentially allows organisations or interest groups to set up their own micro blogging space.

Micro Blogging has now been recognised as a very useful method of sharing information between personnel in large organisations and also with customers. This new micro blogging platform which is called http://status.net allows for greater use of Micro Blogging in many different forms, I have given some examples below :-

- Interest groups wishing to share information about a particular passion or subject such as Ex-Pats living overseas.

- Internally within large organisations such as British Petroleum (BP) or Craft

- Business Community such as http://www.sme7.com where customers, consultants, trainers and service providers can share and communicate in a dedicated environment

- Charities and Social communities

The possibilities for this collaborative messaging are endless. It is also possible to link these feeds with Twitter and Facebook accounts to extend the information outside of the 'closed' group to a wider audience.

Mash-ups

As indicated above the Internet is evolving very fast. The internet is a hot bed of entrepreneurial spirit and new products, services and links to other applications are emerging constantly.

The term Mash-up has been given to the 'joining-together' or linking between web based applications. Some great examples have been fuelled by the explosion of Twitter which at the time of writing this book had reached 27 million subscribers in about 1 year.

API's (Application Programming Interfaces) are tools offered by software developers to allow other software applications to extract information and present in other systems. There are many applications written to provide additional functions that compliment the basic Twitter product such as :-

http://hootsuite.com

http://www.tweedeck.com

These tools allow the manipulation of multiple twitter accounts, the creation of custom views to home in on your favourite fellow followers.

Mash-ups now link many web applications, Twitter can update Facebook automatically. Blogging platforms like Typepad have features to update Facebook, Twitter accounts and other social networking sites.

Mash-ups help us to input information into one application and then have that information replicated for us into our other online services without any manual effort. Once set up our online presence will become one big interconnected information resource with data being exchanged seamlessly between them.

Going back many years the term Mash-up could have referred to the task of integrating business applications so that they talked to each other. Today on the Internet online tools are already going through this integration process. As more and more software products become available in 'the cloud' the potential for bringing together data from a wide variety of sources is very exciting indeed.

Mash-up (breaking news)

Just as I seek to draw a line on what goes into this book, something crops up too important to leave out!

Above I discussed the emergence of a Micro Blogging platform StatusNet.. This is the inevitable production of a service which replicates the features of Twitter but which can be customised for a particular purpose, large company message board, charities, collaborative business information sharing etc. etc. now comes another exciting development...

Social Oomph (http://www.socialoomph.com) has been designed to enable individuals to manage and control multiple micro blogging accounts. There are people, myself included that have more than one twitter account each with a specific purpose. Couple this with participation in multiple StatusNet micro blogging groups (as this grows), it is easy to see that management and control will become a bit of a nightmare.

Social Oomph allows us to bring together all the Micro Blogging channels that we might be working with, including multiple twitter accounts, facebook and other social sites all under one roof.

Tools now exist to filter posts, auto follow people with the right criteria, vet and approve, auto direct message across multiple micro blogging accounts.

Twitter was the first Micro Blogging platform, StatusNet have moved micro blogging on to provide us with Micro Blogging groups, Social Oomph and tools like it will enable us to manage these and no doubt others like it as this exciting area develops.

Blogging in the Future and Live Web

With the announcements that 'Twitter posts would feature in Search engine results the dynamics of the Internet has changed forever'. Why is this statement so important?

Let us consider the pre twitter searching... Web sites were developed and information posted, this is then indexed and made available in search results. All very controlled and content driven.

Nowadays the search results could be heavily influenced by what is being said right now by people on Twitter. Imagine a damning report on a product or service or a report on an event that has suddenly happened in the world... this information immediately enters the public domain... we can all become effectively instant reporters on the web... This has been labelled **Live Web**

If you thought information travelled fast on the Internet already, watch out we haven't seen anything yet! Once **Live Web** takes hold, communication will be almost instantaneous.

Live Web at the time of writing this book was very new, but let us just take a moment to analyse the impact it will have on our lives going forward.

Twitter allows us to communicate from anywhere and push information immediately into a searchable global database. This global database is a living, breathing resource that anyone can use to find out what 'real people' are talking about, doing or want to tell us. This is not News Reporters doing their job, nor is it about topics or subjects that others might deem worth publishing, this is actually what is happening, right now by regular people... and searchable!

Bill Gates the ex boss of Microsoft and the richest man in the world joined Twitter the other day to share with those wishing to follow him what is happening with his charity the Bill and Melinda Gates Foundation.

He picked up more than 150,000 followers in his first 13 hours on the website

Yes.... that is 13 HOURS.... Which means over 3 people every second! No wonder twitter was a bit slow and overloaded that day which happened to coincide with increased activity from those sharing news of the horrors in Haiti.

Using new Search tools such as **twazzup** (http://www.twazzup.com) or **twitter search** (http://www.search.twitter.com) we can find out what is happening in the world right now.

If you want to find out who is saying what about Bill Gates entering the world of blogging on twazzup then follow the link below :-

http://www.twazzup.com/?q=billgates

If we want to find out what people are saying about the earthquake tragedy in Haiti during January 2010 or the continued repair and restoration work taking place there via twitter search then we can follow this link :-

http://search.twitter.com/search?q=Haiti

These tools are giving us direct access into information as it happens from anyone of us choosing to share and this is the first time in history we have been so connected. This is all very interesting of course, but what is the relevance to me and my business you might ask?

With a global search facility we can quickly and easily locate those people who are making news or comments about topics relating to those we may be passionate about (or those that might benefit from what we have to offer) anywhere in the world. Now we have tools to find them, connect with them and to follow them. We can post messages that will appear on their timeline (their lists of activities on their account).

By researching words that people are using in 140 characters we can establish connections to people that could be interested in what we are doing like never before.

There are now tools available that can even automate the process to find and connect to people that are out there in twitter-land… a good example of such a product is shown below :-

twittollower (http://twittollower.com)

This service works on the principle that there are key players in any niche in the twitter-sphere who have very large lists of followers and that by working on getting their followers to follow you, then your followers will grow quickly and automatically.

The link above has an interesting video which includes how Dell have 100 people offering refurbished and second user equipment for sale via twitter and have double turnover to $6 Million. Can you imagine 100 people employed to tweet all day marketing products… that is a significant investment that a major corporation is putting into micro blogging and the live web phenomena.

Websites to view statistics and monitor growth trends for any twitter account now exist such as http://www.twittercounter.com, a useful site that graphically charts followers over various time intervals.

There were about 27 Million Twitter users at the time of writing this book… 27 Million people reporting in on what is going on in their lives, what is 'on their mind ' or interesting snippets of information that they want to share with others. Live Web is about to change the power of the Internet once again.

Why have a Website?

It would appear looking at the advantages of Blogs that the days of having a custom purpose built website are coming to an end.

This actually is far from the truth. The arrival of sophisticated blogging requires us to analyse more carefully what we are trying to achieve and then to choose the most appropriate means of delivering it.

Before we start looking at websites in more detail, let us first analyse what the term Web Site actually means, the actual definition on **Wikipedia** (http://www.wikipedia.org) is :-

A Web Site is a collection of related web pages, images, video or other digital assets that are addressed with a common domain name or IP Address in an Internet Protocol based network. A Web Site is hosted on at least one web server via a network such as the Internet or a private local area network.

So by the definition above actually all Blog Sites are by default Web Sites but those that are created within a defined structure and editable via a series of tools provided to us for that purpose.

Why would we want to create a Web Site then?

Sales Pages

In the first instance the information or Page(s) that we want to 'put out there' on the Internet might be too simple to warrant a Blog. Blog sites are generally designed to serve an ongoing need and be regularly updated, but what if our site didn't need updating and was designed to just serve a specific purpose?

Let's have a look at an example. We want to sell an e-book, the entire purpose of the Web Site (which will only be one page) is to sell the Book. This page will include an introduction to the e-book, describe what is in it and what you will get out it. It could contain a video about the author covering their background and experience which will build their credibility. It will also have some reviews from people who have lucky enough to receive a pre-release copy to read in return for providing a review of the book.

The final element on this page will be a BUY NOW button and a price, followed by additional sales messages encouraging the reader to not delay and get their copy right now!

This Sales Page is effectively a single page web site. People (me included) often think of a Web Site as a complex huge site such as **Amazon** (http://www.amazon.com) where it is possible to spend a whole day and not see everything. But actually the majority of the Web Sites that are out there being put together today are much simpler even than a Blog.

Some good examples of Sales Pages for e-books can be seen below :-

http://www.thesinglesgym.com/relationshipsuccessbook

http://nicolacairncross.com/book/

http://www.in2theclouds.com

Product Sales Sites

When a business has a number of products to sell or would like to have a totally free reign over the look and feel of a web site, Blog sites and their templates may be too restrictive.

Additionally the Web site itself may not require a Blog attached to it, so the major benefits of the Blog are not relevant.

Web Sites offer the designer the creative flair to build the site specifically for the objective and gives freedom to use any emerging tools and gadgets to impress the visitor to the web site.

In such Web Site that I have been personally involved in is that of the **Billbandit** retail site : http://www.billbandit.co.uk

A very simple site to navigate the website is custom designed for its purpose to offer an easy on the eye user experience to find out about the Product, the different ways it can be used and to buy should they wish.

Some of the Key components which are used in the site are :-

Shopping Cart

http://www.totalbusinesscart.com/app/?pr=57&id=130803

Affiliate Scheme

Total Business Cart

Competition Entry

http://www.ipsx.co.uk (via i-Tr@der)

Twitter Window

http://twitter.com/billbandit

Billbandit Video

http://www.youtube.com/watch?v=oFuB-oX5c4&feature=player_embedded

Some or all of these functions could easily be built into a Blogsite, however the key purpose of this site is to offer a small range of products for sale to the UK marketplace.

A Chat facility is a great little addition to a website which enables live chat support to be provided to clients who might have questions prior to placing their order. A great example of a Chat application is **whoson** (http://www.whoson.com) which can be seen on the **Yellow Pig** site below.

Another example of a completely custom site is a business operating in the promotional merchandising field :-

http://www.yellowpig.co.uk

The volume of products on the site and the complexity of printing positions, colours and quantities involved leads to this type of organisation requiring a site with complex algorithms and calculations to arrive at a final price.

Very often custom sites such as this come with a management back end which permits the business owners to add / amend products and images, change descriptions, adjust pricing matrices and most of the other content on the site.

Custom Web Sites within a Standard Framework

Another kind of website is one which is primarily informational, is based upon a template and easy as using a Wordprocessor to update.

Micro businesses, café's, restaurants, Local Caterers even plumbers or tradesman may use this kind of website to get a presence on the Internet. They are typically low maintenance but can provide excellent quality websites, quickly and at low cost.

A good example of this type of product is **PIXIE** (http://www.getpixie.co.uk). This program is an easy to use, very simple, content management system (CMS). In the hands of a competent web designer a web site can be up and running in a matter of hours, all that is really needed is some creative design images and the rest is pretty much 'point and click' to post the copy.

"Your web design company should not use your business to show off their skills. They should use their skills to empower you to show off your business"

The whole ethos behind their business is to get a small business up and running with a great looking website, quickly and empower the Business Owner to make any changes they need as often as they need to at no additional cost.

Specialist Web Site to set yourself apart

When a standard framework just won't cut it, or you want to push the boundaries of the user experience, then a custom, completely unique website is called for.

With a larger budget, longer lead time but with the flexibility to adopt whatever technologies are available on the Internet, Web sites, in the right hands, can become a work of art.

One of the most impressive websites at the time of writing this book that I have seen is the one below :-

http://www.jagermeister.com

Irrespective of the product being sold, what has been created here pushes the envelope of web site experiences and demonstrates what is possible with modern internet technologies. The use of movement, colour, sound and design brought together in a truly memorable visitor experience.

Content Management Systems

For larger clients who need to manage and control many thousands of Internet Pages that regularly change and who need version control, release control, submission and approval management before publishing to the web, Content Management Systems may provide the answer.

This is an area beyond the scope of this book and the Small and Medium sized businesses that this book is targeted towards, however a few important points are worth mentioning here.

The technology behind Web Sites running on Web Servers can be truly on the 'Cloud' i.e. externally hosted (and outside an organisation's network) and these can come in two flavours, Public and Private. A Public version is one where anyone is permitted to access the services, whereas a Private Cloud is ring fenced and available only to those provided with access. Intranets were a forerunner of Private Clouds, where interconnected offices could share Web Services hosted and maintained inside an internal business network.

So the same technology that delivers information on the Internet can be used internally by larger organisations with an Intranet or a Private Cloud solution. This enables larger organisations to provide information, documents and a whole range of services internal to the organisation to increase efficiency and speed up business processes.

Some examples of the type of information an organisation would present through this mechanism include, Induction programmes for new employees, policy and procedure manuals, ISO9001 documentation, Health and Safety regulations, HR documents and services, Holiday requests and even collaborative services for sales people working on large proposals involving many people.

Using Content Management System tools enables organisations to manage their content for presentation both internally and externally easily and effectively, and from anywhere if required. Staff can connect through a simple web portal and access the company's information resource using web browser technology either at the offices or remotely.

Content Management Systems are not however just for large organisations. These types of systems come in all shapes and sizes from a few hundred dollars to 100's of thousands, covering the entire spectrum of business types. They can be used to build simple and complex web sites both for the Internet and the Intranet and are yet another option to consider when evaluating what is the most suitable direction for a business to take.

Social Networking

So far we have discussed the different ways that we can set up on the Internet whatever it is that we want to tell the world. In traditional business this our Collateral, corporate brochures, price list and catalogue, Newsletters and customer updates, although we have much more flexibility online than in the pre-internet days.

Social Networking however is a new phenomena which has emerged as a result of the Internet and was not there before. As mentioned earlier in this chapter, Social Networks are another way people can find us, and how we can advertise our products and services to a specific target market, but let us now take a closer look at how we can use them for our Business.

As we have discussed already 'People buy people first' and now a presence on Facebook, MySpace, Linked In or other Social sites says : I'm up to date with technology, I recognise technology can help my business, I'm sociable too and if you would like to know more about me here are my family, friends and acquaintances and what we get up to in and out of work.

Now not everyone will want to share that level of detail, fortunately social sites have been designed to favour one type of network style or another :-

Facebook quickly adopted by the younger generation but now the largest social site outside of China (yes they have one with more subscribers). Facebook has morphed recently and now has a wide spectrum of users from the young right through to retirees looking to stay in touch with globally extended family and relatives. My Facebook account can be found at

http://www.facebook.com/oglechris

Facebook has recently added the capability to build Business Pages to promote your products and services. The functionality of these increases as you build a solid following. The Business pages allow you to effectively attach additional business related information to your profile. These Business pages are searchable on Facebook and all the features of writing updates and posting pictures are also available.

Business pages therefore are another place where you can expose your business, products and services easily and effectively. Encouraging your contacts to 'Like' your business pages will expand the capabilities of these pages and provide further opportunities to publicise what you do.

Earlier on we were talking about Mash-Ups where applications on the web pass information between them to maximise the effectiveness of updates and minimise the times when we have to login and post the same information in different systems. Facebook allow links to be built between Business Pages and your twitter accounts, so an update on the Business Page will automatically be posted into twitter with a link back to the Business Page on Facebook.

Linked-In is a much more business orientated community. Associating with others requires more information than in Facebook and the terminology and the type of details held on individuals is more geared to business. Linked-in has it's roots in recruitment and as such has much more employment related information than Facebook which was created to share information and pictures amongst friends in college. Linked-In is now used by many companies to find new staff and so searching on skills and experience are key facets of the Linked-In platform. My Linked in profile can be found at

http://www.linkedin.com/in/chrisogle

Ecademy is again a Business Network and started in the UK. Aimed primarily at making business connections there are various levels of membership which entitle the member to use different tools. At the top level it is possible to email all your contacts and with the potential to have many thousands globally this can be a very powerful feature.

Ecademy is very web friendly and Search Engine Keywords feature along with 50 words or phrases that describe your businesses and interests. These are useful tools to promote the business effectively and help to find contacts that might be looking for your products and services or who could provide complementary services.

This is a link to my own ecademy profile :-

http://www.ecademy.com/account.php?id=149131

You Tube is a video Network, where you can add your social profile but also upload videos to support your business or your social life. Other You Tube users can subscribe to your You Tube Channel and receive notifications when you post new video material. Some businesses configure You Tube as their website especially if their business is in the Video Production and media marketplace. A great example of one such You Tube Business website is shown below :-

http://www.youtube.com/richiepic

Other Social Networking Sites there are a great many other social networking sites such as MySpace and Bebo to name just two. Each social site has a slightly different audience and bias and it is worth checking them out to see which ones are most applicable to your enterprise. The Blog site below contains a fairly comprehensive list of Social Media sites :-

http://traffikd.com/social-media-websites/#general

Clearly it is impossible to feature in every Social Network, nor is it essential. A good balance of relevant Social Networking is important however and the explosion in popularity of such Networks suggests that we should not ignore them. The larger Social Networks already provide links between themselves to simplify the updating process and reduce the time it takes so now it is up to us to make the most of the opportunity they present.

We will discuss list building in more detail later in this chapter, but social networks provide us with a warm market audience that trust and respect our suggestions and recommendations. In terms of business generation Warm contact lists perform over 5 times better than cold lists.

What is SEO?

Search Engine Optimisation or SEO has been around now for a few years and anyone with a website will probably have taken a phone call or received an email making claims about 'getting your site at the top of page 1 on Google'.

There is absolutely no doubt that there are techniques and tactics that will improve your rankings, but the search algorithms and methods for delivering results are a closely guarded secret.

Most search engine optimisation is based upon 'trial and error' of what has worked and what hasn't in the past. Let us not forget however that Google, Yahoo, Bing, Ask Jeeves and all the other Search Engines constantly revise and change their Algorithms.

What works one day with the Search Engines may not work the next and so SEO must be used in conjunction with other strategies not relied on solely as a means of generating leads.

Let us now first and foremost look at the goal to reach the 'Top of the Search Engines', and analyse the challenges :-

1. The major search engines use different Algorithms to produce search results, so that what works with one might not produce the same results in another

2. Search Engines take a word or phrase and then produce results. When we are looking to be no.1 which word, words, phrase or phrases are we looking to be top with?

3. Does your Domain name contain the Word or Phrase that you are looking to get to No.1? It doesn't have to but it helps.

4. Search engines look for congruency, i.e. not just the presence of a word or phrase on a website, but whether the pages themselves are relevant to the meaning of the words and phrase being searched on.

5. Hyperlinks (words on a page that allow you to jump to another page) that contain the Word or Phrase and lead to additional relevant content.

6. Image Mouseovers, Hyperlink Mouseover text that substantiates the relevance of the page to the keywords and phrase being used.

7. Page Titles, Meta Tags (these are actually hidden within the web pages themselves and can be populated with words which describe what the page is about and Keywords). Search Engines may or may not use these Tags however why take the risk, they should be setup just in case they are used whilst looking at SEO.

To work through your Site(s) and attend to these 7 items above may be something that can be done internally within the organisation it may not. The approach is also different for Blog based web sites and custom Web sites or Pages. Blogs very often have Keyword and Tag input boxes that can inserted into posts. Blogs also allow Mouseover Text to be inserted when adding Images and creating Links, so with care some of the more technical elements above can be dealt with 'as you go' if your main Website platform is blog based.

If your existing site is a Custom Website and you do not have the skills to change the content and update the site, then you will either have to go back to the developer or seek the assistance of an External SEO specialist to make your site more Web Friendly (be found by the search engines).

But where should we put our effort?

As we have already indicated Search is extremely powerful tool and according to SEO Guru's these are not people just flitting about like perhaps in Facebook or other social networks, they are in Focus mode looking for something. So, in other words compared with other Internet users, Searchers are the most motivated group that will hit a website or blog!

So where should we put our focus and what would we optimise to make the best of SEO for our business?

Off-page elements have the biggest impact on SEO

Take a look at the image below by **SEOmoz** (http://www.seomoz.
org/blog/perfecting-keyword-targeting-on-page-optimization):

Components of Google's Ranking Algorithm

(According to 72 SEOs Surveyed for SEOmoz's Biennial Search Ranking Factors)

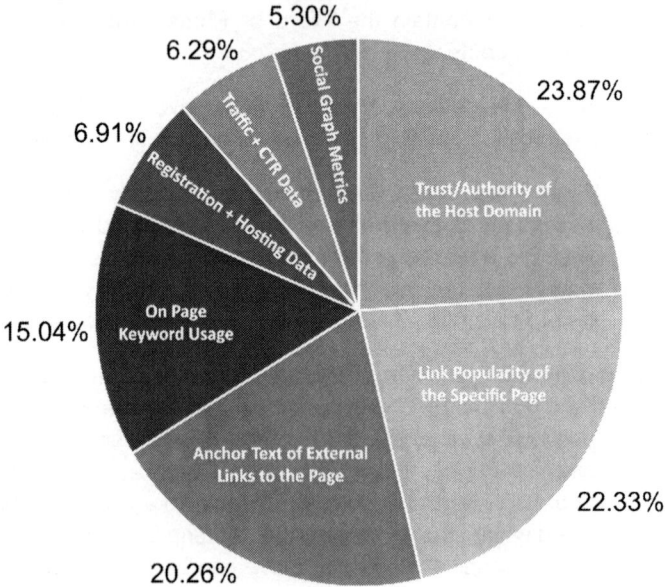

A quick review of the chart reveals that as far as SEO goes, what happens off your site matters more than what's on it.

- 23.87% – The general trust and authority that your domain name builds is the largest indicator of SEO success. As Authority Rules makes clear, what works for search engines is what works with people as well.

- 22.33% – The number of links to a specific page matters a lot too! so think twice about link viability when your content is just out of the gate.

- 20.26% – The text that makes up the clickable external links matters because this is Google's way of finding out what your page is about according to other people, not just you.

In other words, what other people are saying about you, says more about you than what you do!

So to drive the all important visitors to a Website or Blog, the name and respect we have built on the Internet for our Domain, the volume of links back to the site, and what those links actually consist of in terms of words are vital... Once a visitor arrives, then clearly what they experience becomes vital in the sales conversion process. More on this topic of copywriting will be covered later.

A sobering thought. In December 2009 Google announced that they would be extending their 'Customised Search Results' to include all searches not just from those that had an account with Google. Now what did this actually mean?

Ironically the announcement went out on Dec 9th and went largely unnoticed but the effects are extremely profound. A great source for information on searching can be found at

http://searchengineland.com and this particular article at Googles new normal search results (http://searchengineland.com/googles-personalized-results-the-new-normal-31290)

In summary prior to this announcement if two people typed into Google the same keyword they would get the same results. As the article above states, so reliable was this that Businesses used search results in their marketing material... Search on Google for this word and you'll find us, knowing that everyone would receive the same results and find the required link.

After December 9th 2009 this all changed. Now if two people type in the same keyword they are unlikely to get the same result. Google now personalise the results you receive based on your previous 6 months searching history. The idea being that you are more likely to be drawn to the information from similar places that you have searched and visited before.

At the time of writing this book, the new normal search results are now personalised, and if you want to go back to the old normal you have to now click on the 'Customized' link (top right) to find out what has been personalised and change the results.

Fundamentally what results we get back from Google we can't quibble with anyway. If we don't find what we want then we try another search keyword or phrase and 'go again', no one questions whether the results we got are right or not, how would we know anyway!

But for businesses this absolutely changes SEO with Google forever. If now whatever we do with SEO does not guarantee us to end up on the results page because Google is personalising the results, then why are we bothering with SEO at all?

Well the answer is clear, there are no guarantees any more, and like I have mentioned before, we don't make the rules and the rules can be changed at a moments notice without any recourse to us. So, in the future SEO must be looked at from the perspective of …

'SEO will no longer guarantee that we will be found, but it is guaranteed we won't be found if we don't use SEO'

- Chris Ogle

Why has Google changed the search engine results method and personalised them? The theory is that if you went to a library to take out a book and followed a recommendation by the Librarian, then next time you enlisted the librarian's help, armed with the knowledge of what has gone before they would be able to better service your requests. In truth, Google probably recognised that an extrememly lucrative industry had emerged getting people up the search rankings which they were losing out on. By introducing this concept, the only guaranteed method of ensuring a top spot is to use Ad-Words and pay Google advertising fees.

Remember free Cold Business leads via Search Engines accounts for a relatively small percentage of sales probably no more than 14%. Google, at the time of writing this book, had about 36% of the search engine traffic so try and ensure that all search methods are considered. Finally about 30% of visitors arrive via Search results the other 70% will find your business via different methods completely.

In **Conclusion** Search engine traffic is extremely important make no mistake about it, but it has to be put into context with an overall marketing strategy. Regular businesses do not rely on a single marketing approach or campaign nor should we when we move our marketing to the Internet. SEO enables us to optimise, make the best of our web sites and make sure that we don't miss out by failing to use techniques and strategies that are available to us. SEO however, on its own will not guarantee the success or failure of a business.

What is Internet Traffic?

Internet Traffic in simplistic terms is the number of visits to a Web site whether it is a Blog or traditional Web site.

Logically then, the higher the traffic the better, more visitors equals more sales. In principle this is true, however we do need to consider the type of traffic that we receive and whether it is consistent with the nature of the site concerned.

If we are running a social network site or a local community site, then the effectiveness or success of the site can't be measured just by visits alone. The purpose of these sites is to have a large number of active visitors who repeatedly come back to the site, coupled with a measurable percentage of new visitors who we hope will convert to regular visitors. So the Visitors figure needs further analysis to provide us with the feedback we require. There is a section later on that covers analysis tools to measure our Blog and website performance which is crucial in determining our marketing success.

If we are running a business then of course the more visitors we have the better, however let us consider the following scenarios :-

- We are not getting enough visitors

- Visitors arrive but leave straight away

- Visitors arrive but don't buy anything

- No one ever returns to the site

The four points listed above are common place with many businesses online presence. In the following sections we tackle these issues and look at ways of resolving them.

How can I get more traffic?

To be able to measure the effectiveness of our Blogs and Web sites, whatever they are for, we must have traffic. People vote with their fingers online. Assuming our site is serviceable (reasonable response and load times) then what a visitor sees when they arrive and what they do thereafter is crucial for us to understand if we have got it right or not. Web specialists tell us we have no more than 2-3 seconds to engage the visitor after which we will have lost them (probably forever)... the first impression is absolutely crucial to the success of the site.

This section is about making sure that we maximise our potential to get traffic. How can we use the Internet and what it has to offer to make sure we get our fair share of visitors?

Black hat / White hat marketing

As with any new industry and we must remember that Digital Marketing is still in its infancy, there are always those who seek to bend the rules and gain an 'unfair' advantage. Unfair in this case is a loosely used term because the only rules being broken are those that are laid down by the Search engine companies themselves. They decide for themselves what constitutes fair practice and there is little recourse for grievance if you fall foul of their rules.

So let's have a look at the rules then I hear you ask. Well the thing is that there aren't any published rules. So how do we know if we're breaking them? In short we don't know, but through experience we can see who has been black listed and what led to it. There is also a 'gut feel' about fairness. If what someone is trying to do is apply some kind of program to accelerate and propel their website quickly and without doing the legwork then it is likely they will be blacklisted.

Techniques that are used for high speed acceleration up the Search Engine Rankings are called 'Black Hat' Internet Marketing. It is very tempting… to suddenly appear on page 1 of Google or other search engines, score quick wins against rival competitors without having to do a lot of work… a bit like setting up a shop on Oxford Street without having to pay for the privilege.

But… and it is a huge but… if you are caught then your website becomes blacklisted. This means that Domain or web site will never be displayed in that search engines results ever again! Of course content can be moved and a new 'Shop' (Web site) opened and business can continue, but it is from Ground Zero. Would we really want to run this risk?

The problem is that the Search Engine companies know the order of things. They know how a popular website looks like with regard to growth, visits, profile and links back to it over time. If the statistics don't add up, i.e. From the first appearance of the site, the visits are too many too quickly, the volume of links back to the site have occurred too fast for a regular web site, or the website does not contain content relative and in context to the link being used, then the site will be banned.

So what can we do?

Well we can adhere to 'White Hat' marketing. This is where we use all the bonafide methods of promoting Blogs and Web Sites and do not resort to 'get visits quick schemes'.

Coming up in the following sections are some of the techniques that are considered 'White Hat' marketing. We will cover what they and why you should apply them to your Digital Marketing programme.

What is a Web Spider?

I remember being told that if you look at the Internet or the World Wide Web, then the idea of a Spider is something that crawls around that Web (internet).

Well, this is not a bad analogy. The technical details behind Web Spiders are of course vast and not the purpose of this book, but suffice to say, when something moves on the Internet then, as in a real life Web/Spider scenario, the Web Spiders come to see what it is.

So what constitutes a 'movement on the Internet'? Quite simply changes. If something changes on a Blog site or on a Web site then these Spiders crawling the internet come to see what has changed, index the changes, and then re-evaluate the site.

Why is this important?

If we want our search engine rankings to improve, then we need them to take notice of us… often! Making changes brings them back to revisit us and re-evaluate us regularly which tells them a couple things :-

The site is a living, breathing, current and active.

We are adding to and / or improving the site which may lead to our site being presented under different search criteria.

The second thing making changes does, especially if we have subscribers to our feeds is that it encourages our previous visitors who have asked to be kept informed to come back and check us out again.

This is why Blogging is such an important marketing tool. Each new Blog post changes the content on the Blog site and therefore leads to search engines returning to see what has happened and index the new material.

Blogging helps in two ways to improve search engine rankings, it repeatedly re-indexes our site improving our chances of appearing in search results and secondly it increases the visits (traffic) which again is part of the algorithm used for determining our search ranking.

The importance of Links

A link or hyperlink is one of those underlined words that are normally in Blue (or can be an Image) that moves our web browser to a different page or Website.

If we think about it for a few moments… when we are browsing on the Internet all we do is click on links and images to find other things to read, listen to or watch.

There are two very important functions that Link provide for us on the Internet :-

- They enable people browsing to click through to the content that we want them to see

- They perform an important function in determining the search ranking that our Blog or website receives.

   Point 1. It stands to that if we have large numbers of links out there in different places on the Internet, then there is more chance someone will click on the link and visit our web site.

Let us just imagine for a minute that we write an exceptionally good article and that 50 people read it and would like to share this with others. They might post a link to the article into Social sites such as Facebook, Linked In, Hub Pages, Squidoo (more on these later) and many other locations. This would provide a link back to our article and ultimately via the Bio on the article to our Blog or Website.

The next step is that 50 other people or perhaps some of the existing people would then bookmark the article in bookmarking directories for others so see… more links back (backlinks) to our content.

If we were to do this with articles using the Keywords we want to rank highly with the search engines then these Links that have been built will make a big difference to the traffic we receive. More details on this can be found here on Building a Link Farm strategy (http://shareaschnitzel.blogspot.com/2009/04/blog-farm-link-strategy-diagram.html).

Point 2. Links with relevant keywords or phrases as part of the display text (and links with Title tags and images with ALT tags) are regarded by search engines more highly than just pure text. This is provided that the Keyword or Phrase is also present on the page that is displayed via the link.

Let's look at an example of what we mean in point 2 above. Suppose we want to direct a visitor to a specific day on my daily journal blog. The number of ways we could provide that link are infinite, but for the purposes of demonstrating both ends of the spectrum, the two links below can both be configured to point to the same destination address, which is http://www.chrisogle. com/2010/01/day-618---wednesday-6th-january-2010.html. What we can do when creating the link is adjust the text that is displayed to be more friendly, so :-

Click here to see what I did on January 6th 2010 and to see whether it snowed or not in Watford on that day.

Read what Chris Ogle did on January 6th 2010 on his Wealth Creation Blog to find out whether it snowed in Watford on that day.

Now which one is most likely to work best? If we are looking to ensure that Chris Ogle and Wealth Creation Blog feature in search result then the second will work very well we could extend it further to include searches on snow and Watford by the following :-

Read what Chris Ogle did on January 6th 2010 on his Wealth Creation Blog to find out whether we had snow in Watford on that day.

By using descriptive, meaningful hyperlinks and expanding on the words used in the link on the destination pages we can ensure that Blog sites and Web sites are very Internet friendly and we maximise our searching potential.

Getting more links

Now we understand what links are and why they are important, the next question we need to answer is… How can we pro-actively build links on the Internet back to our content?

When our Blog site or Web pages are first published on the Internet they are out there with Billions of others and with the exception of the lucky few we have told about the site (via our business card, email or personally) we are very anonymous.

We may have been found accidentally because someone happened to type a search phrase so unique that ours was the only page on the whole internet with an exact match!

So now the hard work starts… There are a number of avenues that we can now pursue to start building back links and generating visitors :-

Sign up and become a member of Web page recommendation communities

What is a Web Recommendation Community? Well it is a community consisting of individuals all of whom have the ability as members to provide content, and recommend / comment on Blog sites and / or Web sites that they like or dislike. They are effectively a Web site referral community

Of course with millions of visits per week, these aggregation sites act as huge magnets for the Search Engines.

The content on these sites is provided entirely by the members and pages are ranked and indexed by their popularity within the network… it's a bit like a private club where you can vote on other members content and they on yours.

Some great examples of these communities are :-

http://hubpages.com

http://www.squidoo.com

http://www.mybloglog.com

Within these communities it is possible to build your own profile, add pages and provide LINKS to other Blogs and Web Sites that you have. You can build a list of followers and follow other members, much in the same way as Social Networks but it is all about sharing interesting content that is on the Internet.

These sites are a great alternative to locating good quality content on the Internet as all sites are being recommended by people not just served up as results from a search engine query.

With good categorisation and search features within these communities it is easy to find Blogs and Web sites that are recommended by others.

Other referral sites do exist, below are two of the most popular ones. These sites allow the users to experience the internet in a different way :-

http://www.stumbleupon.com

http://digg.com

Each of the above provide a downloadable and installable toolbar that enables the user to simply Tag specific personal or professional interests and then 'Channel Surf' the web by clicking on a button on the installed toolbar. Having clicked on the toolbar link users are then randomly directed to specific websites that adhere to their list of interests. Users have the option to Tag the Blog and Website or with Stumble Upon give it the 'Thumbs up' or 'Thumbs down'. These tags are then added to your profile within the site which can then be shared with others.

These sites can generate back links to your Blog or Web site amazingly quickly. Later in this chapter we discuss putting together a Digital marketing plan and time spent in this area is well worth building into your marketing plan.

Registering on Social Book-marking sites

There are many social book-marking sites all of which have similar functions to Stumbleupon and Digg. Below is a link to a complete list of Social Book-marking sites :-

http://www.social-bookmarking-sites-list.com

The age old issue of Time / Reward needs to be applied here. The more popular social sites are a must and others specific to an industry type could also work well.

Actively comment on other peoples Blogs

There are two sides to this item, the first is making comments on other peoples blog posts, the second is actually sending in a guest post.

When a **comment is made on another Blog** you must leave a name, email address and if you wish a web-site address. This is a route back to your content… provided that the comment is published.

Most Blog comments are moderated and this means read first and then published if deemed appropriate and complimentary to the original post.

Commenting on high profile blogs with good quality posts demonstrates to readers an alternate source of useful information. It builds your credibility and leaves a path to follow and find out more.

Commenting on Blogs that are in your market sector or complimentary to your business will leave a trail back to your business. To find Blogs that are relevant to your business on which to comment go to :-

http://blogsearch.google.com

Facilities for searching on Keywords and Phrases are available to enable you to 'home in' on the blogs that are most relevant for your business.

Guest Posting is where you send in a blog post to put onto someone else's Blog. If you have a unique and useful post that could benefit the intended Blog then it can be a real win / win.

The owner of the Blog gets great content which they did not have to write and the producer of the content gets to put it into a great location (with links back to their blog or web site)

For further details on this and other Blogging ideas visit **ProBlogger** (http://www.problogger.net/archives/2009/02/01/how-to-guest-post-to-promote-your-blog/).

Identify popular Blogs or Web Sites in complimentary markets who would provide reciprocal links

More formal than Guest Posting on other Blogs is where an agreement is entered into between two complementary businesses.

Write Articles

Publishing Articles is a powerful method of promoting your expertise, products and services. The Internet has 000's of article directories that are constantly scanned for new and interesting content.

Articles all contain one very special component a Bio section. The Bio should contain your name, what you do, a few examples of big successes (credibility), contact details and of course a backlink to your Blog or Website.

Articles could be specially written documents or just extended Blogs and can be posted very effectively using article submission web sites that take much of the hard work out of the task. A few Article Submission engine sites / options are shown below :-

http://ezinearticles.com

http://www.submityourarticle.com

Unique Article Wizard (http://www.uniquearticlewizard.com/)

Articles are often re-used and published along with the Authors credentials, Bio and resource box and can have a dramatic effect on traffic.

Paid for Advertising

This can come in various forms but the most well known is Google Ad-Words.

The basic concept is that instead of being part of the free search results set that are displayed for a particular keyword or phrase you can elect to pay to have your link to be displayed right at the top of the results page.

Advertisement campaigns can be given financial limits to prevent costs running away and to fit in with marketing budgets. By carefully choosing the Keywords and Phrases for when the adverts is to be displayed, Ad-Words can represent great value and bring exactly the right kind of visitors to your site.

Google Ad-words has a Keyword analysis tool that enables you to find out which words and phrases are likely to work best for your particular campaign.

There are two main types of Advertisement payment options :-

Pay per Click

When an advert is displayed there is no charge. When the advert is clicked-thru then a payment is taken from your credit bank.

Pay per Impression

Payment is made per '000 advert displays. Each time your advert is displayed on a web page then the counter is incremented. Payment is taken from your credit bank at a rate per '000 displays.

Other forms of **Paid for Advertising** do exist such as the simple purchase of a banner link on a local community website which receives good traffic ratings.

Forums

Participating in Forums that are relevant to your business, products and services is a good way of connecting with others and softly introducing what you do to a potentially large audience.

Forums can become 'moaning central' for those with little going on in their lives so care and attention must be exercised. There is likely to be a number of possible forums for a given subject or Niche and so it might require a bit of trial and error to establish the most suitable.

To locate forums via Google is very simple, just type into the **search box** the forum type you are looking for followed by +forum, a couple of examples are show below :-

cloud computing +forum

table tennis +forum

the results will provide a number of forums that are set up and discussing those subjects.

Forums can serve as a resource for some great benefits to your business such as :-

• Huge variety of comments and opinions from a good cross section of people types

- Other people's experiences with competitive products and services

- Trends about what people are thinking will happen

- Tips and Tricks from those with more experience in a particular field

- Potential new clients

- Potential new suppliers

Blatant advertising on Forums is frowned upon, rather they should be used to build credibility for yourself and the business. Useful and helpful posts will create traffic for your blog / web sites. Most forums permit the use of configurable footers and short Bio's so that other users can easily connect, as well as a direct messaging service if discussions need to be taken outside the main forum posts.

Some Networking companies are now seeing that combining online Forums with live breakfast meetings provides the opportunity to connect online and then also hook up at one of the many weekly network meetings. This formula appears to work well and one of the more popular ones is below :-

http://www.4networking.biz

Copy is king, making the sale

Everything we do on the Internet is surrounded by words which is generically called Copy. There is a bit more to copy though than we might at first think as we may have multiple Blogs and Websites that serve very different purposes and so the style of copy we would use in one place would not work on another. In essence there are two different types of copy, one form is to grab people's attention which is called Copywriting, the other is to build trust and develop a loyal following of repeat customers which is Content Marketing.

Copywriting is one of the most essential elements of successful Digital marketing. Copywriting is the effective use and organisation of words to promote a person, product, business, opinion, or even an idea, to lead the reader into taking some form of action (http://www.copyblogger.com/copywriting-tip/)

Content Marketing is generic term that relates to creating and distribution of useful and informative content as a means of converting prospects into customers and then onto repeat buyers. The main goal of Content Marketing is to obtain a sign-up (permission) to deliver content usually via email over time. Repeated and regular exposure to a good mixture of both useful and relevant information inter-dispersed with offers for products and services to buy provides multiple opportunities for conversion, rather than the "one-shot" all or nothing sales approach.

Copywriting is a skill which must be learned like any other, there are some amazing stories of 'amateur copy' being replaced by professionally produced copy that took sales from zero to many millions in a few months. If there are no copywriting skills in the company and no time to learn them, then this is an area that will require external input.

By just applying the following guidelines you will avoid many of the pitfalls made by 'home grown copywriters' :-

1. Easy to read Font

2. Strong black type for Headlines

3. Clear type for the copy

4. Headlines should be large and bold so everyone will read them and understand the message

5. Pictures used should be relevant to the message and if possible should include the product in use

The actual Copy itself should include the following components :-

1. Describe the problem, get into the consumers mind and empathise with the pain they are in.

2. Why hasn't the problem been solved? Explain to the prospect the challenges that have to be overcome to solve the problem

3. What is possible now? Describe the product or service and deliver all the advantages and Unique selling points to the customer.

4. What is different now? Describe in detail how the customer will feel and what they will experience once the product or service is in and working for them.

5. What they should do now? Call to Action… advise the customer

what they need to do, click here, buy now whatever you want them to do next… remember only one clickable link on the page… no other options, keep it simple.

The most important component of any copy is the **Heading**. If the heading does not grab the reader's attention, then they will read nothing more, the client is lost.

The purpose of this section is not to go into details about how to write great copy but to explain its importance in the creation of marketing materials delivered on the Internet.

There is an 80/20 rule for Headlines, which is that 8 out of 10 will read the headline but only 2 out of 10 will go on to read the content. To find out more about How to write effective Headlines and good copy visit the Blogsite below :-

http://www.copyblogger.com/magnetic-headlines

This site has some really good advice and guidance to enable anyone to produce good quality copy with virtually no expense. The end result might not provide the same results as from a professional copywriter but it will provide 500% better results from an amateur!!

Another source of good copywriting advice and professional copywriting service is **Alan Forrest Smith** (http://www.orangebeetle.com).

The importance of List Building

As indicated above there are really two functions that we produce content for on the Internet, one is to sell directly, the other is to develop a warm market list with whom we can build a relationship.

Before we get into the details of List Building using the Internet first let us look at the typical sales process in business.

1. Lead arrives… this could be from regular or Digital marketing

2. Enquiry is followed up

3. Following Sales process either we get a customer or

4. The Prospect is returned to a not for now status

If an enquiry ends up in the 'Not for Now' bucket, this is not a dead lead, this is a person with whom we can have a relationship with (albeit low volume and not revenue earning) into the future.

There is a saying in sales :-

'there is no way off the sales list except in a pine box'

From personal experience a prospect of mine responded to an email campaign back in 2003. At the time there was not an opportunity to do business.

I put them on my 'keep people informed about developments' list to which I send updates about what is going on every 4 months or so. At the back end of 2008 (November) a new project came to light which we were able to assist my prospect with and today they have 7 separate businesses using our Web based Business Platform.

The power of keeping in touch cannot be underestimated. Personnel change, companies' change, new opportunities crop up all the time, the one thing we do know is we don't know. Methods for keeping people informed are now fairly automated and doesn't require significant resources, so the task is well worth undertaking as my example above proves. I had already built credibility and trust and by just keeping in touch presented myself as worthy of another chance if something came up that we could potentially help with in the future.

At the other end of the spectrum, a colleague of mine was working a sales campaign with a client, the contact of whom was a Dr. De-ath (this is no joke) and ... during the negotiations the Dr. actually did die... In the first instance the name itself created much mirth, but the events afterwards sheer disbelief !

The Internet of course helps us to take enquiries and guide those through the sales 'sausage machine' process, but it also provides us with the capability to build a growing list of people who are interested in being kept informed... a kind of followers list in Social Networking speak.

These 'followers' let us remember have asked us to keep them informed, they were interested enough in what we had to say to register in the hope that other useful communication would be received in the future. The relationship that we build with this list will determine (a) whether they continue to stay subscribed to it (b) whether they are prepared to become a customer later on, or refer us to their contacts.

Useful information, light hearted pieces, tricks and tips even 'thoughts for the day' can be included in these communications. Interspersed in the correspondence can be updates on the Business, new products &

services coming out and even reviews on 3rd party products that have impressed both in the business or personally.

A great example of a publisher who has a subscriber list with whom he communicates twice weekly is Martin Avis. His e-letter named **Kickstart** (http://www.kickstartdaily.com) has a loyal following and Martin publishes very interesting and useful content twice weekly. Martin's audience are avid readers of his communications, so much so that during a recent illness when Martin was unable to publish his readers complained of Kickstart withdrawal symptoms!

What's a Squeeze Page (linking to external systems)?

Internet Marketing has been responsible for the generation of some interesting terminology, a squeeze page is one of them, and so what is a Squeeze page?

Quite simply the squeeze page is where a visitor registers with your Blog or your Web site to be kept informed and join your regular mailing list as described in the previous section.

The information that has to be entered is minimal, normally just a name and an email address. In return for their registration the new subscriber will often receive a free gift which is the attraction to join the mailing list, this might be a downloadable report or even a free e-book.

Some examples of squeeze pages are shown below :-

1. The Squeeze Page for the **SME7 Programme** (http://www. sme7practitioner.com/sme7practitioner)

   This simple squeeze page has a video introducing the SME7 Programme, and a simple registration to join an online Video Conference.

2. Squeeze page for **Keep It Simple Software Training** (http:// keepitsimplesoftwaretraining.com/optin%28WP2%29.html)

   Video training on the popular Wordpress blogging platform plus an offer of a free report, tips and tricks for those who subscribe.

3. Squeeze page for the **Kickstart Newsletter** (http://www. kickstartdaily.com/)

   Sign up squeeze page to receive the Kickstart newsletter twice weekly.

The squeeze page is the secret behind building your warm contact list, and it is highly likely that many of the readers of this book have completed a squeeze page without knowing that is what it is called.

What is a Double Opt-In?

One of the problems with list building and of course email correspondence is how twitchy everyone has got about email, and with good reason might I add... email during the late 1990's and early in the 21st century became the mission critical application of many businesses and yet it was the route into many companies for Virus's and Spyware. Complex anti-virus programs and self protection has meant emailing anyone anything you have to be registered (often called whitelisted) on their email system so that the zealous spam filters let the email through.

Because unsolicited email has become such a problem the recognised and accepted practise for registering on Squeeze pages has been to use a technique known as double opt-in.

What this means is that having filled in your name and email address the name is not automatically included in the email process. There is an additional step before you are confirmed. An email is initially sent out to the subscriber and this normally contains something like what I have shown below:-

> *Thanks for registering on our [Blog/website] for the free [e-book/tips and tricks], there is just one last step to confirm the registration process, please click on the link below.*

Importantly, this email will not arrive if the email address is incorrect, and if the email finds its way into a bulk mail folder, then the recipient will have to go and look for it to confirm their subscription which probably demonstrates real intent.

In any event the purpose of the second email is to weed out those people who only clicked to see what would happen, or those using a false email address, basically anyone that is not serious.

A double opt-in list improves the quality of the database being built, it might reduce the speed with which it grows, but at least it does contain genuinely interested respondents.

What is an Auto-Responder Series (Sales Automation)?

In the physical world if we had sent out a mailshot and one of the options was that the recipient would like to join our mailing list, then this is the kind of equivalent of being added to our database as described in the previous section.

The monthly process of then producing information to send out, printing, putting in envelopes and sending to the subscribers is the manual form of what the Auto Responder does electronically in very simplistic terms.

Of course an Auto-Responder is capable of doing far more than this basic example above and is usually flexible enough to be adapted to different lists, products and markets.

So let's look at the components of an Auto Responder and see how they can be used to automate the sales and follow up process :-

Auto Responder Messages

These are the contents of the email(s) that are sent out once a registrant has requested to join a List. The Auto Responder can be just a single email such as a 'Thank you for joining our List – Click the Link below to confirm that you want to join'. This would be a typical 'Double Opt-in' auto responder email.

That could be the end of the Auto Responder series and in many cases it is. But very often we would want to now build a relationship with our list, providing them with Tips, Tricks, useful information and possibly offering products and services that we might recommend as well.

It is possible to set up 20, 30, 50, 100 or even 365 (one for each day) messages and store them in a single Auto Responder series.

Once a registrant double opts in they join at the first message and then at pre-set time intervals (1 day, 2 days, 3 days, 1 week, 2 weeks whatever the Interval needs to be), the next email is then sent out. Recipients can of course enter the programme at different times and therefore be receiving completely different emails, some might be on message 2 others message 15, 18 and 25 depending on how long they have been on the list.

The list above would be fairly typical for processing a prospect list which has been built or even a 'keep me informed' database. Once a prospect buys something however things can be further automated again...

If we think about the business or person that has now bought something, they have effectively crossed a definite line. They have a level of comfort and trust in the company to part with real money and the auto responder series they were part of up until this point may no longer be suitable.

More sophisticated Auto Responders allow at the point of making the sale to transfer the individual onto a different Auto Responder series, one which is perhaps more suitable for customers not prospects with different information and products.

There is quite a big debate about how wide (how many characters per line) the Auto Responder email messages should be. If you have ever registered to receive regular updates on a web-site or even a blog the chances are that you will have received emails from an Auto Responder series... an example is shown below :-

Dear Chris,

Still looking for your feedback about whether you might be interested in coming to a pretty much free event in London on the 21st / 22nd September, specifically designed for people new, or newish to online business and internet marketing.

You don't have to commit just yet - the VIP Priority tickets will probably go on sale next week, but we are just looking for an idea of numbers right now.

Check this out - watch the video - and put your name and email in, to get onto the VIP Priority booking list.

Here is a great little free text tool **(NoteTab light)** (NoteTab light : http://www.notetab.com) which helps with formatting lines (and a great many other things) to be a specific width for use in Auto Responder series.

Typically Auto Responders are text with some words slightly altered to avoid SPAM filters in the example above fr.ee is used instead of free for exactly this reason. (I have removed the link which was included with this email)

One of the biggest headaches when using Auto Responders is the percentage of emails that are siphoned off as SPAM even when individuals have Double Opted in!

Sign-up Buttons

Auto Responder software provides the HTML Code that is needed to be put onto a web page or Blog that starts the registration process. The buttons are normally underneath the Name and Email entry form and are linked to an Auto Responder series. In this way the same button on different web sites and blogs can enter people into the same database, as well as multiple databases being populated for different types of lists.

Database Manipulation

Most Auto Responder programmes enable the registered names and addresses to be exported and imported. So it is possible to take your lists and load the data into other systems as necessary.

Example Auto Responders

There are a few types of Auto Responders, some more expensive than others. They key is to ensure that the company being used is not blacklisted for sending SPAM email. This has a dramatic effect on the delivery performance of emails. The two Auto Responders service providers that I have listed below are well known, but there are many others available :-

http://www.aweber.com (the largest in the market)

http://www.wizardresponder.com (also very popular)

The one below combines Auto Responder functionality with a leading Shopping Cart to provide a more comprehensive service

http://www.totalbusinesscart.com

Other Auto Responders combine creating professional looking news letter pages with trackable links to other content with scheduled email services. These are more popular when communicating in a monthly / weekly news ezine manner where content is nearly always customised and everyone may receive the same email. A good example is http://www.icontact.com

Auto Responders are a powerful way to automate and process people through the sales funnel. Marketing personnel can set and forget and know that regular interaction is being maintained in a controlled and effective manner.

What are Sales Pages?

A Sales Page is effectively what it says on the tin! A page designed to sell something. This type of page will be used to sell downloadable e-products very often and is used for e-books (such as this book http://www.in2theclouds.com), packages of training, software, reports or intellectual property... anything which can be bought and downloaded instantly works well with a sales page.

There are certain components which are needed to present the product and service in such as way as to convince the customer to take action.

- The Sales Letter formula works something like this:

- Attention grabbing headline in a large font

- Current date (up to date now)

- From the desk of (Author) or similar wording

- The "Dear Friend" salutation

- Pose question(s)

- Offer a solution, describe it, hype it, order links

- Testimonials (Credibility Building)

- Bonuses

- More testimonials and other great news about the product

- Special offer, limited time – call to action!

- Order now link/button

- Signature

- The "P.S" Money back guarantee

There are some amazing examples of Sales Letters some better than others... Sales letters are not available for ever and normally have an Internet shelf life as offers get discontinued and products and services are superseded, there are many reasons. We have saved a few examples that we have uncovered for use in this book enclosed below :-

Text and Pictures Sales Page

http://www.clientmagnets.com

Sales page containing Video

http://www.clientmagnets.com/steppingup2010

Seriously long sales page

http://www.milliondollarpublisher.com

As you can see with Digital and Information products the sales pitch is pretty hard, usually with bright reds, yellows and clear black writing, loads of testimonials and the promise of quite large returns for a seemingly ridiculously low cost....

The whole Internet Sales process follows the following strategy :-

Free Products and Services

This is the Squeeze page as described previously. A giveaway product or service about something in which the visitor has an interest.

Now the name and email is in a database... normally some very useful information or tips / tricks have been provided in return.

Low Cost services, e-books

The next step in the Sales cycle is to try (either immediately) or very soon after to have raised the interest level sufficiently for the visitor to now want to use a product or service, or to perhaps sign up and join a membership site to really get at the 'good stuff'.

This stage is sometimes combined with an e-book, buy the book and then get membership free for 1 month!

Often where there are Web service products such as AutoResponders, Shopping carts or even Online storage services there are low cost 'LITE' (or even free sometimes) options which you can start using straight away but that are bereft of the features that the provider knows you need (nothing new here the Cable TV companies have been doing this for years).

Once up and running and having already put in a fair amount of effort, there is every probability that you will want to upgrade to the main product or service at some point in the future...

Higher priced main products (High profit products/ services)

Once you are in the club, then new features and services will be presented and communicated only available with the premium service and before long… one of these features will be most appealing, an upgrade happens and this part of the sales process has completed.

Let me hasten to add there is nothing wrong with this process it is the natural evolution. The service provider receives a repeat customer using the services, the customer has access to a very useful product or service delivered via the Web.

The issue with Sales Pages which 'let's be honest' are there to deliver a compelling argument and call to action is the inference, certainly with pure Internet Marketing 'info' products that the consumer can earn some staggering amounts of money. The industry (in the USA) is going through a cleanup exercise right now regarding this issue which was / is also prevalent in the MLM (Multi Level Marketing) arena.

Now there are schools of thought that the longer the sales page then the greater the chance of success. I think the jury is out on whether that is the case or not. I have heard this advice given to me and others, but on what basis or science it is offered I am unsure.

Somebody must have proof? Statistics must be available right? And yet I have never seen any… nor on whether Red backgrounds or gaudy colour schemes work better than any other.

The success of any Sales Page must come down to a number of factors such as :-

- The nature of the Product or Service being offered, e.g. is it a technical product which requires detailed performance data, or is it a widget which needs little explanation

- The type of clients for the service or product, e.g. Football merchandise must be sold differently to perhaps Legal services

- The cost of the product or service

Video in a high level of cases will definitely improve the Sales performance of any page, as will Audio and testimonials from happy customers (steer clear of money testimonials however).

From my own experience when faced with a sales page, if the heading grabs me, then I will read on into the next paragraph... I might skim a few of the main headlines looking for something to support my first impression... then I want to know the price... normally tucked away at the bottom of the page... but now being inserted some way up from the bottom to make it awkward to find (that for me is irritating). Then now I know the price... they normally have a few p.s's as the bottom... these are very often read in preference to other items, so these are usually carefully written... a bit like sweet counters located at the checkouts!!

Now I might check out a few of the pictures with testimonials and if I like the look of it... then I'll move back to the bottom and buy the book, service or whatever it is... with higher ticket items I might look on the search engines to see if anything negative has been reported about this particular service, or in a business forum or two... if all is well then the sale is made.

When creating Sales Pages... if the copy is good, and the Sales story well constructed with video, pictures and testimonials located in the correct places it will be a high performing Sales Page, the significance of page length in my opinion is of less import, it needs to be as long as needs to be to cover all the main points. Well crafted Sales Pages are worth their weight in Gold and $5000 to $10000 is not uncommon for the best.

Shopping Carts

The name is fairly easy to understand, similar to a physical shopping cart in a supermarket a shopping cart online would translate into something that is going to be purchased, when you decide to checkout.

Shopping carts are only required if the Website or Blogsite is for the purposes of selling products or services. Online sales requires some careful planning too, not only do you need to select the right shopping cart for the job, but as we shall see later on, which methodology is going to be used to take the money and where is that money going to end up also needs to be thought about at this stage.

There are three basic types of Shopping cart and which is appropriate depends entirely on the nature of the business.

Type 1 - Plug and Play Cart

These carts although primarily used for Digital Products or Info products can be used for Sales of physical products too, typically these Cart solutions are product / service sales functions added to existing websites or Blogs.

The same cart technology is used for example with two products already mentioned in this book :-

Physical product sales (http://www.billbandit.co.uk/billbandit_shop.html)

http://www.in2theclouds.com - Digital e-book product sales

You can see from the first example that the products are physical but the range is not large enough to warrant the set up and configuration of larger more sophisticated Catalogue type systems.

Products can easily be set up within these shopping carts and then the BUY button (and the HTML Code behind it) is provided which can then be put into the Sales page, Blog or Web site.

Clicking the BUY button then adds the product to the cart and takes the visitor to the view cart screen to that they can checkout or return to buy other products.

These shopping carts are now very sophisticated applications offering a wide range of configurable options including :-

Upsell products

Options to encourage the user to by other related products such as spare accessory packs or additional items that will improve the customers' experience of the product purchased.

Wide range of delivery options and pricing

International shipping options, quantity or weight breaks, Courier, 1st class, 2nd class options for delivery, these systems cater for most needs.

Configuration of Accepted Cards and Payment options

Sometimes it is necessary to restrict the credit / debit card options. Other businesses may require repeat monthly auto billing such as a Membership site subscription.

Affiliate Management Tools

Shopping carts provide the tools to build an army of Affiliate Marketing partners.

Imagine a whole group of satisfied customers placing an ad on their high traffic sites recommending your products and being able to earn a commission when product is purchased through the link on their website.

These shopping carts provide automated tools that handle Affiliate Registration, calculate commissions, allow the affiliate to view their sales and download adverts / banners for placing on their blog or websites.

If you reward others for recommending products then it is possible to imagine that there might be a few willing to recommend your products if they have high traffic sites. Some people earn a very reasonable income by recommending other companies products and services only, this is called Affiliate Marketing.

Digital Product Delivery tools

Tools to assist with the security and management of delivering Digital Products such as e-books

Autoresponders

Email and Sales development tools to automate marketing to the subscription database

Ad Trackers

The capability to add tracking code on to buttons and links and measure their effectiveness... This is very useful for evaluating what is working and what is not and adjusting the sales pages.

Reporting

A reporting module that enables a full analysis of the shopping cart visitor history.

A couple of good examples of this type of products are :-

http://www.totalbusinesscart.com also known as

http://1shoppingcart.com

http://www.wahmcart.com or

Google have their own **Google Checkout** service (https:// checkout.google.com/seller/what.html)

In the right business, these are quick to setup and get going and more importantly there is expertise in the marketplace that can configure these applications quickly and efficiently for a small fee.

Type 2 – Online Catalogues

There are many occasions where the requirement is not for ad-hoc product sales or a small range of products added to an existing website or blog but where a more sophisticated user experience is required. The Online Catalogues are websites themselves built around a shopping cart engine.

In these situations it is possible to utilise standard off the self shopping cart systems, one highly popular version of this is **Actinic** (http:// www.actinic.co.uk) which is highly configurable and can produce some excellent looking online sales experiences. Below some example sites constructed using the Actinic shopping cart product.

Off the shelf but, highly customisable and in the right designer's hands retail sites like those above work well both in terms of relatively low development cost but high visual impact and sales performance.

Hosted shopping carts which can be configured online and set up easily are also great value when the site is almost completely dedicated to offering a wide selection of products. One local company I know personally selling computer products uses eUKHost to run and manage his online store :-

http://www.rlsupplies.co.uk **(RL Supplies)**

Type 3 - Custom online shopping

When the business requires a completely original design, an innovative approach or has a specific model for online sales with features specific to the business then there is little option but to put together a custom website. These again fall into different flavours, huge sites where the business is primarily built around the website, great examples of these are the grand-daddy of Internet trading http://www.amazon.com and the online auction site http://www.ebay.com.

The food retail sector has got in on the act as well and all the major chains, Tesco's, Asda's, Sainsbury's, Morrison's, Waitrose as well as all the high street stores have custom built and highly sophisticated online retail applications.

But they are not the only ones... SME's that rely on business which is either wholly or largely generated via the Internet can justify the investment in building a custom online sales front end for their businesses. One great example is a business associate of mine who runs a Stag and Hen weekend business throughout the UK and Europe shown below :-

http://www.maximise.co.uk

This business receives almost all enquiries as a result of website visits and so the aesthetics of the site, operability, flexibility and ability to make changes are all fundamental to their needs. In cases such as this where the performance of the site is tied so closely to the fortunes of the business optimum control over every aspect of the site is essential.

Payment Gateways and Merchant Accounts

With all the service described above we are almost… yes almost in the position to sell something. Just one step remains and this is the process of taking payment.

The previous section contained all the mechanics of Web sites and Blogs in presenting products for sale and building up the contents of the shopping cart. This section is concerned with the connection to the credit card company or the bank and receiving payment.

The actual payment process historically has been one of the major causes for potential customers refraining from using the Internet to buy goods and services. The thought of typing Credit or Debit Card details into a web page and essentially providing access to your account fills many with horror.

The issue is less to do with security risks on proper web sites and more to do with not knowing or being able to detect exactly what page you are on and whether it is real or not.

Let me explain…

- Anyone ever received an email that looks like it is from a friend, with an attachment that then proceeded to infect the computer with a virus?

- I have lost count of Nigerian leaders who would love to reward me with 000's of dollars in return for helping them transfer money from a recently deceased rich relative

- I still receive emails advising me to follow a link and enter all my banking details because they are upgrading their systems and require me to activate something or other

You would think that those responsible for sending out the millions of emails every week would realise that we all know now these are cons. The unfortunate truth is that they do it because they make money doing it, pure and simple. For every million spam or phishing emails that are sent they still catch unwary Internet users who provide security credentials under false pretences and then gain access to accounts and steal money.

This is where the majority of online Credit / Debit card theft arises, not from Bona fide companies genuinely offering products and service in return for payment through Trusted sites.

It is the same as providing others with your passwords and access to business systems, which accounts for some 80% of such occurrences.

Ok... so let us look at the components involved. In most Small and Medium sized businesses payment will be handled by some external payment processing service... These companies have to satisfy rigorous examination and the computers containing sensitive information have to be locked away in secure vaults, protected at all time from attack both physically and electronically.

Some typical examples of these are **RBS Worldpay** (http://www.rbsworldpay.com), **Nochex** (http://www.nochex.com) **SagePay** (http://www.sagepay.com) and **PayPal** (http://www.paypal.com). All the leading banks also provide online payment Gateways as well.

Typically control is passed from the Shopping Cart system when payment is about to be made to the external Payment Processing service. The amount that is being spent is passed to the receiving bank also to enable the credit check / bank balance to be verified and then approved.

It is only on the very large sites such as Government, Utilities (Gas, Electricity, Water, Telecoms), and other very large companies that the credit / debit card details are kept. The vast majority of Blogs or Web sites offering products and services do not have any access to your security information.

Once control is passed to the External Payment Processor you enter a secure environment. Typically the browser will show this with a small padlock image on the status bar (at the bottom) and the site URL is prefixed with https. In simple terms what this means is that data entered is encrypted so that if intercepted it would be meaningless data.

A word about **https**. The ability to use https is granted by a number of 'Security Issuing' authorities. Two such businesses are

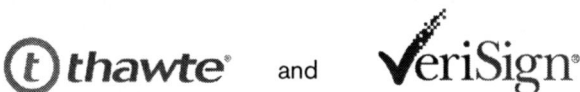

 and

who undertake rigorous accreditation checks to ensure that any business seeking to use a https site is a 'real' business... these checks include independent 3rd party register checks amongst others. What this essentially means is that a site using a security certificate can normally be trusted to protect your data... at least as far as the Internet part is concerned.

The transaction is then verified with the Payment Processing authority and then a result is generated. The result is normally either accepted or rejected, a simple Yes or No, further details are not passed back to the WebSite, Blog or shopping cart system.

If accepted then the Credit / Debit card has the value of the transaction recorded against it and the Business will have its online merchant account credited with the same transaction value.

Charges

There can be three types of charges that are applied when a sale is made.

- Account management fee. This is usually a monthly amount which is billed irrespective of any transactions taking place.

- Transaction Fee. This is a charge for handling the transaction itself. It is fixed irrespective of the value being processed.

- Commission charge. This is a secondary payment which is charged as a percentage of the transaction value. Percentages vary based on the number and volume of transactions that are required to be handled. The higher the volumes the lower the rates and vice versa.

- The fees and commission charges are negotiable in a similar way to regular bank charges applied to our normal bank accounts, however it is important when looking at sales prices to factor these costs into the equation.

Online Chat and Visitor Interaction

For some types of Products and Services especially if they are technical in nature or have complex options, it can be difficult to communicate everything via a product description or even a short video to enable the visitor to buy with confidence.

It is possible that a 'Frequently Asked Questions' section might remove some of the confusion, but if the purchase is quite expensive and there is the chance a client could make the wrong choices, then it might be very handy for the visitor to be able to interact with a customer support agent… in the moment.

This kind of interaction is generically labelled 'Online Chat' and it is now possible to add this functionality to web sites.

In the previous section where we discussed 'Secure Certificate Issuing Authorities' there is a situation exactly like the one described above. Certificates can come with different levels of encryption, 128bit, 256bit, One domain or multiple domains, number of years… etc. etc.

Because of the costs involved and the necessity to match the product with the need very often some advice and guidance is required. Chat both from a Sales and Support standpoint is invaluable here to provide a high level of customer service and ultimately satisfaction.

Chat services for Small Businesses would typically be hosted by the service provider, however for those with technical resources and servers, locally hosted options can be selected.

One service which I have personal experience is :-

You can see this working on the website below :-

Chat services provide some excellent tools to help monitor what is taking place on the website as it happens :-

1. Interactive chat when requested by client, notifies online agents who can elect to pick up the enquiry

2. Ability to actually offer help to the visitor proactively

3. Console to view visits as they happen, see which pages are being accessed and for how long

4. Reports on activity, hour by hour, day by day

When setting up Chat it is possible to include remote workers as Chat Agents, so that this level of client support can be provided from anywhere and by anyone who has an internet connection.

Order Fulfilment

There are five main types of Order, each requires something to happen, but they are very different in the resources necessary to deliver. Let us take a look at the main 5 types below :-

1. **Digital Products**

    e-books, software, online services, information and membership sites are all good examples of Digital products and services.

    The real beauty about sales of this type are that they can be fully automated. The client pays, they receive access and there is no or very little human interaction. Businesses built on this model are 24/7 and potentially global. Sales of e-books can be offered through services such as **Kobo Books** (http://www.kobobooks. com/companyinfo/authorsnpublishers.html) where the author receives 50% of the retail price. Books are then downloaded and read through an application which helps to protect the e-book distribution.

    As we have seen with services such as **Clickbank** (http://www. clickbank.com) and **PayDotCom** (http://www.paydotcom.com) you don't even have to create the Digital Product yourself. These can be good complimentary books or information products that can be added to Blogs or Websites to provide additional value to the visitor or client.

    Digital Products really can be set and forget, so long as the marketing continues in the background. Businesses built on this model can be operated from anywhere in the world and has spawned a new three letter acronym LIP (Location Independent Person)

2. **Other company's physical products**

This can be accomplished in one of two ways. (a) Become an affiliate of the company who makes the products or (b) actually make the sale, then either fulfil from internal product stocks or send the details of the Order to the business partner for fulfilment.

Approach (a) above, requires the company whose products are to be marketed to have an affiliate scheme in operation. Typically they will provide a banner or advert with an affiliate code attached so that any sales made will be credited to that account. In many ways this is identical to a Digital product although commissions are likely to be much smaller. Using this scheme... there is a single transaction per month which would be for the affiliate to collect the commission payment.

In approach (b) the arrangement is more like a distributor. The Distributor is responsible for receiving payment from the customer, handling Credit Control and effectively owns the customer. Delivery can often be handled direct to the client, but it is not unusual for the Distributor to maintain stock especially if the product is sourced internationally.

There are many businesses on the Internet today who will provide custom distributor websites (configured with your logos and colour schemes) for those wishing to work with their product offering. The promotional merchandising marketplace has spawned many Micro businesses utilising this technique as has T-Shirt Printing, Custom Posters, Coffee Mugs and even business cards and stationary. Effectively they are different windows (websites) all linking through to a central production point.

3. **Your own physical products**

Again there are choices in the methods employed for handling your own physical products. If the product range is extensive, then the online Order becomes another method of order placement by clients, but is handled in the same manner as orders received via email, fax or good old snail mail.

For some however if the product is just a single e-book which is now published in paperback form, and needs to be picked and packed, such as:-

http://www.thesinglesgym.com/relationshipsuccessbook

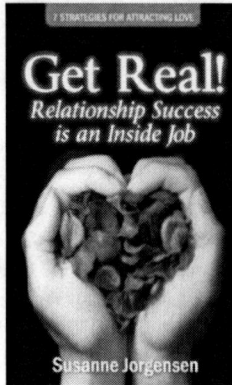

or where there is a small range of products such as on our own **BillBandit** website (http://www.billbandit.co.uk), then a fulfilment company can be used to outsource the pick and pack function.

One company that I have used in the past to provide this service is **Cotswold Handling Services** (http://www.cotswoldhandling.co.uk) who will stock product, pick, pack and ship the product using a variety of delivery partners according to requirements. As businesses evolve using the Internet over the next few decades the demand for offsite distribution will increase **Fulfilment Matters** http://www.fulfillmentmatters.co.uk) is one such company now offering solutions in this arena.

The benefit to small businesses with physical products and using Digital marketing is that the premises costs can be kept to a minimum, so long as the distribution expenses are built into the cost model.

5. Other company's services

Where the sale is of a service nature, then this operates in a similar way to a 3rd party products as described in section (2), the exception being that delivery could be over the web such as training via an Online Webinar, 1-2-1 via screen sharing such as Skype, or indeed in person such as consulting services.

The reward for selling 3rd party services would normally be handled via a commission scheme.

6. Your own services

This would be handled in the same manner as section 4, without the need to make commission payments.

Analysis and Improvement Techniques, the tools you need

The final piece in the Digital Marketing Jigsaw is analysis. Much as we might like to think that what we have created in our Digital Marketing Architecture is superb and right on the nail, the chances are that it is not. The probability is that whatever we have created in the first instance will not deliver the results that we expected. This is not because Digital Marketing is bad, nor that the products we have are undesirable, just the way we have put everything together needs to be optimized!

If a Plane leaves London to go to Singapore, in the first instance it might be flying towards the USA, that's the runway they're using today and it takes off flying west not east. Of course the plane immediately upon attaining a certain altitude makes the correct adjustment and turns to head in the right direction... but the plane is hardly ever pointing the right way to land... until it reaches a few miles from the destination... so it is with our Digital Marketing... we must continually review, check statistics, monitor, tweak, make adjustments, try new things out and see what works best.

There is not a right answer or a wrong answer, there are only results. But by understanding how the results are being derived we can start to increase the performance of what we have put in place.

So let us look at some of the tools which are at our disposal.

Google Analytics *(http://www.google.com/analytics)*

One of the most powerful tools in your arsenal to understand visits to your website or blogsite.

Google Analytics is a web analytics solution that gives you rich insights into your website traffic and marketing effectiveness. Powerful, flexible and easy-to-use features now let you see and analyze your traffic data in an entirely new way. With Google Analytics, you're more prepared to write better-targeted ads, strengthen your marketing initiatives and create higher converting websites. - Google

To use Google Analytics and to get the feedback which you can then analyse a small piece of code needs to be inserted into your website or blogsite pages. Once installed then Google will keep track of what is going on.

The kind of information that is really helpful in understanding how your website(s) or blog(s) are performing are key indicators such as those listed below :-

- How many Visits

- How many unique visits

- How many new visits

- How many returning visitors

- Average number of pages viewed per visit

- Where did the visitors come from

- How long did the visitors stay on the pages

Bounce Rate, how many visitors arrived and then left straight away… i.e. they didn't find what they wanted, weren't interested or perhaps got the wrong site altogether

If the visit was from Google, what Keywords were used and how many visits from each keyword

Although not an exhaustive list by any means over a short period of time it is possible to start understanding the nature of the visits, and making some assessment as to whether this is what was expected.

Clearly a site which has regular updates and provides useful information one would expect to see regular returning visitors, low Bounce rates and high average page views per visit. If this is not consistent with the analytics then something is not right!

If there is an Ad-Words campaign running with certain keywords, then we can begin to see their effectivity using analytics.

Tools such as this enable the Digital marketing team to really start to work marketing much more scientifically than ever before. Plus the results come in hours and days not in weeks or months as it was in the old days with Mailshots and Magazine advertisements.

Google Optimizer

(http://www.google.com/intl/en/websiteoptimizer/features.html)

The link above will take you to the main features list for Google's Optimizer product.

Google Optimizer in simple terms allows you to set up alternate versions of complete pages, or different flavours of the same page and analyze what the relative performances are.

In the right hands, Optimizer provides the ability to optimize web sites to maximise the outcome whatever that is. Below taken from one of the posts on the **Google Optimizer blog** (http://websiteoptimizer.blogspot.com/) some of the key points identified following a successful 'optimisation' where conversion rates were improved from 5% to 22% :-

- Find out why customers aren't converting; don't just guess. If you don't know what their objections are, your chances of overcoming them are very slim.

- Don't "hide your light under a bushel." If your company is the best at something—and if you have proof—make certain the proof is prominently placed on your website.

- Consider segmenting your visitors. How do you know whether to segment visitors? If your most common "visitor intentions" can't be addressed with the same message, you should segment them. Similarly, if you have more than one type of visitor, and they can't all be served by the same message, you'll probably have to segment them. Beware that segmentation can create a lot of extra work, so only do it if you absolutely have to.

- People don't buy what they don't understand. Clearly explain your service, so the prospect is more likely to feel in control and take action.

- Sometimes video is the best medium for explaining things—and for providing proof. Web video needn't cost a lot, as we'll reveal soon. Screen capture videos can easily be carried out using Camtasia (for PC) or Screenflow (for Mac)

Optimizer takes the guesswork out of Optimising your web or blog site. By trialling different options and choosing those that work the best (factually), the online marketing results can be dramatically improved.

Browser Size

(http://browsersize.googlelabs.com/)

Now here is an interesting little tool from Google once again. Over the years we have definitely seen the screen sizes that we use increase significantly (for our laptops and workstations), but there has also been a reduction as the mobile computing drive has pushed on too!

Google's Browser Size program allows you to overlay your website with a template that shows the portion of the page which is viewable by different screen sizes... and what that represents in terms of the percentage of visitors.

Why is this important? Well if your 'call to action', such as the buy button, donate button, register button is not viewable by 30% of visitors without using the scroll bar, then these are 30% of visitors who are less likely to respond. If it is avoidable we should try to do it because this is a problem of our own making brought about by the design and layout of the Website or Blog.

Web Site Statistics

Most Internet Service Providers (ISP's) provide comprehensive reporting statistics on websites that are hosted with them. Blogs will normally either have this information by default or there will be a plug in that can record information for you.

In most cases this information is a repeat of that which is provided by Google Analytics... but there could well be some additional details which might prove useful, so it is well worth asking the ISP if this information is available either online or as a downloadable report that can be requested at will.

In some cases it might not be possible to install the Google Analytics onto the Webpages themselves and if this is the case, the marketing information you need will come from these reports.

Backlink Checker

Earlier in the chapter Hyperlinks, Links and Back links were discussed at length. We now know that rankings in search engines do not depend purely on what we say about ourselves but equally important is what others are saying about us.

What others are saying about us are two things... a link back to us says to Google that our site has something of value on it i.e. it is worth visiting, and the words used on the link tell Google what it should find there once the link is followed.

Clearly an appreciation of how many links are out there pointing back to our Websites and Blogs would be useful feedback. If we have relatively few backlinks then this might be the explanation as to why the search engine ranking is low, and also why low visitor counts are being experienced. If this is the case then a rethink on driving traffic might be required and a strategy to remedy the situation put in place.

There are various paid for and free Bank Link checkers just use one of the search engines using Backlink analyzer or Free Backlink checker

You can get an idea of how many Backlinks you have using the following sites :-

http://www.iwebtool.com

http://seo4experts.com/view/backlink_checker.php

http://tools.seobook.com/backlink-analyzer/

(downloadable tool)

Ad Trackers

An integral part of any advertising campaign is knowing which ads bring you the most visitors, with the Internet we can get a little more scientific than asking the visitor which ad they saw!

There could well be multiple placements of a single ad, or multiple ads running at the same time, what we want to know is which ones are performing the best, so that we can improve the performance of those that aren't or, drop them to concentrate in the highest performing areas.

An ad on the Internet would be a link in the form of words, button, graphic image or banner which normally connects to a squeeze page or sales page

An ad tracking program records when the advertisement was loaded by a browser this is called a page impression. It will record when the URL was clicked and what was the referring URL.

Other information that should be collected at the same time will be the browser and operating system used and the exact time the visitor arrived.

All of the above is compiled along with the total number of hits and also unique hits (takes out any duplicates where one visitor may have clicked more than once) and filed away so that reports can be generated over different time periods... monthly, weekly, daily or in some cases hourly.

Advertising programs like Adwords have their own ad tracking mechanisms built in which you access via their system. But for other advertising campaigns it is necessary to utilise independent ad tracking software.

There are two types of Ad Tracking programs. One type would be self hosted on the website directly the other is an online service.

Self Hosted Scripts

These are normally purchased and then are required to be installed on the Website or Blogsite. The installation would require technical support to install

Online Services

These programs operate completely independently from your own Website or Blog site. The ad code is generated by the service provider and the code inserted with the ad banner or image. The statistics are automatically accumulated remotely by the service provider. Logging into the system provides access to the reports and marketing information.

Some Shopping cart providers like **Total Business Cart** (http://www.totalbusinesscart.com) provide Ad Trackers as part of their overall package which helps to reduce the number of cyber partners needed.

Information overload!!

I have to confess if you have got this far then you've done very well indeed!! a huge pat on the back is required. What we have done is walk through the vast majority of the components that make up Digital Marketing which is a BIG task!

At this point it is worth mentioning that it is not important to understand how and what to do in every part of Digital Marketing. What is important is to have gained an appreciation of the size and scope of what is possible and to be able to come back to this book as a source of reference when establishing your own Internet strategy.

It took a good 8 months or so for me to be familiar with all the main components and put them all in their pecking order (and that is with a technical background and a day job!) and in the next section we will examine what things need to be done first and which can be left to one side for later on.

Digital Marketing is one of those subjects where everyone wants to pass on a mass of information immediately and in our eagerness to learn it can be tempting to attend seminar after seminar and get wrapped up in the whole euphoria. There is a good balance between learning … (especially what you need to know to get started) and actually making progress… moving forward.

Most of the work that will be undertaken is likely to be outsourced or delegated to others, so for the business owner it is not about doing the job rather which parts are relevant and how to integrate them into the sales and marketing process.

As part of the process of learning Internet Marketing and to save writing down URL's (web addresses) on scraps of paper which were later lost, we put together a series of **Internet Marketing Help Pages** (http://www.internetmarketing-help.com/help_BriefOverview.htm) that explained many of the services that are available ranging from Blogging platforms through to professional Voice Over Artists for that special audio or video. These have all been conveniently categorised into the areas to which they relate for example, Driving Traffic, Internet Tools, and Social Networks. This is regularly updated and provides a handy Index to most of the popular services that Businesses need.

The problem facing any business when discovering Digital marketing for the first time is, where on earth do we start? Most companies will have some web presence or other but the chances are it is not really doing anything other than providing an electronic brochure for the business (for those lucky enough to find it) or worse still just a handy place to get directions to the office.

What I needed and what most Business owners want to know is how can they embrace Digital Marketing and move forward? What is the first step?

In the next section we will walk through the process of developing your online Internet – Marketing department for your business. Notice the hyphenation in the in the Internet – Marketing department. This is intentional we are not 'Digital Marketing' in the strict sense of the word which is more to do with the development and sale of Digital products online. We are applying Internet Marketing techniques to develop an online (Digital based) Marketing Department for what is probably a predominantly offline business.

Getting started

I think this is one of the big hurdles for most people entering Digital Marketing at any level is... why am I doing this? Why am I posting content onto Blogs, twittering, when no one is visiting anyway? I'm not reading my other 1000 followers tweets, so I am sure they are not reading mine! If I'm the only one reading what I'm writing I'd sooner not bother! 2 Blog posts a day, why? for what? What am I going to say? What difference will it make?

We expect those new to Digital Marketing to blindly accept that

'you should get a blog, you should use Twitter and join Facebook... trust me... you will see the benefit, later on everything will be much clearer...'

Here then is the issue... of course signing up to these services, Blogs, Twitter, Facebook, Linked in or any other social media platform is not in itself going to make any difference to a business. Just the same as printing some leaflets for a mailshot and leaving them in the garage, or attending networking meetings and not talking to anyone, these won't make much impact either.

The facts are that Digital Marketing is a complex business. It performs the functions of building individual's profiles and credibility, Brand awareness and product / service sales via one medium. Each of these areas requires different techniques, services and strategies online, but you can't go about this in a half baked, apathetic manner. Digital Marketing has the ability to transform businesses, enable small companies to compete with the 'big boys' and build new enterprises from nothing but not by making one blog post a week, or the odd twitter tweet now and then and then complaining that sales haven't increased yet!

So what is the reality? The reality is this, that Digital marketing provides the ability to reach 100,000's of people and quickly, but it won't happen without effort... A LOT OF IT!

Most Small Businesses are owned privately, very often by the entrepreneur who found a niche, designed a new product or took advantage of an opportunity. These individuals are often technical people and suffer from the old 'Feast and Famine' syndrome that finds refuge in Micro and small businesses. When we're in Sales mode we are extremely busy, when servicing customers, our prospect lists dry up... then we're found scratching around for business again which happens, eventually, months after we needed it.

A Digital Marketing department can help smooth out the Feast and Famine issues and with regular, consistently applied effort will bring in a steady stream of qualified prospects, week after week, even when busy with other Customers.

Now typical business owners don't think of themselves as sales people and will readily admit they don't like this part of the business and yet without it the business can't survive, but let us divorce Marketing from Sales and look at each of these separately for a moment.

Marketing is encouraging people to consider your products and services... visitors if you like, whereas Sales is the matching of the customer's requirements to your offerings. At no point in this is there any persuasion or manipulation... better still, much of this sales process can be automated with Digital Marketing. Marketing requires an audience to market too... sales requires us to provide information, substantiate our offering and provide a method to engage with us.

My recommendation is that if you are serious about introducing a Marketing department into your business whether it will consist of existing staff in the company or services provided by outsourced resources a funding budget will be required. To set up a traditional Marketing department would cost $10's of thousands, an Internet – Marketing department will cost less but it will cost! Some words of caution… if the investment is little the return will be little… if the effort is small and erratic the results will be little as well. Remember the Internet has not changed the basic rules of business… but it has changed the mechanics of how it happens.

Here are three useful links covering successful Digital Marketing campaigns and also those that were not so successful. Although undertaken in the main by very large organisations we can learn a lot from the approaches they have taken and adapt them for our own marketing strategies.

> **8 Good online PR Campaigns** (http://www.in2theclouds. com/8%20Good%20online%20PR%20Campaigns.htm)

> **10 Social Media Campaigns that Rock** (http://www. in2theclouds.com/10%20Social%20Media%20 Campaigns%20that%20Rock.htm)

> **10 Online PR Failures** (http://www.in2theclouds. com/10%20Online%20PR%20Failures.htm)

Enough talk then, let's now get into the meat of what we need to do to start building our Internet – Marketing department.

Your Internet Strategy – The planning stage (Exercise 1)

Before we actually embark on the exercise of deployment we need to analyse our business in detail and look at the message and image that we want to promote. This is no different to an offline business; everything we do from a marketing perspective must contribute to the 'master plan' if it doesn't then drop it.

Key milestones in this stage include :-

- **What are we promoting?** This might sound obvious, but in our own business we are promoting 3 key brands. **Chris Ogle** (http://www.public-cards.com/chrisogle), **SME7** (http://www.sme7.com), and i-Tr@der our business platform. They are of course all interlinked as we would expect, but whatever we do ties back to these key brands.

- **Defining your ideal customer.** This is more important than you might think. Without understanding who we think is the type of client who will best benefit from our Products and Services how can we expect to deliver a compelling message to them.

- **Where are our customers?** This can mean physically where they are in terms of local, national, or global. It can also mean what industry sectors or vertical markets, such as business to consumer or business to business e.g. retail, business services, engineering, construction, education, healthcare etc. it might be that clients transcend different markets.

- **The Message(s)**. This is dependent on which client, which product and which market. If the customer is Business to Consumer then the message might be very different (even if the product is the same) to the one used for Construction companies. The message has to be consistent with what you want to happen next... it needs to be clear, easy to understand and have very few options... maximum of three choices.

- **The Sales Cycle**. We need to define the process that a new contact will go through to eventually become a client. What happens at the first contact? how and what will we use to build rapport and develop the relationship with them?

- **The Products**. Identify the products and services that the client can buy as we build trust and credibility with them.

What is the end result (Exercise 2)

Start with the end in mind! How many customers are we looking to find, what will they buy from us and what will be the increase in turnover? In chapter one we looked at belief systems, here is our chance to imagine the new customers, experience how it feels, and sense the excitement from the success of our Digital Marketing.

We need goals, we need a target and it is extremely important with Digital Marketing. I have heard countless stories of individuals caught up in the buzz and excitement of earning a small fortune, doing very little, with no overheads and minimum expenses, easily and within a short time frame. This is about as likely to achieve as winning the lottery... no, unfortunately success is a result of the application of a four letter word – WORK, and it applies just the same here as anywhere else...

"you won't get success when you want it, only when you deserve it"

Let's do some simple Maths... If we believe that every 500th visitor to our Website or Blog generated 1 sale, and we were looking to make an additional 100 sales, then we can calculate the number of visitors required. If we worked on the premise that only 3% of message recipients (whichever form these took) responded and clicked on the link... then the following is true :-

100 sales x 500 visitors / 0.03 = Total number of contacts

= 1,666,666 contacts required.

That looks like a huge number, it is a very large list indeed... but let us just apply some other ideas to this number....

5 people with 60,000 on their lists, sending out 5 tweets per day... this could generate 5 x 5 x 60,000 contacts = 1,500,000, already this is almost enough...

... now suppose some of the 60,000 re-tweeted their lists... lets say 100 people re-tweeted and their lists had an average of 5,000... this is another 500,000 so now added to our existing 1.5M we now have 2M contacts being made.

This is just a simple example with Twitter... and as we have discussed before there are many other sources of lists. The important point is that you don't necessarily have to do all the work yourself, and if the message, products or service is good others will come on board recommending and advertising for you, compounding the initial effort.

Identify some Key Partners (Exercise 3)

Of course the above example has an element of Joint Ventures and / or Affiliate Marketing (where others are assisting promoting your product or service) and this is the great strength of online marketing... collaboration, co-operation and working with an abundance attitude.

Working together significantly widens the potential audience (prospect list) and will generate increased sales and benefits for everyone. Take a simple example in our own business, by developing a close working relationship with **4Networking** (http://www.4networking.biz) (a networking group) and by group leading our local meeting and putting together our 'what has 4N done for us' blog

GoOgle4N

GoOgle4N.com

http://www.google4n.co.uk (GoOgle) we achieve a number of objectives. We promote the brand Ogle with the amusing Google connection and naturally on the blog we promote our own products & Services; **SME7** (http://www.sme7.com), i-Tr@der and **in2TheClouds** (http://www.in2theclouds.co.uk) but we also heavily promote 4Networking too!! The 4Networking Business is receiving in effect free publicity to all our visitors whilst we see increased traffic as people enjoy our ongoing live testimonial explaining how 4Networking has helped our business. This is a mutually beneficial and highly effective form of Marketing unavailable to us in the conventional world but that is open to those who are prepared to think outside the box working online.

Online Inventory Check

If the above exercises have been completed, what we will have is a good idea of our key brands, our typical ideal customer, the markets we want to sell into, some goals to aim for and some potential partners who we can approach to help us get there more quickly.

We now need to take stock of the existing collateral that we have on the Internet. What are our existing online websites and resources and what are they doing for us if anything? It is also a good idea whilst this exercise is taking place, to obtain a list of the following company assets which you may need going forward :-

1. Domain Names the business has registered

- Where are they hosted?

- When were they registered

- Who owns the domains (sometimes the website provider may have acquired them and they are registered in their name)

- Where are the websites hosted (this is often the same place as where the domain is hosted, but not always)

You might find the following website useful for finding out this information **Whois Domain Search** tool (http://whois. domaintools.com)

2. Login credentials for Hosting companies

If the Domain has been registered with an online company such as **123-Reg** (http://www.123-reg.co.uk), **BlueHost** (http://www.bluehost.com), **Hostgator** (http://www.hostgator.com) or **GoDaddy** (http://www.godaddy.com), then there should be Usernames and Passwords associated with the account. These are essential to make changes to Web Site or Blog site hosting details, and will be essential in the management of the collateral in our Online Marketing Department.

3. Choosing the right Domains

If the Business does not have a website, blogsite or any online collateral or if it is a new division, product or service which requires its own resources then the following items need to be considered straight away :-

- Domain Name (for the website or Blogsite)

- Twitter Account (Micro Blogging & List building)

- Facebook or a Facebook Page (Social Media)

- Linked-In (Business Networking)

- Potential other networks e.g. ecademy

- You Tube (Video Posting)

Clearly when deciding a name for the Business, Product or Service it is highly important to find a domain name which is relevant to what is being offered. Going back a few years 3 letter acronyms were hugely popular, IBM, BIC, KPM... but actually although short and easy to type, unless they are household names they are not much use for search engines to establish what the Business, Product or Service is.

It is now accepted that if the domain has a keyword or two relevant to the business, then it will fare much better... remember it is rare people type Domains anymore, they use search engines to look them up and then click on what appears in the results set.

We have seen already some examples of this before and a few of them are listed below where this is true :-

http://www.kisstrainingonline.com

http://www.chrisoglewine.com

http://www.watford.tabletennisblogs.com

http://www.internetmarketing-help.com

There is little doubt that from the Domain names above we can get an idea of what the business is about... no surprise then that the search engines can do the same, so it is important to consider this right at the start. It maybe that existing Domains do little for the business and now might be a good time to rethink the whole strategy. This is vital to get right at the outset and sets the stage for everything that comes after with Digital Marketing, get this right then it will save hours and days of rework later on.

Tying in a Twitter account, Facebook account, Linked-In account, You Tube account using the same basic philosophy as described above is beneficial also. It may not be essential to start setting up all the profiles right now but get the account opened and later on these can be revisited.

To register a Domain is very easy compared with a few years back, and this can be done online by anyone these days. I have already mentioned 4 Websites where you can do this and get the domain validated and purchased quickly. Here they are again...**123-Reg** (http://www.123-reg.co.uk), **BlueHost** (http://www.bluehost.com), **Hostgator** (http://www.hostgator.com) or **GoDaddy** (http://www.godaddy.com).

When selecting where to host your domain I can safely say that those above or indeed any other that you might be using are fine for Domain Hosting... but a word of CAUTION here, not all hosting companies are the same when it comes to providing other kinds of services. I personally really like 123-Reg for hosting Domains and have found their website simple to use... I have also found BlueHost to be great for WordPress Blog hosting and would thoroughly recommend them for this... the last Wordpress site we set up took a matter of minutes and was completely trouble free!! So if in doubt about who you are using check with someone in the know first and get their advice.

What is the last bit of a Domain name about?

The last bit of a Domain name such as .com, .co.uk, .net, .biz, .ltd.com, .info, .org, .eu, .tv etc. etc. there seems to be so many options, what is the difference and which would be best for a business?

Well there is no right or wrong here the first domain names that came out were .com which was to indicate that the website was a commercial website, rather than a government or educational one.

The endings have been growing ever since as the demand for Domains has been increasing. There are really two types of domain, Country specific domains and then global.

A country specific domain such as .co.uk for the United Kingdom, .hu for Hungary, .ie for Ireland here is a Full list of country Domain Name extensions (http://www.iana.org/domains/root/db/).

In general if the market for the products and services of the business is country specific then it is better to choose a domain name with the country extension... mydomain.co.uk for a business located and selling into the UK marketplace. Google and other search engines will rank regional / country specific site content relating to the enquirers country higher than more general domains, so this is worthy of consideration.

If the Business is global or international then it might be preferable to pick a .com, .net or .biz domain extension as these are specifically targeted at business. .eu extensions might be more beneficial if the business targets primarily the European Union.

Commercial businesses should steer clear of .info and also .org which are more closely aligned with charities and public information sites... similarly unless the object of the site is very video and TV orientated choosing .tv might not be wholly appropriate.

Check with your SME7 Practitioner or Digital Coach to help on choosing the most appropriate Domain name(s). This is how the online content will be found, referenced and information stored about the project of Business it is much too important to get wrong.

Making life easy

Now before we go any further... there are a few FREE products that are worth subscribing to and/or downloading (for those actually working on your Digital Marketing Project)

Here I go... One of the real issues for me when first learning about Digital Marketing was the number of URLs (Web site addresses) that people kept bombarding me with. As fast as I wrote them down, more came... in the end I had no idea what the web sites were supposed to be for... lost my notes and then they were forgotten until someone else reminded me later on. For real internet Newbie's who would like a simple to use desktop with all the main applications clearly listed to get you up and running quickly and easily at for FREE, then register at the Bronze Level on the site below :-

Internet Marketing Help (http://www.internetmarketing-help.com)

When you get to the page, on the top right, fill in your name and email address and you after a confirmation email (Check your bulk folder) you will receive a Username and Password. Once logged in there is one click access to all the main Digital Marketing tools... also the ability to download some other neat software applications that will come in handy later on, these are located in the Resources link, under Internet and then the Software folder :-

NVU

Open Office

FileZilla

NoteTab

Tweetdeck

...and

Roboform... now this product is pretty essential. Free of charge up to 10 passwords (you will soon exceed this), but after that for a one off fee this product will remember all your passwords for all your different Online accounts. At the last reckoning we had somewhere in the region of 120+ online usernames and passwords. The problem is that us humans are lazy and often use the same Usernames and Passwords for online activities, this is both insecure and dangerous... but, if they are all different we have the problem of remembering them all... Roboform gets rid of this problem. The Roboform password feature can also be implemented on a Memory stick so that you can use any PC or Laptop and still have all your usernames and passwords with you!!

From the FREEDOM desktop you have a workplace from which you can initiate your Digital Marketing department. Built within the Favourites section are handy links to additional really useful Internet tools. The resources section is constantly being updated with extra tips / videos / links and essential information that can help get your Digital Marketing department off the ground.

Architecting the Solution

The Easy part is over

Until now things have been quite simple, up until now there will have been no need to enlist the support of an Digital Coach, but... if you want to move quickly now, then the best advice would be to find someone who can help architect the main components of your Digital Marketing goals.

What do I mean by this? And why do I need a specialist?

In order to build an Online Digital Marketing Department, in effect we are linking together lots of independent services that have been created by different service providers. Now the Internet is still in its infancy we have to remember this. So there are literally thousands of gifted entrepreneurs building great solutions which solve specific problems, e.g. Shopping carts, Affiliate Product Banks, Autoresponders, Payment gateways, email marketing products, keyword tools, blogging platforms... the list goes on and on.

Now the problem is that these modules have to be joined together and the Internet Industry is some way off providing a common data exchange model that would allow each of these applications to be plugged in to a single central system. But the idea is coming, just take a look what iPhones and the App Store have done... a central engine and, as long as you play by the rules, your application can just be plugged in... These are simple stand alone Apps though... for these systems to exchange data then they have to present information in a standard format that others can recognise and pick up...

Wordpress Blogs look like they are paving the way towards this model but we are still a long way off... so that is the future! Today we have to join these modules together ourselves, this requires some significant technical knowledge.

To illustrate this point we are going to focus on a much simpler exercise than building a companywide Digital Marketing department and how it all links up, we're just going to focus on what is involved in a simple launch of an online e-book... can't be that tough can it?

Ok so below are the steps that we will have to follow :-

A Blog or Website

We must have a domain registered for this... if we use this book as an example, then the domain is in2theclouds.com. The next task is to link that domain name to a Website or Blogsite. This requires the DNS (Domain Name Server) settings to be amended to point the Domain Name to where our content is being stored.

Sales Page(s)

The next task is to create a Sales Page that will promote the book. We have discussed these in a previous section, but for this the following skills are needed, HTML (or be familiar with a software program that creates it), Copywriting (the words on the page), Video and or Audio production, and Image manipulation. You will then also need to know how to arrange everything on the page in an aesthetically pleasing graphic design style and then upload the page and any supporting images, videos and audio files along with it.

Buy Button

The Buy button, needs to link to a shopping cart system, this will require a PayPal or Internet Merchant Account setting up and the Shopping cart system will need the product (the e-book) adding and configuring to deliver all the custom pages such as 'Thank You' and the instructions for downloading the book, as well as taking the money.

Affiliates

If the book can be offered for sale by other people who might like to promote the book, then an Affiliate programme will need setting up. This will handle all the affiliate registrations, provide them with a unique ID, and handle all their commission payments. Affiliate Advertisement images and banners will need to be created so that the affiliates can use a pretty image as an advert for the Book.

Product Bank Affiliate Marketing

If the e-book is to be offered for anyone to resell on the Internet, then two of the main companies providing Product banks are Clickbank and PayDotCom. Any Internet Marketer can browse their product libraries and choose complimentary products to promote and sell. These services need to be registered and configured if required.

Google Ad Words Marketing

Ad Words enable us to get listed at the top of the Google Search engine for keywords or phrases that we want to found with. We can be very specific about the Keywords, we can define that we only want the advert served up from Country specific searches, we can limit our daily spend and there are a multitude of other options to target precisely the audience being sought. There are many stories of Ad Words being used and significant sums of money being effectively wasted because of poor set up and not working through the configuration options carefully enough. This can be a fantastically powerful tool in the right hands but equally, expensive in the hands of the novice.

Are you getting the picture now? The above requires an extensive set of skills and know-how and is often broken down into a number of specialists all performing their piece of the overall jigsaw.

This of course all presupposes… we know what it is we are attempting to do in the first place? …in our case above this was just selling a simple Digital product, once we start to combine this with other products, services and a companywide message things can quickly get complicated.

To clear the fog and put together a comprehensive plan for the Digital Marketing Department identifying which Online Products and Services are required to deliver everything in a coherent fashion is a consulting task. This requires an excellent understanding of the business goals, wide experience of Digital Marketing, and up to date knowledge of products, services and tools available on the web.

From this consulting process will emerge a report of what Online Products, Services and Tools need to be included to deliver on the plan, and how they will all fit together. To execute the roll out will probably require a multi disciplined group of resources, anything from a Video production team, copywriting specialist through to a Blog configuration specialist or HTML programmer. The great thing about the Internet is that it provides us with choices. In this scenario we have a choice to make. If we have 'In-House' staff then we can retrain as necessary to undertake the various rolls, if not then we can enlist the help of external professionals and Outsource some or all of the tasks.

The build – Collateral, web sites, memberships, books

Collateral used to be Corporate Brochures, Product specifications,

Leaflets, Flyers and other printed matter to assist in the promotion of products and services.

Our collateral from a Digital Marketing Department perspective is what we send our Visitors to look at. It could also be deemed to include anything that we offer free in exchange for a name and email address via a squeeze page such as a report, mini e-book or tips and tricks.

Collateral comes in all shapes and sizes and different media, it can be online information via web pages, audio, video or a downloadable PDF (Portable Document Format).

The nature of the collateral relevant to any particular business varies of course, there may well be a whole raft of it already in existence from previous Internet projects. The important point now is that the 'Grand Plan' the architected Digital Marketing Strategy should highlight the collateral that is required to deliver on the goals.

In the early stages of setting up the online marketing many more hours are spent on architecting the Marketing platform and putting together the collateral that is going to be marketed. There is no point in generating traffic if there is nowhere to deliver the traffic too is there?

So building a Digital Marketing department (depending on the complexity) is like building a house… it can seem like hours, days, weeks and even months are being consumed with very little to be seen as the result. What is being done here is building the foundation, get the design right, put in the hours making sure that what you do is good and in line with the overall objectives of the business, then the rewards will come… no doubt, guaranteed! Once the collateral has been built (the foundation put in place) then the rest of the marketing can take place pretty quickly.

It is at this stage that the Look and feel, Branding images, Fonts and Colours that are to be used all need to be considered, before any real work is carried out.

It may well be possible when looking at the scope of the total project that it can be completed in bite size chunks that can be prioritised. Breaking down the project in this way, is desirable and allows parts of the Digital Marketing to get started whilst other elements continue to be put in place.

As discussed above it is important that you have a clear understanding of the overall plan so that short term mini projects will find themselves as part of the bigger picture later on.

> *A good tip that I was given early on is to get good pictures of the key players that are going to be used on the Web sorted out. What is the image that you want to portray? A single image should be used for each person, this makes them instantly recognisable, breeds familiarity and strengthens the connection with the brands.*

Super Tip: For those businesses using Wordpress (and other web tools) a great free service called **Gravatar** (http://gravatar.com) enables the uploading of image(s) to associate with email addresses. Then, whenever a comment is made on a Wordpress blog or other membership site using the 'Gravatar plug-in' it will automatically display the image for the email address!

Getting Started

Where do I Start?

Putting aside collateral for the moment, which is likely to require technical personnel and specialist skills, the first task is to sort out what resources you have at your disposal. These resources will be required to transact on the Internet… that is, they will be updating information, putting up Blog posts, using online services to actually do the marketing work.

The project timescales will need to be looked at too… if the time to get everything sorted is critical, then in the first instance Outsourcing might be the only way, but with training being run in parallel for internal people, the maintenance task could be handled with existing staff members.

As the Digital Marketing department grows then so does the amount of updating, posting and prospect building activity. Before all that kicks off though there are many other set up jobs to get stuck into whilst all the main Web / Blog site work is being carried out.

1. Become an avid learner

There is so much to learn in the early days but, concentrate on some of the basic social media platforms and getting comfortable with putting information out there to start with. See what others in a similar position to yourself are posting and begin to strategise on the way these services can be embedded as part of your ongoing Digital Marketing platform.

MD's of very large organisations use Twitter and Micro Blogging to keep in touch and deliver important information to their trading partners, customers and even as a means of providing support... so it does need investigating carefully to optimise the benefits to the business.

PLEASE NOTE: You will be registering and signing up to a large number of online sites. These will cover various functions; to create a Trading Account, Social Media / Advertising Account, An affiliate account and accounts to use for free services. Care is needed when deciding what Usernames to use. In some cases it will be important to make it absolutely meaningless, but in others such as Social Media sites it is part of the site name and how your information will be found... if in doubt consult your Digital Coach.

2. Write 3 or 4 various length Bio's for your key people, 50 words, 100 words, 200 and 300 should cover most situations.

The majority of us (not all) are a bit sheepish when it comes to blowing our own trumpets. It often feels a bit 'big headed' and 'brash' to declare oneself as an expert or say how brilliant we are at one thing or another.

But we don't want to deal with people who aren't the best do we? Well why should others engage with us if we don't tell them we're the best? No one else is going to say it. The Bio should be carefully crafted and include clear statements on :-

- Who you are, What you do (position), where you live and favourite hobby

- A bit of history / credibility why you are able to perform the functions that you do

- Details of Business Associations belonged to and any Industry specific accreditations gained

- Notable success stories personally involved and proud to have taken part in

- It should also be written in the 3rd person as well

My own bio goes like this… which has all the main bits in… but it's not necessarily perfect… just a guide :-

Chris Ogle is Managing Director of Internet Power Systems Ltd, has lived in Watford near London in the UK for most of his life and is a keen Table Tennis player in his spare time.

Chris has worked in the computer since leaving full time education and has both a technical and commercial background which is unusual in the IT field. Having worked with 000's of companies both large and small alike Chris now uses this experience to deliver his web based business platform to Small and Medium sized companies.

Chris has recently completed his first book 'in 2 the clouds', which draws on his 25 years experience and helps businesses adapt for the exciting challenges of the 21st century. Not content with just business, Chris is also applying his knowledge to community projects, such as revolutionising the development of his sporting passion, Table Tennis.

Chris Ogle's home page:-

http://www.public-cards.com/chrisogle

3. Start to build Social Networking Profiles

We have discussed in considerable length earlier in this chapter about the why's and wherefore's of these sites. The bottom line is that they engender credibility and provide a human face to products and services… in effect the lady or the man behind the persona we see and read about in the normal marketing spiel.

If new to this and entering the online social domain for the first time, it will all be very confusing at first but familiarity comes with use after a few weeks, mastery arrives soon after, only a month or two down the line.

What is key here is to start building a list of contacts and to start communicating with the world at large… I know of many, many people who have reconnected with people from the distant past as a by-product of introducing this into their daily activity and has therefore been rewarding on multiple levels.

4. Establish a Twitter presence

It is **Twitter** (http://twitter.com) today it might well be another Micro Blogging platform that is dominant in the future. This is a means of broadcasting to an audience of many thousands in an instant. There are countless online learning programs to learn how to use Twitter to engage with and follow those who may be interested in your products and services or even who might share a common leisure passion.

The key here is to get off the ground and start following some interesting people and then being followed yourself. Initially Twitter users used their names as Usernames, but more recently this has been replaced by more business orientated names such as http://twitter.com/trainingloopy or our own http://twitter.com/sme_7.

A word on Following and Followers. As the number of people being followed grows, the amount of time that a tweet remains in your timeline reduces... once could spend all day looking at tweets, organising, unfollowing (removing someone being followed) and generally administering the account... the net earnings would be zero... with the exception of Media Superstars with zillions of followers and who are following less than 50 the rest of us either have to spend time seeking out those worth following or engage the services of an automated service to take some of the tedium out of it.

Tools for managing your twitter accounts

Automated tools come in a variety of flavours from the follow anything that moves variety to those that apply some science and rules to the process... one such automated product is **Twittollower** (http://www.twittollower.com) and has resulted in around 2000 followers in 3 weeks of activation.

There are some great utilities out there for Twitter to help build and manage your Twitter accounts. Disseminating information for sales or any other purpose is a numbers game, pure and simple, some of the people who follow a Twitter account will latch on to the message, send again, and a different set of people will see it. So if it is a game are there any rules?

Yes there are some rules, not too many at this time, but remember, fall foul of the people who run these sites and they can close you down without an recourse or grievance... so play clean is the best motto.

One of the rules on Twitter (at the moment) is the magic number of 2000. You are NOT allowed to follow more than 2000 people until you have more than 2000 people following you. Why? Well this prevents people following millions of people, then unfollowing everyone that hasn't followed back, leaving a huge amount of followers behind. So what is wrong with this? Well, it can be automated, causes huge amounts of work for the computers behind the scenes and is against the principle of Twitter which is a mechanism to communicate between people not just to blast out spam to zillions of people.

So Twitter accounts need to be managed, the good news is there are tools to do this. I've mentioned **Twittollower** (http://www. twittollower.com) above which is an automated tool that handles the growth of followers automatically for you in your selected niche, but there are other products that you can use that permit the same level of management but they are a bit more DIY (Do it Yourself).

There are two great tools for this, the first is **ReFollow** (http:// refollow.com), this FREE online service allows you to find an individual operating in your target market, look at all their followers and then select and follow their followers. Now there are some great additional features to refine the selections but in principle... if these people are following the big names in your niche... you have a tool here to tap in and get that list (or a percentage at least) to follow you too! Do this with many of the big names... and what a following you could end up with!

Now... the key here is to keep the number of Followers and those Following in line... i.e. not too far apart in numbers terms... so there is a great tool called http://thetwitcleaner.com/ that enables to you find people who aren't doing anything much with Twitter and unfollow them automatically... this is weeding out the spammers, or those that are not using the service very often etc. So we could select all those that don't have an avatar (image) or all those that haven't tweeted in 3 months, or those that have a huge discrepancy between followers and those they are following, and, en-mass unfollow these accounts. This way we can then follow more suitable twitterers and build our following with real people. To build your twitter list... just do this over and over again... with each twitter account that you have.

Twitter Lists also enable us to categorise people who are posting regular good information into groups that we can set up ourselves… this is invaluable as a method of catching the good stuff from an ever faster moving timeline. I have a Money Gym list for example and I can quickly keep up to date with all their posts just by accessing that list. All their posts are neatly stored there under a single link. All the Twitter tools that link up with twitter allow similar and even more comprehensive facilities to maximise the efficient use of twitter which is more than this book aims to cover.

5. Sign up and register for useful tools

Check out the **Internet Marketing Help** (http://www. internetmarketing-help.com) site, you should definitely sign up for Hootsuite, SocialOomph or another Twitter management tool. There are some great aggregation products out there that bring multiple feeds into a single timeline such as 'FriendFeed' which might be applicable. The list of online services is huge and growing all the time, get on board with the key ones to start with and commit to learning what different sites can do for you… for example what is the difference between **StumbleUpon** (http:// www.stumbleupon.com) and **Squidoo** (http://www.squidoo. com) and how might they be used in the overall marketing strategy.

6. Sign up for all the different products and services that the business is going to need

These may include some or all of the following :-

Shopping Carts, Blogging Platforms, Hosting services, Emailing and Autoresponder services, Membership platforms… if there is money involved; merchant accounts or PayPal, Product Banks (Clickbank, PayDotCom)

It may not be necessary to activate or start some of these services just now. Some however take a while to put in place. Merchant accounts with some banks at this point in time necessary for regular monthly billing can take 6 weeks for some reason, so if this is required it makes sense to kick it off quite early on.

The amount of time it can take to 'set up' the basic infrastructure to support all the online activities can run into days or even weeks if there are multiple products and services involved. The set up is a once off investment, although there will undoubtedly be updates and additions over time. Experienced Internet Marketers will complete the above activities much more quickly for sure, but if the management is to be in-house then the learning experience will be invaluable during this phase.

Routine Activity Schedule

The Digital Marketing department are primarily concerned with three main activities :-

- Keeping the Digital Marketing platform fed with updates and new content

- Running Campaigns and Product Launches

- Providing Marketing Statistics and Analysis reports

These activities can be further subdivided into regularity. Below I have provided an example of how this activity might break down into daily, weekly , monthly and annual time buckets.

This provides a scalable model for Digital Marketing. One full time person may be able to handle all the marketing activity for 3 products. To manage 6 products may need 2 people. As all of the activities are Internet based these functions can easily be outsourced providing flexible choices on staffing for the business owners.

Every day activity

So what does a Digital Marketing department do on a daily basis?

Twitter (30 minute workout)

- Send out 3 social chat messages as you go about your day

- Share 3 things that you have found that you want to share with others

- Retweet 3 messages from others, that you wanted to share with others

- Send out 2 messages that demonstrate your expertise or knowledge

- Spend time replying to anyone that messages you

- Spend time answering any questions around your area of expertise

- Spend some time recommending other peeps to follow

- Answer any direct messages that are not spam

- Invite a daily question on your area of expertise or knowledge

- Spend time in the Search, listen & then engage when you can add value

The above represents activity that would be pertinent to a single Twitter account... 6 accounts = 3 hours.... every day. Of course if following tools are being used then some elements of the above may not be required.

Managing your Twitter Account

At the time of writing this book there were a few (but not that many) rules about what you can and can't do in terms of building your lists as we discussed earlier in this chapter.

Work on building your followers every day using a tool such as **ReFollow** (http://refollow.com) or if you want to automate the process **Twittollower** (http://twittollower.com). Each day find a Big List owner in the niche and work on their list to build your following. To find Big List owners use the Twitter search tool **twitter search** (http://search.twitter.com) or **twazzup** (http://www.twazzup.com).

Then using a tool such as http://thetwitcleaner.com/ sort out the real accounts from the spammers and clean the list from yesterdays activity.

** Great new service **

You can start to produce some quite clever feeds from information being collected via Twitter these days... here is a great example the **Chris Ogle Daily** (http://paper.li/chrisogle) which is automatically formatted each day on posts made by myself and those people who I am following... now it is real people making the News!

Facebook

Linking Facebook with Twitter accounts is a great way to share information automatically with your facebook contacts without any additional effort.

For those wishing to expand contacts and use Facebook more actively then link Business pages with Twitter accounts. Updates posted onto Business pages then get automatically posted onto the designated Twitter account. Another feature of Facebook that can encourage connections is to set up a Group. Both Groups and Pages allow postings to go out to all the members. Used to encourage debate and provide valuable help to others will create connections, trust and then opportunity.

If using Business Pages and custom pages, then each day we should be responding to wall posts, discussion groups, posting questions and inviting responses. This regular interaction will develop and strengthen the budding relationship with those who 'Like' these pages. Remember these posts are appearing on the timeline of each follower.

This is the **Facebook SME7 Business Page** (http://bit.ly/SME7) which has been built to add value and promote discussion around Digital Coaching with Facebook fans. This is a great way to meet new people from across the globe, harness new ideas and improve the end products and services to clients.

Great new features are being added daily to Facebook especially with Business pages e.g. Newsletters (check out Nutshell below to find out more)

*** *top tip : get all your updates from Facebook, Twitter, myspace and linked in all into your email inbox plus lots more with :-*

http://nutshellmail.com/

N.B. A word of warning, there is a huge amount of 'Noise' (sales activity and just general marketing) going on with Social media sites, and it is growing as businesses seize the potential. There is likely to be a backlash at some point... to avoid being hidden from timelines or unfollowed it is prudent to flavour activities in this area as **'Relationship Building'** as opposed to Marketing... people are not daft and want to be connected to people and treated as a person not just a sales prospect.

Blog Posts

A blog post should be written and posted in the early days at least once per day. Many new to Digital Marketing complain bitterly about the frequency of blogging and that they could not possibly find that much to write about or indeed the time to do it. The Digital Marketing departments' responsibility is to request content from those in the business who can provide it… or… go find interesting content about their market sector on the Internet somewhere and blog about that. Of course when using other people's content there is a requirement to provide a backlink back to the originating blog.

The marketing department might find **EzineArticles** (http:// ezinearticles.com), **MyBlogLog** (http://www.mybloglog.com), **StumbleUpon** (http://www.stumbleupon.com), **Hub Pages** (http://hubpages.com) and **Squidoo** (http://www.squidoo.com) sources of interesting content that can easily be turned into Blog posts if the in-house team come up a little short on the creativity front.

Blogging and fresh content brings search engines back to re-index your content. Consistent usage of the keywords being used to promote and market the business need to be included within each blog post and this serves to consolidate their understanding of the main functions and purpose of the site(s).

This reminds me of a gem of advice from a boss in the past…

> *Success is about doing things which others won't do. Most work is boring, but consistently and persistently doing the basics better than anyone else, more often ends up with success.*

… and so it is with Digital Marketing whether it is done by the business owner or delegated it doesn't matter much, what does matter is that it gets done regardless. Check back to Step 2 in this book… it is not our responsibility to do everything or enjoy all the tasks that are involved in our respective businesses. Most important is that we document what needs doing into a process and then delegate the task to a resource competent to carry it out.

Social Bookmarking

This is an activity that needs to just become part of the routine. As we locate interesting sites and pages on the web we should start to automatically bookmark them.

We are all used to adding things to our favourites on a web browser, well a bookmark is a similar thing just not on your web browser on your machine, but filed on an online account which you set up with one of the bookmarking sites... here is a few of them

Delicious (http://delicious.com)

Diigo (http://www.diigo.com)

Digg (http://digg.com)

StumbleUpon (http://www.stumbleupon.com)

All of these have slightly different flavours... most of them have toolbars that you can plug into your browser as well to make storing and retrieving them a simple click away, and you can access these libraries of favourites from anywhere.

Why would we use these? Well these are essentially communities where people are sharing web pages and information that they have already screened and liked. So it is effectively another method of consuming web content, another way to find information that has already had approval and been found to be worthwhile.

By bookmarking sites, once again we are building up links and social networks, credibility and contacts. **Diigo** (http://www. diigo.com) is really handy as it allows you to annotate the web page information you have bookmarked with your own notes. Stumbleupon is an advanced social network which can become a great publicity tool and generate traffic back to your content, so this is well worth exploring.

Forums

Forums, especially those that are allied to your business can provide a fertile breeding ground for opportunities. They can also be a general moaning zone for habitual negative people and so caution is required when participating.

A review of recent posts, commenting on those where it is relevant and a useful personal contribution can be made. Reply to any PM

(Private Messages) that have been received.

Weekly tasks

Write an Article

Articles are really powerful for both the authors' credibility and for a solid regular volume of backlinks to your content. **EzineArticles** (http://ezinearticles.com) provides a great place to get registered and to start building an expert status in your field. Between 10 and 25 published articles will improve the status and accelerate the speed of articles being published.

There are ways to publish articles globally across the Internet. By writing different version of the same paragraph, programs can spin article sections and deliver a wide range of versions of the essentially the same article. With 10 paragraphs and 5 versions of each the permutations are vast and unique articles can be posted on thousands of article sites without duplication. A great example of such as product is **Unique Article Wizard** (http://www.uniquearticlewizard.com/), this product has around 11,000 article and blog sites available to post to and will increase backlinks to your site by the hundreds!

Weekly Ezines

All Digital Marketing Departments should be building a database of businesses / people that are interested for us to keep in touch with them. Generally an 'opt-in' list is built as a result of offering a free report, a guide or some tips, perhaps even a mini e-book as is the case with SME7.

The weekly ezine is a tool for keeping in touch with the subscribers. There are various methods for delivering an ezine, from plain text through to full colour html pages with feedback on who has clicked on each link in the ezine. There are arguments in favour for both types. A good example of one online service is **iContact** (http://www.icontact.com).

Review months marketing campaign / launch and adjust

Each month should contain a positive marketing campaign. Of course this is not essential, but it is like running an offline mailshot or perhaps a telephone canvassing campaign.

In order to continue to drive traffic new ideas such as free product offers or online competitions will create genuine proactive interest that will lead to further subscribers and new leads.

The progress of such campaigns should be measured weekly and adjusted if necessary

Review programme for next month's marketing campaign

During the current month the planning and development of next month's campaign should be monitored and checked to ensure that is will be complete in time for the start of the month.

Forums

Start a thread on each of the forums that the business is participating in, remember that whoever is posting is representing the business and these posts should be cleared for publication by an authorised individual within the business before they are submitted.

Networking

Plan to attend one networking event every week. **4Networking** (http://www.4networking.biz) in the UK works well for us combining online forums and regular meetings held in a number of towns within a 30 minute drive from our locale. There are a good number of these now operating, all with a slightly different format, it's about picking the one that is right for you, BNI is another that has a good following. There are also Women only groups catering for Women in Business and operating in a more 'family friendly' manner, one which always has a good turnout in the UK is Women In **Business Network** (http://www.wibn.co.uk).

Contacts Database Update

Enter all the new contacts met this week with appropriate information about what they do into you business CRM system. If you don't have one, then it is my recommendation that you get one. This information will become crucial for the business going forward. A Cloud based system as discussed at step 3 provides the best in flexibility, even if this is not apparent right now. Do this activity weekly it is much easier to do little and often than face the prospect of days of mundane data entry and trying to remember who the people were!

Twitter

Don't forget to (Twitter) follow any new people you may have met at Network meetings, been given their business card or have spoken to on the phone.

Facebook

If you are using Twitter to feed directly into Twitter then administration of Facebook ought to be at the PAGES level. A post on the Wall per day giving an update on developments.

Locate and find new people met during the week at Network meetings and add them as friends with a short welcome message

Linked-In

Locate and find new people met during the week at Network meetings and add them as connections with the details of where you met with them.

KBI Statistics review

In any Marketing endeavour there will be key business indices that give us an indication of performance. Digital Marketing is no different, although what these indices are will be different between businesses, actually even between different functions. The weekly check would be just to ensure no catastrophe has taken place on the key indices... such as number of visitors for the week compared with previous weeks...

If we take a look at our local **Watford Table Tennis Blog** (http://www.watford.tabletennisblogs.com) it has 87% of visitors that are returning and only 13% new. This is fairly typical because the visitors are checking the league tables and also reading interesting new blog posts.

These results would not be sensible for a site which is promoting a new product or service... the statistics for that site would need to be the other way around. If this was not the case then clearly something is wrong.

We might also consider 'New Registrations' for the Free e-Book and joining our ezine list an important statistic to monitor weekly as would be the number of e-books sold.

The monthly analysis would look at these statistics and into the heart of the detail such as where did the visitor come from and which adverts resulted in most sales of the book etc. etc.

Monthly actions

At the end of each month, set aside some time with your Digital Coach (certainly in the early months). This time should be used to review progress and to learn the necessary analysis skills. Activity will generate a series of results already touched on it the weekly action list, now we need to get more comprehensive.

For an initial period the Digital Coach will be able to run the reports off (they are all web based anyhow) and collect the analysis data which should form the basis for decision making in the monthly marketing meeting.

The list below should form the basis of the Agenda, obviously chopping out the bits which aren't relevant and adding in specialist items maybe not covered here.

Review Profiles make sure they are still current

Check all the online profiles, of which there will be a few and make any adjustments or amendments as appropriate. With multiple profiles in an organisation the likelihood of changes goes up with the volume. Seek to keep these as up to date as is possible and in line with the business and people as things change.

AutoResponder series

If the business is using autoresponders for developing ongoing relationships with the opt-in list, check frequency of email sends, unsubscribe numbers and check take up or sales of any products that might be offered via this mechanism. I have often been pestered incessantly by overzealous Autoresponder series and whilst it might be acceptable in the purist form of Digital Marketing in the business world this would be viewed as harassment and end up with unsubscribe numbers being high. A good balance of quality information on a regular but not too often basis is the spot to aim for... some tweaking will be needed to get it right... personally my view is once a week would be just about acceptable.

Often autoresponder series need to be revisited and honed over time, the capability to see what is happening and rectify as soon as we spot undesirable actions is a great facility. It is likely that there will be the need for multiple Autoresponders, those for

Prospective clients and others for those which have now become clients.

Check Backlinks

In a previous section I went into detail about the importance of Backlinks. These are other website links that point to your content. A large number of backlinks is interpreted by the search engines that there is something worth visiting and sharing, which is good news!

With a solid article submission program and by using products such as **Unique Article Wizard** there should be a significant increase in the number of backlinks pointing back to the websites and blogs.

Backlinks can be counted automatically by online programs and are listed again for convenience below :-

http://www.iwebtool.com

http://seo4experts.com/view/backlink_checker.php

http://tools.seobook.com/backlink-analyzer/

(downloadable tool)

This should be done monthly to monitor the effectiveness of the articles and to measure the increased exposure. This will translate into increased visits to the websites and Blogs. If Sales are not increasing even though visits are up, then this would suggest that work needs to be performed on the copy. It means people are visiting but not voting with their wallets. OK, this is a problem, but at least now we know and are able to do something about it.

Review detailed KBI's

As we have seen above the Internet provides us with amazing quality feedback that has never been available in the offline world. We are now able to measure and monitor just about all our online activity, within a matter of 24 hours and then make adjustments and go again.

What is crucial is to define a set of Key figures that are a good measure of different aspects of the Online Marketing, and then put these into a spreadsheet. Over time, this raw data can be represented in graphs to and annotated with activity that can explain how and what has happened. Time to get scientific with marketing!!

Monthly Newsletters / Ezine

The monthly ezine like the weekly one explained above is a tool for keeping in touch with subscribers. It is unlikely that the same products or business areas would have both, although within a business there could exist a weekly and a monthly ezine covering a different subscriber database.

In our own business we do not operate a weekly ezine. The monthly Ezine provides a summary of all the articles and blog posts that have happened in the month in a short but succinct professional looking email. The subscriber can then link through and read any of the posted documents which catches their interest.

We provide links to one or two of our own products and some useful 3rd party products (those that we have used ourselves and are happy to recommend) to add an extra dimension and colour to the Ezine.

We use i**Contact** (http://www.icontact.com) as well as our own in-house Contact Management system (which has a built in email campaign module) to send out both the regular Ezine and special announcements and promotions to our main business / customer database.

This Ezine should be on the monthly marketing Agenda to review the content, presentation and ratified ready to send out.

Review JV Opportunities & New Contacts

At the end of the month it is important to table the contacts we have met in the month. Opportunities happen when people meet. Networking on a regular basis gives us a chance to discover new people with new skills who could supply us with a product or service, help out someone we know, or indeed if the timing is right open up a new profit centre.

New contacts made during the month should be discussed at this meeting to evaluate any potential. With our own **SME7** (http://www.sme7.com) business, almost any contact could become one of the following :-

- Someone offering a valued service a contact or acquaintance I know may need, so I can refer them

- A member of our monthly database and be kept informed regularly about what we are doing. We never know something might be of interest to them later on

- They may wish to engage with us and take advantage of one of our service offerings

- They may wish to join the **SME7** (http://www.sme7.com) network and want to deliver the 7 Step programme to their clients increasing their earning potential

- They might have an idea that they would like to discuss and possibly joint venture with us

Actually what I do know is that I don't know, and it is always important to never be attached to the outcome. I always seek to learn as much as I can about a new person so that at the very least I can become comfortable with the individual and I can perhaps help out in some way.

Bringing these contacts to the table enables us to categorise and annotate their contact record in our system properly. This improves the quality of our contact data and ensures that we communicate with these businesses / people in the most effective manner.

Launch this months Marketing Campaign

Keeping our business fresh, innovative, new and exciting is one of the roles of marketing. There are some great online services now that provide us with tools to keep customers coming back to our site time and time again :-

- Ad Words (http://adwords.google.com)

- Product Launch

- Surveys & Questionnaires (http://www.surveymonkey.com)

- Collect votes on a subject with Poll Software (http://www.surveypopups.com)

It may be time to start an AdWords campaign. This requires both care when planning and perhaps even the services of an expert who will earn their keep in no time, providing good sound advice, guidance in picking the correct words and phrases, setting the project up and making sure you maximise the ROI (Return on Investment). Check out June Cory – **My Mustard** (http://www.mymustard.co.uk) who explains Ad Words in a 'user friendly' language and has a well respected reputation in helping clients get the most from their ad-words campaigns.

If you have a Product launch coming up, substitute this months campaign for the Launch. We'll come on to Product Launching in a bit, but there is plenty to keep occupied on this without contemplating more marketing activity for the month.

Surveys, Questionnaires and Poll software products (and there are others out there) engage with your audience and can also provide useful feedback and direction. Announce these surveys on Twitter and the social networks to get real feedback from real people… information collected in this way can be invaluable for both product development and also for increasing the business profile.

Define the measurement criteria, how will you know if this campaign has been successful? What is the primary purpose, increase visits, new subscribers or sales? what tools will be used to report back the results? What would be considered a **good** campaign and one that would be run again in the future?

Review this months Marketing Campaign, analyse reports and keep a spreadsheet of key statistics

Take time out to review how this months Marketing campaign (that has just finished) has worked out.

The statistics should be available for the meeting and reviewed against the criteria set for this campaign. Later on in this chapter we review the Analysis tools available to us, but with products such as **Google Ad Words** (http://adwords.google.com), **Survey Monkey** (http://www.surveymonkey.com) and **Survey Popups** (http://www.surveypopups.com) they provide excellent graphical statistics of activity.

Digital Marketing tools provide such a comprehensive feedback loop that we can quickly make changes to our online materials from what we learn. Prospects, Clients and in fact people in general are always willing to pass on an opinion. Use these tools to encourage our online network to talk to us and help us get more in tune with our audience. Once the world at large sees that their opinion is valued this provides a stronger bond between the business and the site visitors. Use the results of campaigns as Blog posts to explain what happened with the feedback, this communicates that the time spent completing the online questionnaire / survey by the respondents wasn't a waste of time.

Annual reviews

This is the time when we need to take stock. Annual targets whether they are monetary or activity related are crucial, not so that we can haul individuals over the coals or even beat ourselves up but so that we can set some idea of how things are progressing. Why are Targets... or shall we call them **Business Plans** important?

Well because we have to plan, it doesn't matter if we're wildly wrong about our expectations, but what we need is to have thought about what would we like our business to look like at the end of the year?

It maybe that this is a number of books that have been sold, or the number of new clients we have signed up to one programme or another, or even how many paid for delegates on training courses in the year... the good news is that no one is telling you the answer you can make it up! But be honest, be realistic and use all the information you have at your disposal to come up with the best possible guess...

You might ask quite reasonably, and, as a business partner of mine (who still is, and now does a business plan) asked of me, what's the point of creating a plan if I've made it up?

Well the answer is this, the best person to make a forecast about your business is who? It is you of course, if someone wanted to invest in your business, or you wanted to borrow some funds to develop your business, how would those people assess the worth of your endeavour? It would be based on what you think, you are the only one capable of delivering a competent forecast about your business and if you can't do it then no one can, and no one is going to lend anything. The only way is by looking at your Business Plan. Ideally it should be an 18 month plan... projecting out into the future how you expect the business to pan out.

Now what is in a Business Plan? The purpose of this book is not to go into the details of a complex business plan, however it should contain 3 or 4 sections.

1. Expected Revenues. Sales, broken down across your different products and services

2. Costs. All the business costs, right down to phone bills, heating costs, stationary etc.

3. Sales Volumes. This explains the how the revenue is broken down into actual products and services

4. Salary Analysis, which breaks down one of the major cost lines into more detail.

Now once loaded into a Spreadsheet (Click here for a spreadsheet example which can be used if desired) you can start to see based on your projections the retained earnings and profits from your business.

There is nothing so rewarding as looking at a Business plan and increasing the various numbers to see what extra sales can do to the profits... your earnings, or indeed looking at price increases and how that could affect the bottom line profit.

Ok... armed with our new tool, we are in position to start to analyse what we have. If completed correctly the costs should be pretty accurate perhaps with the exception of a few scalable items, however the real variable as we know is the predicted sales. That is why it is so important to have a business plan, if only to see when the business might actually start to make a profit.

The business might of course already have a comprehensive business plan, if this is the case then what is needed is what we are coming onto next, working out what we need to do online to get the (increased) sales results that we are looking for.

To predict Sales volumes we need to come back to our marketing. To get any real concrete figures we have to start by how many sales we want to make, then apply percentages up the line to find out how many contacts we would need to make. Let's see what that might look like for a particular product. Again let us use this e-book as an example in this exercise :-

Let's assume we want to sell 5,000 books in the 1st year. Seems like a reasonable target. If we were to sell the book for $27 dollars and $15 dollars was paid out to affiliates, then we would make after all fees approximately $10 per book. So the revenue stream would be $50,000, looks good...

So what would we have to do to achieve this?

Lets assume that for every 100 people who visit the sales page we convert 1 into a sale... so to sell 5,000 books we would need to divide this by 0.01 = 500,000 visits.

Now we know that to get 5,000 book sales we need 500,000 visits that is 41,667 per month or around 1,389 every day! We have to now look at how we can derive those visits. In the section coming up 'The Marketing Mechanics' we will be looking at the different tools that we can use to drive traffic to our Book Sales Page / Blog.

Now the percentages above might be wrong, they could be too optimistic or pessimistic... we won't know until we start the process, and we may have to adjust figures accordingly. It is highly likely that different traffic from different sites will generate different sales percentages and Ad Trackers should be used to identify where the sales have come from... Now why would different sites produce different results, how can that be?

Well let us say that we have are working hard in the Networking arena and these contacts are mostly business people which is definitely our target audience. We send those interested in knowing more about us directly to the book sales blog... the sign up for the book here is coming from personal interaction and a genuine business interest, the percentage might be as high as 10%. In another situation the visit may have come via Twitter a much more generic suspect population... here the headline may have caught someone's attention but on arrival there is a much lower conversion rate into a sale compared to that of the networking environment.

The two situations above highlight the terms, warm market and cold market. The best conversions are found in the warm market, the trick is to work therefore in your warm market... or work with others on their warm market.

What I am trying to do here is show that there is a bit more to planning and annual review than a blind leap of faith, finger in the air, stab in the dark approach. Of course the first Plan will be hopelessly wrong, but as the results come in, so the plan can be adjusted and improvements made all the time.

The annual review gives us a great opportunity to look at the year as a whole, where it went wrong, where it went right, and set the plan for next year, although we won't be waiting till the end of the year to make adjustments right? (If a monthly review demands it?) So what drops out the bottom of this planning exercise?

ACTIONS… lots of them!! Actually results and sales come from doing things, lots of them, over and over again. The reason for planning is so that we know how many things we need to do, allocate the necessary time, and plan who will be doing them… what we are saying here is that from the plan actually comes all the daily marketing activities that we need to perform.

The other key thing here, is that this is exciting stuff and we need those who are going to undertake the tasks to be involved in the planning stage… accepting a discussed set of plans involving the individuals concerned gets a 'buy in' and assigns a level of 'responsibility and ownership' and the commitment to carry out the action… giving people a target discussed from 'on high' with no involvement = under performance, every time…

Launching Products & Campaigns

Product launches and campaigns are different from the regular updates that take place on daily, weekly and monthly cycles. These are one of projects that are run to illicit a response.

That response might be to get feedback on a current service or product, or to canvass from clients some indication of preference about something still in development.

This is an opportunity to sell and promote the company all in one go, and involves a considerable amount of resource. There are really six main elements to a Campaign (whether this is a product or information type campaign the approach will be similar).

1. Planning (2 days)

2. Collateral (1 week)

3. Pre Launch (1 – 2 weeks typically)

4. The Day before the launch (1 day)

5. Launch period (typically 1 week)

6. Post launch analysis (1 day)

Our Campaign should adhere to the themes and styles that we have introduced at the global marketing level for continuity. Once again let us take the **in 2 The Clouds** e-book as our example. This is a simple product launch that fits into the scope of our much wider Internet Marketing Digital Marketing project. We can take a simplified view of the activities that were required to get things in motion right up to the point of the launch; they are steps 1 through 4 above :-

Planning

Registration of Domain

Visited **123-Reg** (http://www.123-reg.co.uk), checked out domains and secured both the .com and .co.uk flavours of the In2TheClouds domain.

Decide how the Book is to be launched & promoted

How was the book to be launched and in fact how anything is to be launched is probably the most difficult part of any campaign. To get the book out there in the first place and to encourage people to read it we decided that offering the e-book free if registrations took place before a certain date would perhaps work well for us. It would also give us a fixed point in time to work to (goal) and enable us to promote to our lists up to that date. After this date we would then revert to a different approach... there would be a book blog/web site which would handle the ongoing sales of the book. Being a blog would mean that I could easily post book updates and new links as they are discovered, and complement the book and which could later be rolled into a new revision, but make these updates available for visitors and subscribers as they happened.

The initial Sales Page which actually is a squeeze page (read more about squeeze pages earlier in this chapter) provides a free chapter of the book now and the e-book for free before the launch in exchange for a name and email address.

After the launch this squeeze page will be adapted for other uses but still operate as a sign up / registration page.

Enlist help of others for promotion

If the business doesn't have an existing database of any size, then we have a few options, to create one, buy one or borrow one (or two). In fact our e-book is complimentary to many companies that we have a working relationship with. Partnerships such as this can give the launch of any product a welcome boost. We agreed to create a special version of our page for one such company so that when they registered we could identify from which list the lead originated and therefore pass control back to them for follow up.

Who is going to do what?

The plan is in place, the next challenge bearing in mind the timeline is who is going to do what? With just 4 weeks to go before the launch we have time constraints so the delivery ends up with the following list of contributors :-

- Sales Page – Internal

- Set up Google Analytics - Internal

- Twitter marketing – Internal

- Email Marketing – Internal

- Ad Words – (not utilised on our campaign)

- Supporting Articles – Internal

- Facebook publicity – Internal

- Forums – 4Networking – Internal

- Other Membership sites – Internal

- Product Bank set up, Clickbank, PayDotCom - Internal

- **Total Business Cart** (http://www.totalbusinesscart.com) set up and configuration (Autoresponders, subscribe form) – Internal

- Book Formatting – External **Suzanne Barnett** (http://suzannebarnett.co.uk)

- Revised **In2TheClouds** e-book Sales Page (http://www.in2theclouds.com) post launch - External **Claire Raikes** (http://www.claireraikes.com)

Some of this is Collateral build; the Sign up for the free book and the revised sales page, however the majority of the work on this project revolves around the marketing and getting the message out there.

Notice however the final two items the Book Formatting and the revised Sales Page for post launch. These we elected to outsource, why? Because it was the most cost effective method of getting the jobs done!! Internally we were struggling with time and expertise, more on this in the next chapter 'Outsourcing'.

Collateral

1. Sales Page

Having defined the process, the next step is to build the sign up page. To achieve this we will use a number of tools, NVU (free HTML editor), **Total Business Cart** (http://www.totalbusinesscart.com) to store the registrations for the book, Filezilla to upload the HTML page and Images to the web server. Image manipulation software will also be needed for testimonials and to make the page look as good as possible.

There are sales page generators (http://saleslettergenerator.com) and headline generators (http://instantheadlinegenerator.com) that can be used to produce elements of a Sales page. In our company we are familiar with HTML and comfortable changing the pages directly, but for many these tools can speed the process up, lighten the load quite a lot and produce good results without the need for technical knowledge.

The Sales Page is our shop window... this is our one time opportunity to produce a compelling argument that convinces the visitor that they need to take action, so if this page doesn't deliver everything else that has gone before has been a complete waste of time!

Set up Social / Media sites

We may already have established Social Media accounts and Live Web functions such as Twitter which can be used to generate traffic to our Sales Page. Depending on the product there might be a need to start fresh clean accounts. In the example of this e-book this is complimentary to the **Chris Ogle Facebook** account (http://www.facebook.com/OgleChris) (as I am the author) and so the addition of an **in 2 The Clouds - Facebook page** (http://www.facebook.com/pages/In-2-The-Clouds/287441351921) is sufficient for us to have a presence there and to be able to build up a fan base for the Book. These connections are either friends or associates who have expressed that they wish to have you on their radar and you on theirs and will normally be receptive to what you want to tell them.

Twitter on the other hand is a different proposition, in the example here of the book, this is a much slower burn opportunity. We have a number of twitter accounts already and building up a list of followers for the book in its own right won't really help for marketing and will take a lot of effort too. We can leverage off our other Twitter accounts to market the book.

One thing to think about here is Twitter account names. If your staff are promoting your business under their own names and their own social networking accounts there are a few issues to consider. (1) that your product or service is also associated with the friends and connections of your staff member and things that go on in private lives can cross over into Business (2) If a member of staff leaves the business, they disappear with all their connections too! This can be a real pain for the company losing the individual, but interesting marketing potential for the new employer / business venture. Certainly this is an area which will become quite important when looking for new marketing staff and what they can bring to the table in terms of contacts.

3. Decide on post launch collateral

In our example campaign of this book, once we arrive at the magic day when the FREE sign up is complete the rules will change. The book sales will be handled by a different site which will inherit the In2TheClouds domain and the sales page that has until now been collecting registrations for the free pre-release book will be adapted for a different function.

After the e-book launch we want to offer three options for visitors to engage with us :-

- Download the 22 page free chapter and join our regular ezine subscriber list to stay up to date with all the news on the 7 steps (potential future client rapport building)

- Purchase the book and learn the secrets to more time and

more money (low cost but highly valuable)

- Get on the fast track to taking the business forward and talk to a qualified **SME7** (http://www.sme7.com) Practitioner (longer term projects and commitment with a large Return on Investment (ROI)

- So to deliver this we would need two further blog sites and a reworked Sales Page!!

Notice though that although much more work, what we have achieved here with a simple book launch is to merge it with the much wider scope of our ongoing Digital Marketing strategy. This is essential as mentioned earlier in this section, that everything we do ultimately feeds into and fits into the bigger picture.

As part of our overall strategy to provide SME's with a Blueprint for taking their businesses forward, this book is critical in the transfer of knowledge to the SME marketplace and provides every business the opportunity to consider the relevance for their business.

4. Acquire any products or services that may be needed

To enact the plan we needed to :-

- Acquire a Domain

- Purchase a Wordpress Theme (for both **SME7** (http://www. sme7.com) and the new post launch **in 2 The Clouds** (http://www.in2theclouds.com) sites)

- Hosting company for the Wordpress websites

- Engage the services of External outsourced resources, fees, timelines etc.

- Pay for Product lodgement in Affiliate product bank service providers Clickbank and PayDotCom.

- Ad Words campaign (in this particular case we didn't use this service but it could be relevant in other situations)

Of course the above depends on what services can be handled internally and whether the collateral is already in place, but is an indication of the type of expenses which may be incurred.

Pre-Launch

1. Run pre-launch activity

This is the transactional element of the plan, where we promote and engage with our 'Lists' to market the e-book offering the product for free until the closing date which was the 21st February 2010.

We ran a two week schedule of Twitter posts, Facebook posts, Blogging, email campaigns to our own and a 3rd party list. We posted on forums and networked the book at breakfast meetings. One thing quickly learned with Digital Marketing is that once is not enough. Calls to action need to be sent out a number of times... this is very true with Twitter and Facebook where the audience needs to be at the right place at the right time to see your message. Email marketing needs to be used with much more sensitivity as recipients quickly become tired of being battered with the same or similar message.

Now there are two interesting questions here... (1) If we are notifying people then they must be already on one of our lists so we're not gaining any new information... what is the point? (2) Why is the book free in the first place? Why not sell the book for a reduced price – special offer, are we not leaving money on the table?

I think the answer to both of these quite valid questions is the nature of the book itself. In other examples if the book was for entertainment and leisure then there would be no need perhaps to present such a favourable offer. The Harry Potter books for example were never (in their regular retail form and with the exception of supermarkets) discounted from the start or offered for free!

In our example the book is educational and targeted at Small and Medium sized business owners. The book covers ideas and concepts which are specific to the new 'Internet Web2.0' age and beyond. Business owners may find the information in this book useful, but might never recognise this. The only way to reach these people and to have them find out about such a book is to have it recommended by a trusted and valued friend.

In other words, we need people we already know to read the book, who in turn will discuss it with business associates and then encourage them to read it too! The book is an education tool, a facilitator of Action, it promotes thought and encourages business owners to revisit their situation... and... if appropriate make adjustments for the 21st century.

Our pre-launch activity was designed and aimed at building a reasonable number of 'initial readers' who in turn would carry the message to others who might benefit from it. The pre-launch was never considered as a money earning opportunity from the outset. The pre-launch list exceeded 100 subscribers, which we believed was an acceptable number to get the ball rolling.

2. The Day before the Launch

The last 24 hours before the launch

With 100 or so registrations already in we set a new target for the last day to get to 130+. As with any campaign people are busy and although the intention to register was there, the close date is some way off, and so it gets left as a job to do later on.

The last 24 hours introduces a sense of urgency... it has to be done now... but only if people are reminded. Armed with the U-Factor (Urgency) the aim is to provoke another 1/3 to register.

The following list of actions were organised to run towards the end of Sunday 21st February and then again Monday 22nd February before Noon GMT (which is when 21st slips away in the far reaches of America and the Pacific).

- Email campaign to our Internal Contact list

- Twitter posts on both **sme7** (http://twitter.com/sme_7) and **Chris Ogle** (http://twitter.com/chrisogle)

- Posting on our Google Groups (Money Gym and Money Gym Mastermind)

- Request to other Friendly Internet Marketers to Re-tweet to promote the book

- Facebook posts to encourage others to sign up

- JV Partners encouraged to 'send out emails' to their lists once again, warning of impending deadline.

So what was the result... a further 35 registrations... just proving that the last day is a special day when running a campaign…this should be a full on marketing day, as you can see the results are very significant indeed and well worth the effort.

Personally I like to try and operate everything we do with Integrity. I find the whole concept of 'The promotion has been such a success we've decided to keep it running for a further… n hours / days' or 'We don't know how long we can keep this price… but' all a bit distasteful, no one really believes this stuff anyway… what we are really saying is 'it hasn't been so successful' and 'buy now before we put the price up, even though we know this won't happen and they'll be glad of the business at this price' they have been proven to generate business, but at some cost in my opinion. Would you want your customers feeling this way about your promotions? Be straight and honest is the best policy, don't treat clients as idiots… they are not!

As promised at 12pm Noon GMT on the 22nd February the Free offer was removed. Subscriptions afterwards would of course be able to receive the Free Chapter and receive the ezine going forward, that promotion will continue.

Launch Day

3. The launch period

Finally… launch day! Except for the frenetic last minute sign ups with 24 hours of countdown marketing which yielded a further 35 registrations… in our situation it was a normal day. The marketing completed, the Offer page was replaced with a sign up for the Free Chapter plus registration for the monthly Ezine.

We are Professional users of the **Total Business Cart** (http://www.totalbusinesscart.com) product and with this comes a Digital Products secure download service that prevents unauthorised distribution of the download link to the e-book. This is an ideal mechanism for the release of the **in 2 The Clouds** (http://www.in2theclouds.com) e-book.

Five post launch activities now take place in the 2 weeks ensuing from the launch, distribution of the e-book to those that subscribed pre-launch (1-2 weeks), changeover of the Sales Page to the new e-book Wordpress blog sales site and introduction of the eZine / Free chapter squeeze page accessible via the newly released **SME7** (http://www.sme7.com) site and a thorough review of how the Pre-Launch activity went, what worked and what didn't, how it could've been improved and document which parts we will do differently next time!

The **in 2 The Clouds** (http://www.in2theclouds.co.uk) Blog site will also double up for us as a membership site. Those that have purchased the book will be eligible to sign in and to view updates that we have released for the book. Being a 'technology' book, new ideas and concepts are coming out all the time and these would normally be updates to be included in the next edition of the book. The Blog provides us with the vehicle to file these ready for future inclusion but offer to existing customers the chance to keep up to date with the supplements as they happen.

Post Launch Analysis

4. Did we get the results that we expected?

In our example we were looking for a sample readership for the book and to receive feedback from a sufficiently diverse background.

There is a good mix of subscribers :-

- Those already involved in Digital Marketing who will find this chapter very useful

- Others are already seeing the potential to offer Digital Marketing services to Clients

- Business consultants who are either already or looking to assist SME's in business development

- Business owners who want to understand how the business map is changing

In hindsight what have we learned from this exercise? The results that we received working with others through their lists could have been greatly improved with a more strategic approach. We dealt with this in a rather haphazard manner and so it wasn't as effective as it could have been.

We were unsuccessful at tapping into other high profile Twitter users who could have exposed our campaign to a much wider audience. More time and effort could have been spent in this area.

We could have introduced some 'Paid for' advertising such as 'Ad Words' or 'Facebook' however it was decided this money would be better invested after harnessing further positive book reviews rather than at the initial launch. Spending money when there is a potential monetary return on the investment sounds good too!!

Lets have a look at the analysis statistics for the campaign, we had the sign up page hooked up to Google analytics (covered a little bit later on) and a summary of the percentages is listed below :-

- 70% of visits were direct i.e. via Email campaigns or where a direct link was entered into the browser

- 7% of visits were via Twitter (cold market)

- The remainder of the visits were split amongst other referrers including :-

- Our Website

- Facebook

- Google (via In2TheClouds – Keyword)

- Ezine Articles

- Ecademy

The percentage of visits to sign up was an amazing 40%, which is heavily weighted because of the warm market nature of the Email list. The majority of those that would click the link would have done so to sign up. With nothing to pay and the chance to read a book by a person known to them already the offer was a good one.

The number of visitors to the page was not that large, amplifying the fact that we do not have high traffic volumes to our other websites as yet, which one might expect as a significant source of visits if traffic volumes there were high. The Digital Marketing for these sites is still Work In Progress and if running a similar campaign in 12 months time the profile of the results might look very different.

This has been an Interesting experience, and the difference between cold and warm marketing clearly visible in this exercise.

The campaign achieved its target of establishing a good initial reader population.

How much work is involved in just releasing an e-book product? Hopefully this has shed some light on the activities and effort that needs to be put in. Certainly this is less than what would be required for a real hard copy book, but significant nonetheless. Of course not every product launch is the same, every campaign needs to be thought through and carefully 'engineered' to deliver the results expected to suit each situation.

The Marketing Mechanics

Having built the Digital Marketing Department (or some of it), now it's time to tell the world, so, how do we do that? What tools and techniques do we have at our disposal? What are the methods we can use to encourage new contacts to engage with us? How can we keep them interested and coming back; going forward?

Below I have listed the main ways we can 'transact' on the Internet, and drive traffic to our Content (collateral). Many of these we have already touched on elsewhere in this book... but bringing them together under one heading will provide a useful reference point.

1. PR – Traffic via Backlinks

Put your News out there onto the Internet using PR sites. Search engine friendly containing all the right keywords PR sites help make the most of launches and announcements submitting them to all the popular news sites! Google News, Yahoo News, ASK and Topix all visit PR sites to get the latest updates and news about Business. Two popular PR sites are below :-

PRWeb

(http://www.internetmarketing-help.com/help_PRWeb_2.htm)

Pressbox

(http://www.internetmarketing-help.com/help_Pressbox_2.htm)

These sites are also frequented by Journalists, freelancers, reporters and research specialists all looking for inspiration and news items worthy of reporting on. Submissions drive traffic straight back to business websites and can result in significant back links and traffic.

Some PR sites require a monthly subscription others remain free.

2. Articles– Traffic via Backlinks

Invaluable for Backlinks to your content and breeding credibility on the Internet, articles are a must. An article can be about almost anything and is typically longer than a blogpost.

Articles gives an opportunity to educate and inform about a specialist subject, so personally I have posted a number of articles on ezinearticles (http://www.internetmarketing-help.com/help_ezinearticles_2.htm) and you can read those at Chris Ogle's ezine articles here (http://ezinearticles.com/?expert_bio=Chris_D_Ogle).

Articles are not an advert or promotion for a business, but rather a chance to provide access to your expertise to a wide audience. Articles should be keyword rich with all the major keywords that have been identified with the business. Along with each Article is your accompanying Bio plus a resource box. The bio is an important item as it provides details about you, the company, main achievements and builds credibility. The Resource box inserted at the end of an article is the reward for providing this expertise for free and is the blatant opportunity to sell, including any websites and other useful information for the article reader.

Articles contain great content written by experts in their field and are hot property. Other Businesses, Journalists, Bloggers and industry specialists are constantly on the lookout for new and interesting items to share with their audience. Articles can end up being used globally on a large number of Web sites and Blogs… ensure that the Keywords, Bio and Resource box has everything within them to maximise the effect of every Article written.

One of the big problems that I found when writing articles was trying to make sure that all the relevant keywords to improve the performance of the text were in the Article. How do you do that? Answer : **Web Content Studio** (http://webcontentstudio.com/). This product takes the hard work out of the keyword research for your market and then provides the tools to embed these within your new articles… If you write articles or planning too in the future, this product is guaranteed to make a huge difference to their performance.

There are problems with plagiarism on the Internet, people copying articles and using them as their own. The Internet makes an attempt to prevent this with Articles submission software checking to see whether the article has been posted elsewhere. Of course with our own articles we would like the article posted in as many places as possible so long as it links back to our collateral. The site Unique Article Wizard makes a very good attempt at helping us achieve this. By writing 3 different version of each paragraph or section and then submitting these to Unique Article Wizard it will post to around 11,000 article and blog sites directories automatically. All these posts will be unique and provide those incredibly useful back links to your site, by the hundreds!

Click this link for more help on Article Marketing (http:// www.internetmarketing-help.com/help_BriefOverview. htm#GettingTraffic)

3. Ad-Words – Traffic via Paid Advertising

Google has a huge percentage of the search engine market, and was named Britain's Number One brand in 2009.

When a user searches on Google, relevant ads are triggered as "sponsored links" on the right side of the screen, and often above the main search results, these Ads are collectively called Ad-Words.

These ads have no impact on where your website appears in the normal hierarchy of searches but this global PPC (pay per click) programme delivers highly targeted and totally measurable results and is one of the most important marketing tools in the world.

Ad Words has found some negativity out there with companies that have had poor results, or found this approach expensive, but this will have due to been badly planned campaigns, with poor execution. With the correct setup and configuration this is highly targeted, highly effective and at a budget you set.

Here are some major organisations that use Google Ad-words to get more customers, Bupa, Direct Line, o2, Estee Lauder, Halifax, Dell, BBC.

Podcasting

What is Podcasting? You may have heard the term from Radio 1 or other radio stations. A Podcast is literally a downloadable

Audio recording in a format that you can put easily onto an iPod or computer and then listen to at your leisure. So in simple terms it is a digital Audio recording in a file, e.g. myPodcast.mp3

The radio stations use these Podcasts to provide a compilation of all the best bits from a radio show and then place then on the Internet as a link to be downloaded and consumed by the listener at a later date or time.

How could we use these then to drive traffic? This medium is great for Interviews, for recordings of Webinars, training materials, even snippets of this book could be recorded and then sent out as audio adverts… now that's not a bad idea! It is a different medium and allows us to connect with busy people who may be out on the road and where listening to an audio file is a good alternative to reading and watching.

The Podcast files can be placed on any web site or blog as just plain links or they can be hosted on different websites such as **Hipcast** (http://www.internetmarketing-help.com/help_ hipcast_2.htm), **Audio Acrobat** (http://www.internetmarketing-help.com/help_AudioAcrobat_2.htm) and **Pod Cast Pickle** (http://www.internetmarketing-help.com/help_PodCastPickle_2. htm). These sites provide nice looking customisable mini players that give, stop, start, pause, rewind and restart functions that can be located onto Blogs and Websites. These players look highly professional and enhance the visitors experience on the site.

Direct links to podcasts can be sent to anyone in the world! Use Audio to provide rich content on your sites and marketing campaigns and stand out from the crowd.

Video Promotion

The capability to put Video onto websites and Blogsites used to be the domain of large companies only. But with Digital video cameras being low cost and so easy to use such as the **The Flip** (http://www.theflip.com/en-gb/) or even Web Cams it is now possible to take good quality Video at any time, upload to a You Tube account and then embed the Video directly into a Web or Blog site.

Corporate Videos of 2 minutes can now be put together for $00's of dollars not $000's and this is bringing alive the Internet. The amount of information that can be communicated in a short video is so large compared with written text or audio it is no wonder that this is becoming the technology to master.

Products such as **Camtasia** (http://www.internetmarketing-help.com/help_camtasia_2.htm) enable the manipulation of the video that has been recorded, the overlaying of music or different sound tracks and the ability to record what is being displayed on the computer screen along with recording voice (picked up via the computer microphone). This can be amazingly powerful for demonstration clips, showing others how to do things in a training environment.

Video is beginning to pop up everywhere and web sites such as You Tube are removing the fear of experimentation and enabling anyone with the desire to create them.

There is still a place for professionals, businesses that can produce high quality video to communicate the right message on Web sites or blogs, but in many other situations a simple low budget Video can vastly improve communication. Here is an article which provides some useful ideas & tips on using You Tube for promoting your business (http://www.informit.com/articles/article.aspx?p=1016107&seqNum=1), and another that gives 10 top tips for using You Tube for business (http://bit.ly/awRUul).

Some examples of how a Video can be captured and used in your marketing campaigns :-

Demonstrations this could be how to put a simple product together, how to make something, or even how to operate a computer programme. The quality does not have to be professional necessarily (using something like Camtasia and a web cam is often enough, remember the resolution being used to view the video is no more than 320x240).

Depending on the audience the message might need to communicate 'I could do that' to the viewer, so an amateur video can sometimes be most effective.

Meetings and Spontaneous Events

Get creative, start to record spontaneous events or snippets of discussions with Customers. Clearly we don't have to use everything but behind every video is a story. Small testimonials of how a product or service has solved problems for customers are invaluable and with their permission can be used over and over on Web Sites, Blogs and marketing campaigns.

If the business hasn't started a You-Tube account then make sure it has one, then, join up with **Tube Mogul** (http://www.tubemogul. com) which is a web site that will post Videos to other video sites like You Tube. When the account is first set up with Tube Mogul it is a bit laborious as accounts have to be created in all the other Video sites, but once completed... a video submitted to Tube Mogul ends up in all the others too!

A brand new service has just been started by Lilach Bullock called **Network Waves** (http://www.networkwaves.com), this service makes uploading video content to the main Video hosting sites such as You Tube, Viddler and Facebook a one click operation and can save a lot of time... well worth checking out if Video promotion is key to the business.

Viral Video

Videos, especially amusing ones can be an extremely effective method of marketing. If the video grabs the attention of the viewer then there is a high possibility that it will be referred on to others.

This is an excellent method of marketing, check this advertisement for a furniture company (http://www.youtube.com/ watch?v=X7MVtgXMcll) which holds your attention and is very amusing too! Adverts like these can reach hundreds of thousands of people with a very modest investment.

When an Impression counts...

If you need to make that all important first impression, whether it be a corporate video, customer testimonial or to promote your brand and products then DON'T try and go it alone, DO enlist the help of those that know what they are doing... This **BillBandit Video** (http://www.youtube.com/watch?v=_W40hT6Y3SE) was produced fairly inexpensively by **Richie Pic** (http://www.youtube. com/richiepic)... people who really do know their business and the quality is good enough for Television use!

Whether your video requirements are like the above or abstract, 'production houses' are now emerging, serving the market for web delivered video.

Viral Marketing

The theory is... if you can create enough buzz, with enough

momentum to get the ball rolling then... the marketing campaign will continue on its own accord thereafter.

Perhaps best conceived now with the help of Video, if the moment in time with the right material can be caught then the rewards are often off the scale. Who can forget the examples of Paul Potts and Susan Boyle, just two situations where the exposure could not be stopped even if they had wanted it to.

Invariably these campaigns pull heavily on our emotions and with an element of something extraordinary or special. Although after the event we marvel at the reaction and the scale of the results, very often there is collaboration, planning and a lot of work to seed the project in the first place.

Seeding is a systematic approach to pushing content in all the regular communication channels whatever it is being published. Ad-Words, Adsense and other auto insertion ad placements, Twitter posts, Facebook, email campaigns, Articles, You Tube and other social platforms are effectively loaded over a campaign that might last 3 months. This 'feeding' of information continues until a critical mass is reached and then if successful will take on a life of its own.

ELetters

Eletters, Ezines, Newsletters all come under the same banner. These are one of the most important tools in the Digital Marketing Department. These are the communication tools between us and those in our list.

Opt-in Subscribers have supplied us with their email address normally in return for a free product or service. The ELetter is one method we possess to communicate not only with these subscribers / prospects, but in addition our customers that may be on a different list. It could be that the message for the two groups needs to be different, but it is a good idea to ensure that we communicate regularly with our lists.

** A point on lists. Customers will already be in our main business system as we are selling products and services to them. Prospects are potential clients that we are engaging with directly or those that have already subscribed to an entry level service or product. Suspect are contacts which have registered an interest, but have not yet warmed up enough to buy one of the products or services, so this is our 'Double Opt-In List'.

It is the responsibility of the Marketing Department to understand the nature of the lists, who is on them and therefore the nature of the correspondence that is to be sent to them. Data can be exported and imported into Emailing programs quite easily and/or updated for the purposes of monthly newsletters. List management is quite an important task of the Marketing team.

The Eletter or Newsletter is our chance to update prospects and clients about what has happened over the past month. This can be fairly easily compiled from information published during the month and formatted into a very professional document using some great web based tools.

Lets have a look at a pair of products that allow us to send out professional documents to our list of contacts and see what kind of feedback we can expect to help with our ongoing promotions.

Constant Contact (http://www.internetmarketing-help.com/help_ConstantContact_2.htm) is an online tool that enables the creation of professional eLetters / Newsletters but comes with a swathe of usability features such as Templates for a multitude of different business types. Drag and drop features, images and total control over the look and feel provides ample scope for tailoring the newsletter to the business house style.

Reporting on what has happened with the email is where products such as **Constant Contact** (http://www.internetmarketing-help.com/help_ConstantContact_2.htm) and **iContact** (http://www.internetmarketing-help.com/help_iContact_2.htm) come into their own. Once a Newsletter has gone out statistics will indicate, how many were opened, which recipients clicked on different links and how many times each link was viewed… this reporting gives the marketing department unrivalled 'as-it happens' visibility on the status of the Newsletter. Many businesses 'need' this feedback which is invaluable to the sales team to identify 'hot leads' or indeed those that have 'gone cold'.

Live promotion, Events, Webinars, Teleseminars and Video Conferences

Does your business run Events, Online Webinars or Teleseminars? then there are excellent online tools available to Host, Promote, Book and take payment.

So what are the differences between these three types of functions and how would we use them. Let's start with the event, this seems simple enough, it could either be something that is happening offline, i.e. a bootcamp, workshop or even a classroom style training course. A Webinar is typically where a set number of delegates join an interactive session via their PC and are in the main watching the Webinar instructor. These are typically demonstrations and online training classes. Teleseminars tend to be for larger audiences and involve participants phoning in to a central conference call arrangement. These can be configured to allow participation by the delegates or not.

What has all this got to do with marketing? Well online events as well as offline events need to be promoted. We have another opportunity to communicate with our list(s). Events work in much the same way as product sales! Earlier in this chapter we looked at product launches... an event, Webinar or Teleseminar is a product, it may be a free product (but it is our chance to build a compelling argument to buy something), but there is a great deal of work with any product launch.

Event promotion and booking... we have just spoken about **Constant Contact** (http://www.internetmarketing-help.com/help_ConstantContact_2.htm) in the previous section, we can revisit this product again now as it has an event management module which will earn its keep in no time. Now although there are subtle differences between the 3 event types being discussed, ostensibly they are all events, something that takes place at a point in time. Constant Contact allows the creation of events, setting of max number of attendees and will manage the whole email promotion of the event... it will also take care of payment online (uses PayPal too!) and deal with confirmations... Set up and use is very easy, and the events booking pages can be customised with the businesses logos and colours.

Another great FREE service that allows the creation of a e-Ticketed events and then take payments easily and effectively is Event Brite (http://www.eventbrite.com/). Simply sign up, add your event, put in the details, venue, pricing and even hook up with Google Analytics. A small commission is taken only when tickets are sold.

If you are running Teleseminars then don't forget to inform delegates to use low cost telephone services such as **Tele Discount** (http://www.internetmarketing-help.com/help_Telediscount_2.htm) to call in, or use Voice Over IP services.

Post Event / Webinar / Teleseminar, what do we have? Well if the event took place online using one of these tools, **Instant Teleseminar** (http://www.internetmarketing-help.com/help_InstantTeleseminar_2.htm), **Go To Meeting** (http://www.internetmarketing-help.com/help_gotomeeting_2.htm) or **Go To Webinar** (http://www.internetmarketing-help.com/help_gotoWebinar_2.htm), then there will be a recorded copy of the whole event. This material can be used just as it is for another webinar of the same type… effectively on Auto Pilot, or it can be sliced and diced and used for marketing purposes to encourage other prospects to come on board. Snippets posted on **Tube Mogul** (http://www.tubemogul.com) will accelerate visits to the sites as will blog posts with testimonials from happy delegates.

Don't forget to take Video and/or Audio testimonials from delegates that can be used in next months eLetter, ezine or newsletter!! Make the most of the material that is being produced as a result of running and managing the business to generate further customers and prospects.

Don't miss a trick with Webinars though. If anyone has been involved in arranging live seminars where we gather into one room a group of people to listen to a presenter we know just how hard it is to get 'bums on seats'. We know that if we put the effort in and that we manage to get the delegates there that we will definitely make sales.

Well welcome to the Webinar… it is exactly the same as a seminar except that no one has to travel anywhere… and with a few clicks and the power of the Internet the practice perfect presentation can be going out nationwide or even globally. Think of the power of being able to have your best performer, talking to all the delegates wherever they are in the comfort of their office or even at home!

IF YOU WANT TO USE WEBINARS TO HELP BUILD YOUR BUSINESS (http://www.in2theclouds.com/howtousewebinars.pdf) READ THIS ARTICLE

One of the key uses of a Webinar is to offer some great free education and tips on a particular subject, it could be 'how to use a product better' or it could be a 'whet the appetite', 'setting the scene' for all the secrets and detailed knowledge that the delegate can have when they buy the paid for product or service... We are all human... when we know there is more that we know will be useful we just can't survive on half the information... the bits we now crave are always included in the paid for item... of course they are! It is the same with Lite versions of software... these are free but they build the need for the features which are only available in the 'professional' or 'non-free' version.

By the time we have invested our time and energy to learn about the product, service or software system, we know enough to know that we need the rest... and it is a natural upgrade progression.

Using Webinars to attract an 'audience' for free and then delivering a compelling reason why the delegate needs more, then ask for action... ask for the Order... that's the bit most people shy away from and the biggest mistake! Here we have a captive audience wanting to be informed, listening and receptive to our message... do not waive this opportunity to help them take action and buy!

Video Conferences

Video Conferencing is another way to engage even more strongly with your audience. Everything that applies to Webinars also applies when delivered through a Video Conference. No one can argue that being able to present in the comfort of home or at the office to a number of people remotely via a Webinar is extremely powerful, but to actually see your attendees, gauge their reaction, and view responses to the message is another level of engagement.

Video Conferences used to be the domain of large corporates but in the Digital Age affordable solutions are now available for much smaller SME businesses. I have been using the services of **MegaMeeting** (http://www.megameeting.co.uk) to provide up to 10 seats in video conferences that we run and will soon be extending this to 25.

Video Conferences have typically been used to reduce travel and connect people across large distances who are working for the same organisation or perhaps collaborating on large projects. We have already found many uses for Video conferencing in our small company including :-

1. Internal meetings, we run a virtual business (walk the walk)

2. Sales Presentations instead of Webinars

3. Client training

4. Business Meetings with collaboration partners

5. Online Virtual Boardrooms for problem solving for groups of businesses

6. Mastermind group sessions

This form of communication will just get better and better going forward. The capacity to speed up business decision making, collaborate and communicate more effectively coupled with removing the time wasted travelling will guarantee the success of these tools.

Internet Radio Shows

What is an Internet Radio show? In simple terms this is where one or more people dial into a teleseminar service and speak together. With services like **Blog Talk Radio** (http://www. internetmarketing-help.com/help_BlogTalkRadio_2.htm) you can set up your own Internet Radio Shows and then advertise to your 'Database List' that you are now broadcasting a radio show, informing them of the date and time.

Listeners can 'tune in' via the invitation link in the email, or go via the Blog Talk Radio website… alternatively those that can't hear the show live can download it later on in the form of a Podcast as all the shows are automatically recorded.

A good online friend of mine Louise Barnes-Johnston (**Frontline Results** - http://www.frontline-results.com/) runs a regular radio show via Blog Talk Radio, and here are a couple of shows that I took part in…

Is Cloud Computing the Way Forward?

(http://www.blogtalkradio.com/louisebj/2009/07/13/is-cloud-computing-the-way-forward)

Just how secure is Cloud Computing?

(http://www.blogtalkradio.com/louisebj/2009/09/07/flr-32-just-how-secure-is-cloud-computing)

The great thing about Radio shows is that they can be publicised and marketed before they take place, recorded, and then marketed again afterwards on how good they were...

Finding great experts as guests provides your listeners with highly useful material much in the same way as a guest blogger does on a blog site. An added bonus is that guests will often provide a link to the radio show and blog about their appearance providing further traffic back to the main Website or Blog. Finding the right guest which is complementary to the business provides added value to clients and opens the door to further JV (Joint Venture) opportunities.

Radio shows are not the first item on the agenda when setting up the Digital Marketing Department for a business, but can quickly set a business apart from others when done well.

TV Streaming

The next step up from Radio shows is breaking into your very own TV Channel. How does this differ from a Radio show? Well the equipment used to start with. Now we introduce the computer Web Cam and microphone as essential tools. Clearly like the Radio show this is perhaps not something that we tackle with the Digital Marketing department on day one, no, this comes later when we have already mastered many of the other areas to generate traffic... but we should plan this into our overall strategy... at some point it will become appropriate.

So what would we use a TV channel for? Well much like the Radio show it can be promoted beforehand... the show can be carried out and then the show can be used as collateral to drive traffic to websites and blogs.

You can set up a TV Channel using free software such as **UStream TV** (http://www.ustream.tv), under this channel you can then broadcast directly from the Web Cam either live or record the programme for showing later on. With other great software tools such as **WebCamMax** (http://www.internetmarketing-help.com/ help_webcammax_2.htm), you can bring others into the TV show using communication products such as Skype... So in effect with these tools, an Interviewer could be chatting to a guest on a video phone call over **Skype** (http://www.internetmarketing-help. com/help_skype_2.htm) from anywhere in the world and using something like **WebCamMax** (http://www.internetmarketing-help.com/help_webcammax_2.htm) the two participants can be merged into the one Web Cam window and then this can be broadcast live Via Ustream TV over the Internet... all for no cost!

How amazing is that? Now I know this is exciting technology and it will get even better. The service is not professional quality, but for free you could hardly expect it... but experiment with this technology because once it is on the radar it changes the way marketing, sales or just plain communication is thought about forever!!

The Money Gym Live - 10. 29. 2008.
GMT+0000   16:02:03

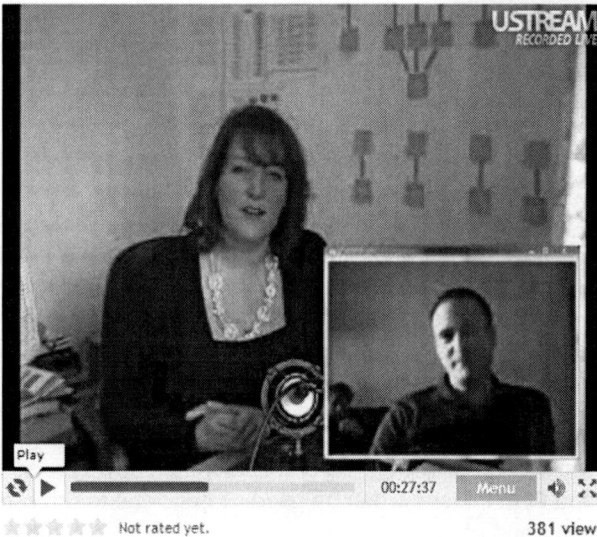

UStream TV video example: Nicola Cairncross interviewing Chris Ogle live via Skype video phone call using WebCamMax to integrate the images into one Video feed.

Users include :-

bloggers, podcasters, radio stations, DJ's, citizen journalist, talk show hosts, celebrities, rock bands, entertainers, comedians, churches, political candidates, government officials, conferences, event sponsors, record labels, television networks, colleges, university organizations, fraternities, sororities, charities, community groups, websites, civic groups, priests, monks, bird lovers, ghost hunters, dog watchers, weddings, life casters, professionals and amateurs.

Adapting and setting the course for your Digital Marketing Department requires an all round knowledge of what is available, whether a TV channel is right for your business today, in the future or not at all it doesn't matter, the important part is that it is available!

Mobile Marketing

At the time of writing this book, Mobile Marketing has just emerged into a form of marketing worthy of its own name! The Mobile device is always on, always with the owner and demands instant attention… hence its appeal to Marketers.

The Pubs, Clubs, Restaurants, Automotive sales, repair and servicing organisations have switched onto SMS as a means of driving business for some years already now… but the advancement of Browsing technology, applications on Mobile phones and the future predictions means that, well placed advertisements on the mobile handset will be a massive market.

Predominantly B2C (Business to Consumer) this market is estimated to be worth $24 Billion by 2013. It is an emerging market where traditionally advertisements have had to be constructed to suit the wide variety of phones. With the development of standardised mobile platforms like the iPhone iOS, Android by Google, Windows Phone 7 Series by Microsoft and other manufacturers beginning to emerge there will undoubtedly be new standards put in place.

Support on Smart Phones for java script has now increased the ability to monitor when a mobile device is being used to access web sites which is now producing some interesting stats.

During 2009, it was reported that one per cent of all UK e-commerce sales were conducted via a mobile. The US reports similarly small numbers with three to five per cent being the generally accepted level. However in the more forward-thinking markets of Asia such as Korea and Japan scores of 30-40 per cent of all transactions are recorded as being via a mobile device. These are very impressive statistics indeed and with phones becoming ever more sophisticated and capable ensuring that our online content can be accessed over this technology and we don't miss out is a must for us all.

The use to which Mobile Marketing can be put is still in its infancy but two examples that recently came to light are :-

Footwear Manufacturer

Ran a series of adverts that promoted the ability for mobile users to take a photograph of something with a colour they liked. This image could be sent to the company who would then produce a set of shoes customised with this colour within 7-10 days.

KitKat

Ran a mobile campaign with a cleverly placed advert on a Mobile home page and saw sales quadruple.

Mobile Marketing might not apply to every business and the truth is right now we might not even imagine how this technology could be applied to our business. The inclusion in this book is to highlight that this is likely to be a huge new arena for advertising and whether relevant or not it demands to be on the Agenda for discussion every time, only if, to keep up with what is happening in the market and subsequently discount it. Mobile Marketing is part of the Digital Revolution along with Digital Marketing and is the future so we need to ensure that we are ready to take advantage at the earliest opportunity.

Mobile Marketing brings a whole new dimension to the marketing arena in that you know exactly where the handset device is. For the first time this opens up channels to market locality specific products and services to the individual.

This is so new and revolutionary that the implications of this marketing approach have not yet filtered down into deliverables, but it remains only a question of time before we see the initial experimental ideas emerge.

Location Based Marketing

If Mobile Marketing deserves a mention then so does Location based maketing. The bald fact that a mobile phone is rarely more than 3 feet from its owner has grabbed the attention of the Marketeers out there! It has been suggested recently that over 60% of us would rather lose our wallet than lose our smart mobile devices!!

Watch out for the explosion of Location based Marketing and the emergence of products and services like **FourSquare** (http://foursquare.com) and **GoWalla** (http://gowalla.com) as the business world wakes up to this new massive opportunity.

It is yet another paradigm shift... marketing based on where you are therefore your Smart Phone are... right now!

These services are able to recommend a local coffee establishment, a restaurant, vehicle repair outlet or even the nearest cash point, all based on where you are according to your smart phone. Expect in the future to receive tips and guidance when visiting an area on the 'best places to go'. Location marketing will expand rapidly over the next 10 years as innovative solution providers rush to provide services to hungry, 'ahead of the curve' businesses looking to capitalise on a new way to reach customers. If your business operates in an area... or is regional you need to get up to speed on this technology.

It's happening already big Pizza brands and Coffee franchises are offering FourSquare Mayors (people who most often 'check-in' to a location) free Pizza's and Coffee's as reward for their loyalty... many more ideas like this will emerge as this technology evolves.

Competitions

Everyone likes something for free... the opportunity to win a product or a service will normally evoke a positive response.

The simplest competition might be for example, win a free day's consultancy on Digital Marketing ... something topical and easy to deliver. What we would need to do to get a competition such as this up and running? What do we need from the person entering?

Well we will need to be able to contact them, so a name and an email address would be the absolute minimum. Hang-on doesn't that sound like a squeeze page? Well yes absolutely, we can use exactly the same mechanism to run a competition as we might to launch a product or run a campaign.

A little thought though... as only one of the entrants will actually win the prize anyhow can we collect any other useful information at the same time that would help us to identify any other real prospects that we could then go back to and perhaps offer some discounted services too??

This reminds me of a funny story :-

A farmer's donkey had died, and he approached his neighbour who had a donkey and asked how much he would sell it for. The neighbour replied $900. The Farmer agreed to take the donkey, paid the neighbour who arranged to drop the donkey around the next day.

Anyhow during the night this donkey became ill and died as well. The neighbour was beside himself and went around in the morning to tell the Farmer the donkey had died. The Farmer said no problem just give me my money back and everything will be ok.

Well the Neighbour said that is the problem I have already spent the money... so the farmer thought for a moment and said, ok well bring the donkey around anyway. The neighbour said, what will you do with a dead donkey, the Farmer said it is mine, I'll do with it what I want.

Anyhow a few weeks later the neighbour once again met the Farmer and queried him about the donkey saga. The Farmer said, oh that, it was fine... I raffled the Donkey for $50, and ended up making $700 profit after the $900 I paid to you.

The neighbour was horrified... you raffled a dead donkey, what did the winner say? He was disappointed of course but I just gave him his money back.

Of course we are not running a competition like this but it demonstrates the point that there is only one or a handful of winners. Running a competition increases the profile of the business, generates traffic, encourages referrals, and can be used afterwards for further promotion with the winner, who is likely to agree to the publicity.

We also have generated a warm list of names and email addresses from businesses or individuals who have registered an interest in our products and services.

Polls, Surveys & Questionnaires

These three items can be used in different ways, but they all provide great feedback on what you are doing or what you might be thinking about doing in the future.

Polls are a great way to engage with your Members, Clients and Prospects. Let's imagine we have a new product coming out. It could be that we want to get our various lists to look at the new product which we are featuring on our brand new home page. But rather than blatantly lead with the product, we can engage with our lists on a topic of getting their valued opinion on a Poll.

Everyone has Opinions! It doesn't matter whether we agree with them or not, we are building valuable feedback from the marketplace. Would we rather be making business decisions with input from our target marketplace or not? Of course with, this is hugely valuable information and with Digital Marketing the task is made even simpler!

There are some great products out there which allow you to create Polls, Surveys and Questionnaires easily, and run them as campaigns, as hosted applications (on the service providers website) or even locate simple ones straight into your own Website or Blog. Take a look at **Constant Contact** (http://www. internetmarketing-help.com/help_ConstantContact_2.htm) which has an excellent add on module for Polls and Questionnaires. **Survey Monkey** (http://www.surveymonkey.com) is highly configurable and used by all the Fortune 100 companies. Survey Monkey covers a vast range of uses including, Customer Feedback, Employee Reviews, Market research, popular opinion, Event attendance, Guest preferences, Course Evaluations and even Thesis research.

Forums

Forums come in many different flavours but can be a great asset to the business if used properly. There are thousands of forums so finding the most appropriate for your business and identifying those with the most potential is a matter of working with them, and sorting out those that work the best.

Forums are a place to air opinion and to view others opinion on a wide range of topics. It is not direct marketing and they should not be used in this way.

Forums provide a vehicle to demonstrate your core competence and build a reputation, not to sell. Those that share your opinion might well go on to seek out further details about you, your business and how they might engage with you.

All forums provide facilities to complete an Online Profile where you can go into details about the business and your credentials. Normally a footer accompanies all posts as well, this footer usually can contain links and images to the products and services that you provide.

Posts with footer backlinks (images and website addresses) are indexed by the search engines and provide additional verification of the business and can improve rankings.

Although the posts themselves must remain neutral, there is scope for developing good credibility, trust and therefore opportunity.

Our business is a big fan of **4Networking** (http://www.4networking.biz) which has developed a very active business forum environment coupled with a Breakfast networking community. Not only can people participate online and share opinions and views, but are also able to book into offline meetings and arrange to meet face-to-face with those people with whom respect and credibility has been built online.

Of course there are forums aimed specifically at special interest groups which have a more targeted audience, and you can check these out by using the following search techniques from within the Google search box :-

cloud computing +forum

table tennis +forum

A word of warning: Forums can fast become a habit and a friendly place to hang out, full of supercharged ego's full of very self opinionated people…. Ask yourself this ?

'Do you want to be right? Or do you want to be rich?'

Forums have their place, but they are 'another' string to the bow, they are an important part, and, if business comes from them it is a bonus… use these sites for credibility building… never argue…

'First seek to understand, then seek to be understood'

put your case and justify it… accept others are not always wired the same... that would be boring now wouldn't it!

We have found that it is important to designate a time slot perhaps twice daily to check forums, respond, and start threads related to your own business activity. Hours can easily be whittled away on forums where that time invested elsewhere could be of greater benefit.

Business Groups (vertical markets)

Leading on from the section above with Forums that can be aimed at specialist business sectors, e.g. Pets, Raw Food, Self development, Coaching etc. etc. we can find that in our own businesses we have developed specialised knowledge for one of more industry sectors.

It might be that your business specialises in dealing with the legal profession and that success has come with the knowledge of their challenges and how these have been overcome in other client situations.

A friend of mine, who designs and build websites for the Limousine Hire Industry (e.g. **A1 Stretch Limos**) (http://www.a1stretch. co.uk/limo-hire-london.html) has now made a name for himself providing services into this sector and has a large niche portfolio based on his experience combined with his photographic skills.

Most industries have some sort of governing body, an institute, federation or organisation which lobbies government and 'looks out' for their particular sector... examples of this type are shown below :-

Federation of Small Businesses (looking after SME's)

(http://www.fsb.org.uk)

British Promotional Merchandise Association (BPMA)

(http://www.bpma.co.uk)

British Medical Association (BMA) (http://www.bma.org.uk)

The Law Society (http://www.lawsociety.org.uk)

Not so much a tool but a series of marketing options, these organisations are keen to offer 'value for money' to their subscribing members. Membership of professional organisations is usually not a free service and the more benefit members can derive from their subscription the better.

There are opportunities to (1) advertise on their websites, (2) Build a list of email addresses, companies and contacts for a marketing campaign, (3) Form a Joint Venture programme with the organisation rewarding both parties and perhaps feature in the monthly newsletter to the membership.

The Internet provides us with aggregation sites like the one above for most industry sectors which simplifies the data collection process and enables us to develop markets in which we have already demonstrated our capabilities. No one ever wants to be the first to use a product or service in an industry sector, references in this context are worth their weight in gold.

Email & Autoresponders

As far as Digital Marketing is concerned Email marketing is the oldest weapon in the arsenal… unfortunately also the most abused. Unsolicited email is considered to be SPAM email. This means that if a request for emails has not been made then email should not be sent to those email addresses.

The Squeeze page technique which has the 'Double Opt-In' feature helps to get around the SPAM problem. Registrants have to provide their email address and then confirm in a separate email that they definitely want to receive email correspondence however, this does not guarantee that the emails will ever be delivered to them.

The problem is that we are all so well protected with Firewalls, Anti Virus and Spam prevention software that unless we actually 'White List' (a technique for approving an email address) an email address then it will end up in the Junk folder probably.

So we need to take a careful look on a regular basis to those single 'Opt-In' registrants i.e. those that never completed the verification process. Of course the email address might have been invalid, they may have signed up by accident, or thought better of registering… however it is worth checking.

As a point to mention, there are now Spam prevention programs which detect a 'Non White Listed' email address and then send back an email to the sender to manually confirm that this is a human at the other end, not a SPAM engine. Once a Human verifies this email then the Email address is automatically 'White Listed', a good example of this is **Spam Arrest** (http://www.spamarrest.com) which can be applied to regular email accounts. Please ensure therefore that the sending email address is one which is monitored often because these emails will be replied to that senders address.

There are four main types of Marketing emails. Let's have a quick look at each of these :-

Mass emailing

Generic email sent to a large list, this would normally be sent to a 'Suspect' list, the top part of our Marketing funnel consisting of a large number of recipients. Emails are not followed up.

Targeted emailing

This is effectively the old marketing Mailshot synopsis. The list is clearly defined, the message specific to the recipients and the emails will be followed up by a telephone call.

News letter / Customer Update emailing

This type has already been covered earlier in this section

Autoresponders

An automated series of emails that are pre-written and sent out at regular intervals to a recipient database that has 'double opted in'. Recipients can enter this process at different dates and times and normally do so after registering for a free product or service. Once registered they will start at email no.1 and then they will progress through the series of pre-written emails.

N.B. It is possible to have multiple autoresponders running at any time. An autoresponder series may contain a simple single email saying 'Thank You' for subscribing and nothing more. Autoresponder series can be set up to be relevant to different lists, i.e. a list for Prospects and a list for Customers. Registrants can be moved automatically from one list to another based on an event taking place.

The Digital Marketing Department will probably handle a mixture of all of these emailing techniques.

Marketing is driving people to look at our content and continuing to engage with those 'Prospects' until they buy something, hopefully either now or in the future. Marketing is also about 'Farming' the existing customers to make them new customers once again… spend more money with us.

The collective name for those people who are not yet customers is the 'Sales Funnel'… there also exists a Sales Funnel for existing clients but like the Autoresponder series requires a different approach.

In actual fact without knowing it or analysing it there may be more than one sales funnel… if the product or service applies to different vertical markets then the sales approach and lists may well be separately maintained as would the ongoing marketing.

It also stands to reason that the more sales funnels we have, that the more business we are likely to write…

The marketing technique which causes the most difficulty with Digital Marketing is the Autoresponder series. One of the main reasons is that it is different from what we have encountered before. The attraction to Autoresponders is that it can build a relationship with your contact list on Auto Pilot whether the marketing team (or you) are there or not… it is literally set and forget. BUT and it is a huge but, Autoresponders are a challenge to write.

An autoresponder series could be 20-30 emails being sent out over a 6 month programme. Each email has to be crafted individually to help nudge the prospect a bit further down the buying process… each email has to build on the previous and begin to create a compelling story. The emails must be interspersed with Tips, Tricks, Interesting Stories, useful and amusing content, otherwise they will not be read, worse still the prospect unsubscribe.

So this requires us to think…

> *'the problem with thinking is that it is the hardest work we ever do and that is why a good many of us don't do very much of it'*

… or you could enlist the help of your SME7 Practitioner (or Digital Coach) who will be either able to help directly or locate someone who can provide this service.

Don't overuse Autoresponders. How can we know where the line is? The secret is to put yourself in the position of the prospect. There are many emails that I now receive as a result of subscribing in the distant past which I never read. The reason that I never read these is that all they want to do is sell something else to me, the next best thing...

It is an incredibly fine line between being informative and helpful and giving the impression that all you want to do is flog some more stuff. Few get this right, many get it wrong.

The Internet marketing industry worked on the basis that if there are 10,000 on a list and 5% look at the email and a further 1% go onto buy and the profit is $50 per sale, then this is $250. Do this 3 times per week, 12 times per month, this is $3000 per month.

The numbers look very impressive and this can all be dealt with by a clever Autoresponder series on Auto Pilot... if we were wildly out and it was only 10% of this then it would still be $300 per month, not bad as a supplementary income.

Where is the flaw? ... sounds great! It may have worked in the past and I am sure that for some products and services it will still work in the future... but for the vast majority of regular offline businesses the model for massaging the prospect database requires a much lighter touch. The pure 'Internet Marketing' days when the number of people in it were much smaller needed the model described above... it was all about educating the market... by and large the process of selling to 'would be Internet Marketers' has created 10's of thousands of individuals who have self funded their own education. A lot of people got rich... a lot more people didn't.

We now move onto the next chapter using the knowledge to engage with the Business community and turn Internet Marketing into a professional 'grown-up' business which is Digital Marketing. There is a huge amount of work to do and nowhere near enough Digital Coaches with the pre-requisite knowledge for the task in hand...

JV's

Joint Ventures is a word which has far more significance today than at any time before. The Internet has opened up the possibilities for collaboration that transcend spatial distance and it means we can effectively work with anyone on the planet!

How can a Joint Venture help us with Marketing?

Going back to Chapter 1 when we started to work on the mindset, there is a need to understand that (1) there is plenty of work out there, (2) that we can't do it all.

This is called an **Abundance attitude**. By taking this line of thinking what actually happens is that we divorce ourselves from the outcome. That takes the pressure out of the sales process, that then means we're not selling we're informing, this leads to a much more palatable interaction with potential clients and contacts… which ironically leads to more business. We could never make up the client's mind for them anyway so why worry about the outcome… we do our best and see what happens.

An **Abundance Attitude** also opens the doors to sharing business opportunities. What is the biggest difference between you and your biggest competitor? The answer 'YOU' so if the client picks them then they cannot have your knowledge, expertise and the relationship that goes with it…

Working with others accelerates progress, builds knowledge and spreads the word faster. JV's develop a sense of 'Urgency', in the market… there is a shared responsibility and actually it creates more customers than the combined JV partnership could probably handle… and certainly more than if they had worked independently.

In our own Industry sector of Cloud Computing, the big guns of Google, Yahoo and Microsoft have spent millions on advertising their cloud solutions. The newspapers and press report on the revolution which is in the clouds! There is now a massive movement to learn, understand and adopt Cloud based solutions… and our business never spent a cent getting that message to the masses. Now their market is not our target market but the audience understands the term 'Cloud Computing' and is now receptive to looking at solutions in that space.

In practical terms, a JV relationship needs to be mutually beneficial and the most common forms of a JV are when both parties bring something to the table. Typically the arrangement is between the creator of a product or service and a Sales network list owned by the other JV partner. One provides product, the other sales exposure – the vehicle.

A great example of such a partnership could be a new ebook which is relevant to the membership of an organisation or an industry sector. By forming a mutually agreed financial arrangement the author can make sales of the book to the membership with the support and promotional assistance of the organisation.

The Organisation benefits both financially and by endorsing a product that has value to the membership. The members benefit by being able to read a book which could influence their businesses going forward and the Author makes book sales and builds credibility in the marketplace, a win / win / win.

When we come onto Chapter 6 in the book we can see how Joint Ventures can not only be used for existing businesses but new ventures as well. As our businesses begin to function without us around and we move to 'working on the business not in the business' we can start to take a look at new ideas and business relationships.

Become an Expert - write an e-book

One of the best ways to stake your claim as an expert is to write a book about your passion or Business area. What is the difference between an expert and another person who has the same knowledge but is not considered or recognised as an expert?

The answer is… putting oneself forward and taking on the role publically. The person who puts their hand up and offers to be an expert will be known as the expert… that is it… that is the difference.

By writing a book, this is the first step on the road to being labelled 'an expert in your field'.

Apart from self gratification or a huge ego trip, what else can come from writing and publishing a book?

Earlier on in this chapter we discussed the Brands that relate to a business… without doubt one of the biggest brands is the owner of the business… take a look at some of the biggest companies in the world today… Bill Gates (Microsoft), Steve Jobs (Apple), Larry Page / Sergey Brin (Google), Mark Zuckerberg (Facebook), the companies and the owners (figureheads) are almost as important as the Brand itself... the same is true in every industry, fashion, music...

Experts get invited to speak at events, experts get to go on Radio and TV, experts get asked for comment and opinion... expert status helps to build businesses.

Conclusion

There are many ways and many tools available to the newly established Digital Marketing Department. The message is clear understand what is available, but do not try to run before we can walk. Some of the areas like UstreamTV and Radio shows are very exciting, but it is important to build the department steadily from the bottom up.

Get the basics in place, get the collateral organised, start building lists and then building relationships with those subscribing to your content. A rock solid foundation with a clear understanding of what is available coupled with short and long term goals will ensure that the business gets the most from its Digital Marketing department.

Results, analysis and Tuning

How are we doing? How is the marketing going? Are we getting any more visits these days? How did that campaign go last month?

All the questions above are very valid and if we turn back the clock to the pre-internet days how would we answer them?

I think personally that Marketing as a profession has struggled to gain respect certainly with the SME marketplace. The SME owner knows that they need to undertake marketing but the vagueness of the results and the costs have made it an unpalatable meal.

The good news is that with Digital Marketing we can pretty much analyse everything to death, the bad news is that it is accountability time. The reason for lack of respect for Marketers is not that they are necessarily bad at their job... it's that no one could measure what they had achieved in any scientific way. With sales it is easy... here is the target... what did you do? Plain and simple... with Marketing it is all about activity, tasks, and where the leads came from... if the information is being collected at all. Here are some other interesting questions...

was it the artwork that was wrong? Was it the copy? Was it the target audience? Do we know if anyone actually read it?

Welcome to Digital Marketing. There are three crucial tools that help us to understand what is going on with our content and message, **Google Analytics** (http://www.google.com/analytics), **Google Optimizer** (http://www.google.com/intl/en/websiteoptimizer/features.html) and Ad Trackers.

Let us just have a recap... sales are when we convert visitors to buy something... marketing is when we drive traffic to our content by whatever means we have used.

The key information that any business might want to know when looking at their marketing is the following :-

- How many visits did we get in the month (per website / blog)

- How many visits were new?

- How many visits were returning?

- Of the visits how many left immediately (bounced)?

- Where did the visitors come from (referring URL)?

- A list of the top referring sites

- Of the visits from searches, what were the words or phrase used that resulted in us being found?

- How many registrations did we get from our squeeze page as a percentage of visits

- Where did the visitors come from that went to our squeeze page

- How many products did we sell and which pages generated the sales

- Which was the best performing sales page

- How many affiliates signed up this month?

- Which is our top performing affiliate?

- Can we change some of the words and/or images and measure the difference in performance

- What if we change that entire page for a different one, then go back to the old one and see the difference

Of course there may be a lot more questions, and some of these may not be relevant at all to the business concerned. These are the types of questions that as a business owner I would want to know the answers to.

Digital Marketing and two products in particular, **Google Analytics** (http://www.google.com/analytics) and **Google Optimizer** (http://www.google.com/intl/en/websiteoptimizer/features.html) can provide answers to all those questions above. You will need to configure your websites and blogs to collect the data, but once this is done, this data is available on a daily basis!!

The interpretation of the results and what they mean will be different in every case, but it is absolutely vital that businesses start collecting this data. Most SME's are driving the ship with the blindfolds on as far as marketing is concerned. With this level of detailed marketing feedback, everything can be analysed...

Are you getting visitors but not converting them to sales? Your copy is probably rubbish or the website is not saying what you think it is to your visitors... time to look at the content.

Are your visitor numbers low? Then the marketing department needs to get busy generating traffic to the web or blog site.

Visitors arriving at the squeeze page but not signing up? Is it the copy or are the visitors of the wrong type? Swap out the squeeze page with some different graphics and copy and measure the difference... try offering some other product for free and giving that another week or two... all the while we are collecting feedback to enable us to hone and improve how are marketing materials are working for us.

One sales page is working but the other one is not... is it that one is receiving more visitors than the other... is the advert location on the wrong site? Now we can check everything this gives us the power to put things right!!

There is another tool that is very useful that should feature as part of your analysis and feedback loop, **Google Alerts** (http://www.google.com/alerts). Would you like to know who else is mentioning your products and services or talking about you or your company? Would you like to get regular updates about specific topics being discussed on the Internet relating to your business sector or market sent everyday to your inbox?

If the answer to the above is yes... then select some key words, phrases or topics that you want to monitor and set up some **Google Alerts** (http://www.google.com/alerts). We monitor things like 'Cloud Computing', 'Chris Ogle', 'BillBandit' and 'SaaS', to see what is being posted and keep up to date with what is happening in the marketplace.

As we begin to utilise and expand our engagement with social media platforms such as Twitter, Facebook and Linked-In it becomes increasingly important to track what is being said about our brands, business, individuals and products or services... how can we track what is going on across the social media platforms? Why should you be interested? What if you are only dabbling and not really using these services yet?

The internet is like a vacuum, if we do not feed it with our own positive contributions, then we will find that others will populate it for us... if we are not saying something then it does not mean nothing is being said. Part of the marketing ritual must be to find out what is being said about us, even if we're not pro-actively saying anything.

Talking to a colleague who visited a multi national company on the very subject of Social Media, he asked them who had started their facebook page... they looked puzzled... we don't have a facebook page... oh yes you do! my colleague replied and showed them a facebook page dedicated to slating their products and canvassing other peoples contributions who felt the same way... this cannot be avoided any longer... ignoring and abdicating responsibility in this area is a dangerous game to play these days.

Check out the following sites which may provide some of the facilities required to ensure you monitor what is happening on social media platforms relating to your online Digital presence.

Social Mention (http://www.socialmention.com)

Addict-o-matic (http://www.addictomatic.com)

UberVu (http://www.ubervu.com)

Talk to your SME7 Practitioner or Digital Coach and start collecting the raw data upon which some meaningful decisions about Digital marketing for the business can be based.

Step 5

Outsourcing

We have now covered four of the Seven steps to having the business you really want… if you are still reading at this point having negotiated the gargantuan previous chapter on the Digital Revolution then you have come a long way already!

We are prepared for change, are looking to deploy best practice processes to streamline and automate the business, implementing a Cloud based business platform so that we can manage the business from anywhere… and now we can begin to effectively market the business and increase sales using Digital Marketing strategies…

At quite a few of the steps along the path identified above, the resources required will not be available from within the business. This means that external professionals will be required to deliver a whole raft of products and services. Before we get too excited, this is no bad thing. The more we can contract to businesses to supply according to Service level agreements the more time we save and the more flexibility we introduce into the business. Of course there are some items that will never be outsourced, but IT services, bookkeeping, cash collection, even Digital Marketing can probably be outsourced at less cost than doing it internally. Let's look then at the area of business outsourcing…

What is traditional outsourcing?

What do we mean by Outsourcing? It is a word which has been abused over recent years especially with the opening up of Asian markets and the old Eastern block as well.

Well in the dictionary the word outsourcing is defined as to either 'subcontract (work) to another company' or 'to buy (components for a product) rather than manufacture them'.

Outsourcing has manifested itself in business in a variety of ways already and below are some examples :-

In house outsourcing is where an external resource is brought into a company to perform a function. This could be a simple 'Temp' type role in an accounts clerk capacity or it could be a whole department such as IT Support in larger organisations, where the external staff actually work within the procuring company premises.

External Outsourcing is where a task or a function is provided by an external business. The services to be undertaken are agreed, the fees for the work are agreed along with schedules and or timescales. This is often Accounting or Bookkeeping functions, legal work or IT services in the main. Expertise is the main reason for this type of Outsourcing.

Offshoring or Offshore outsourcing is where the work is actually outsourced typically to different lower cost base countries. Contractual agreements are the same as for external outsourcing described above.

The most widely used functions which have attracted this type of outsourcing are call centres and IT support services from very large organisations seeking to lower the cost of service provision. Cost is the primary reason for offshoring adoption.

Although much of the outsourcing described above would seem way beyond the reach of SME businesses, we are outsourcing a good many routine tasks already. Common outsourced functions for small businesses are Payroll, Management Accounts, Shipping (Fedex, DHL), Web and IT services and even Direct Marketing activities. Many of these services are acquired because we don't have the infrastructure to perform the function, others because it saves money, but for what other reasons might we outsource?

What and why might we want to Outsource?

Cost effective (person sharing)

There are two main reasons why Outsourcing can save money and therefore be cost effective.

The first is where the task that needs to be done is insufficient for a full time person. Typically these tasks end up being dumped on someone who doesn't like the task or it is not their main job function and is undertaken with a half hearted attitude at best.

Outsourcing to someone who does that job day-in-day-out will be far more efficient and focused and consequently more productive than a regular member of staff. A real example of this is a few local businesses I know who outsource their bookkeeping to **KD Accounting** (http:// www.kdaccounting.com) for exactly the above reasons. They want to focus on their business growth not spend time recording what goes on...

In the same way we outsource our Payroll... saves all the hassle of worrying about legislation changes and is all seamlessly taken care of. It is not expensive and removes a tedious but important job. Also it is offsite and secure elsewhere.

The second example of how using an Outsourcing service can save money is best demonstrated with an example of Pick and Pack service we use. The **BillBandit** (http://www.billbandit.co.uk) is a physical product and sales of this product are managed through the website. To ship this product requires storage, picking, packing and then shipping by registered post. By outsourcing to **Cotswold Handling Services** (http://www.cotswoldhandling.co.uk) who are a specialist in Pick and Pack we could bring down the cost of each shipment. Cotswold Handling Services buy packaging in large volumes and being that our product is small there is minimum overheard in storage charges.

Staff changes

Staff 'come and go' that is a fact of running a business, but by adopting some of the practices outlined earlier in this book combined with an element of outsourcing it doesn't need to be as disruptive as it has in the past.

In chapter two we discussed the merits of defining proper business processes and documenting roles and responsibilities. With this blueprint for running the business actually most roles become easier to learn. Outsourcing now becomes a viable option, the choice is at least there... if the business is going through some restructuring or there are business changes, the management team can now outsource and continue to operate the business which effectively defers permanent employment decision till later on.

New Projects or Ventures

From time to time tasks appear which are important to the business but that which could distract staff or may even be developments not ready for disclosure internally within the company at this time.

Examples of such tasks could be writing the Policy and Procedures manual, ISO9000 accreditation, exploring new avenues for the business or even implementing 'Cloud computing' solutions. An additional profit centre or complimentary new product may be lead to employees 'taking their eye of the ball' and so this is another area where outsourcing may be beneficial.

Although it is possible to utilise internal resources to address many of the situations described above there are spin off benefits from bringing in an external resource. Access to additional knowledge and experience can often question some of the operational elements or plans and consequently lead to a better overall final solution. Using internal resources may cost less but it might also lead to insular 'in-the-box' thinking, distraction from fulfilling the normal day job and delays in completing the new project.

Efficiency

'Not invented here Syndrome' or NIHS is a common problem in Small businesses. As Creators and Entrepreneurs a good many of us believe we can do things better… we don't want to let go of the reigns and find it difficult to delegate. I did suffer from this problem once upon a time, until the realisation hit home… I can't know everything, 'Jack of all trades, master of none' is not the road to excellence, and there are only 24 hours in a day and I'll end up working all of them and then some!

To be excellent at one thing is a full time occupation so if you are trying to be an expert in Sales & Marketing, Product Development, IT, Business Processes, Finance, HR and the Legal profession there is no time to do anything else… like run and manage a business.

The business belongs to the SME owner, so they can do whichever job they want to do… choose the role that best fits his / her skill sets and then build a team, internal and / or external to support and underpin the business.

To recognise our limitations is one of the great 'revelations' for a business owner. Once accepted that 'to do it all' is both impossible, inefficient and will result in an inferior end result we are then liberated. Free and focused to deliver on the roles we have assigned ourselves and enjoy safe in the knowledge the other tasks are being looked after by people who are the best in their roles.

The next Step on Ideas will lead us to find those people who can work with us to greater levels of achievement.

Specialist Skills & Expertise

An extension on the previous section, there are time when specialist skills are going to be needed. Typical examples of this are Legal representation, Translation work, Copywriting or Graphic design.

In relation to the contents of this book 'In 2 The Clouds' many of the areas are new and as such which require outsourcing to 'get the job done'.

It is highly unlikely that within the business there is a member of staff who is Digital Coach with the wealth of Digital Marketing expertise required, or any of the resources that are required to put the marketing collateral online.

We have probably outsourced a fair amount already however these historically will have been companies and treated as Suppliers in the conventional business model. In the coming years SME's will engage with more virtual, independent service providers that engage with us on a much personal level.

There are three examples I can cite here, one is **Claire Raikes** (http://www.claireraikes.com) who is in effect our Marketing Director and provides us with social media advice, configuration and set up and the second is Suzanne Barnett - **Kiss Training Online** (http://www.kisstrainingonline.co.uk) who is helping us to develop our online training programme(s).

The 3rd specialist service we have used was on a legal matter when pursuing a Trademark registration. We enlisted the services of **Surjj Legal** (http://www.surjjlegal.co.uk), a specialist in Intellectual Property and with a wealth of corporate Trademark experience now available (and affordable) to SME's like ourselves.

Employment hurdles

It doesn't seem to matter which country we live in, governments want to know about our employees. Of course they want us to collect their taxes for them, health contributions and lay down a myriad of other regulations that we must comply with. Welcome to employment law!

If an individual works full time or almost full time and has no other employment then of course this is an employee relationship and quite rightly so. If a job function however is erratic or part time then it is much more suitable to utilise outsourced services. This enables the services to be switched on and off, fixes the costs and avoids all the shackles of setting up employee relationships.

There is another benefit to Outsourcing here… we still need to manage the work to and from the Outsourcer, however from a people / team management perspective or 'red tape' (where the contribution to the business is negligible) this is drastically reduced. We agree a task and a price and a delivery date… how this is achieved outside these basic details is not of our concern, we can simply get on with other things, safe in the knowledge that what has agreed will happen. It is in effect an item crossed off the 'to do' list.

Lower cost labour markets

It started with Hong Kong and Singapore many years ago, then moved to Taiwan on to Thailand, Korea, Vietnam, and has now reached China, India and the Eastern Block (as it was). We are of course talking about the movement of production to follow the low cost labour markets.

Outsourcing is no exception, only that any market is available to us, so long as the resources have the knowledge and experience that we need then we can engage with them.

Web sites such as **Freelancers** (http://www.internetmarketing-help. com/help_getafreelancer_2.htm) provide an opportunity to post a task and then receive quotes for doing the work, once accepted a contract is formed and payment only made to the outsourcer upon satisfactory project completion.

The Internet has enabled (and partly been responsible for) an army of English speaking IT resources in India to find customers in Western Europe and the USA. By 2020 China will place a further 300 million English speaking people into the marketplace (making it the largest English speaking nation in the world) so the outsourcing battle will not end anytime soon!

Punch above your weight

Outsourcing can be useful when there is a need to give the impression that the business is bigger than it really is. Small companies cannot afford the luxury of dedicated Financial Directors, Marketing Directors, HR or Operations Directors but these functions can now be outsourced for a fixed monthly fee giving access to the same level of expertise enjoyed by much larger companies. A few hours input on the phone each month from these key individuals is all that will be required to keep the business on the right track.

SME's are much more agile than their larger competitors and often the same advice and guidance can be actioned and deployed far more quickly leading to that all important competitive advantage.

Outsourcing as a business

As we have seen above with Freelancers, outsourcing and managing outsourced contracts is actually a business in itself.

An SME7 Practitioner is a prime example where working with a business may need to call on a whole range of outsourced services. It is highly improbable that one individual could possess all the necessary knowledge to take a business from Step 1 through to Step 7 as outlined in this book. But working with a number of proven outsourced resources the SME7 Practitioner has the virtual team to meet the company's objectives.

Do we recognise any opportunities here to inject a little extra pace and zip into our newly invigorated growing enterprise?

Business Revolution

A few years back it was mooted that the Internet would change lives beyond our wildest dreams. These visionaries were perhaps given some airplay but largely thought of as a bit close to the edge. The truth however is that they were right and the period between 2010 and 2020 will see the biggest change in business since the industrial revolution.

The Vehicle - Internet Highway

So what has changed? Well the tools and applications that are now available via the Internet truly means that our business are completely portable.

Anyone can connect to anyone, anywhere and manage our business accounts, do quotes, process orders, file and access documents... we can run sales campaigns, digitally market our products and services, offer support and assistance, run presentations for audiences attending from any location...

With the exception of physical product handling the majority of activities can be delivered via the Internet.

... and as the speed and size of the bandwidth (how much data and traffic can pass through) expands so the usage will grow to absorb it. High definition Video and downloads will replace low resolution and poor quality and in the same way that roads miraculously fill up with traffic as they are built so will the Internet Highways.

The Driver - People evolution

So... if people can work just as effectively, reduce wasted time and save money (and the environment) by travelling less what will they do? They will want to do more of it of course! Now this won't happen overnight... there is a cultural change that needs to take place, but change it will.

Why spend 2 hours travelling back and forth to the office every day? Think about this question for a minute... is it the social element of seeing the people we work with? The being part of a team? Is it the gossip or company politics? Is it getting out of the house and away to a different environment? Or is it something else?

The fact is that we have been conditioned to work the way we do, by the very limiting nature of our previous technology. The Internet provides us with liberation; we are no longer constrained by the boundaries that tied us to the 'Office'.

In contrast, if we are able to amble 10m from the bedroom to the kitchen, to the workstation (study / home office), if we are able to slot our work around our families, if we can work at times which suit us better than the regular 9:00-5:00, and if we can do this in a location that makes us happy and content... would we not choose this?

If we could then combine the above and apply our skills and knowledge to work with clients whom we choose because we like them and enjoy working with them... then perhaps this is the face of 'working' in the Digital Age.

It is estimated that by 2020 over 1 Billion people will be working from home... that is 1/6 of the entire world population... probably 1/3 of the working population... that might be an overestimate but if it was even 30% wrong the number would still be staggering.

The Destination - The changing 'Business Model'

So where are we headed? To evaluate the impact of the enormity of this migration to a different way of working and what affect that will have on businesses of the future, let us first look at how far we have come already.

30 years ago everyone went to the office, there were no exceptions, and people just had to travel to their place of work. Actually, those that attempted to work from home to find some solitude to write a report or proposal were often frowned upon or labelled shirkers and work

dodgers. There was a knowing smile 'oh working from home are we?' as if to say… that's just another excuse for a day off, we know you won't be working!

How far have we come already? Today 3.5 million or so people in the UK already work from home and the number is rising. 60% of new businesses in the UK are started from home. Vastly higher numbers of field workers like sales reps and engineers are expected to work from their remote home offices and only go to the office for meetings and presentations. It has become accepted that it is effective for both the employee and the employer or us to work in this more flexible manner, as we discussed in Step 3.

The Internet and broadband connectivity has of course facilitated these changes and enabled people to work from just about anywhere at very low incremental costs, making it financially viable as well.

So what are the businesses of the future going to look like?

The demand for dedicated traditional office spaces has to reduce, as more people put their homes to multiple uses.

Interestingly there will be much greater demand for flexible business space and shared resources. Not everyone has the discipline to work from home (at least not every day), some will miss the companionship of others in the office environment and for others it just won't be practical for whatever reason to operate from home.

Micro businesses offer specialised services examples today include Business consultants, Digital coaches, Graphic Designers, Bookkeeping and Marketing services. These services are offered to conventional businesses but also to other micro businesses like themselves.

Consider this… a regular business consists of Finance, Sales & Marketing, the Managing Director, IT, Administration and Production (of the product or service).

- What if none of these people actually worked full time for any one business but performed their role for a 'few' businesses?

- What if each of these people lived at opposite ends of the country?

- What if these people came highly recommended through connections on Facebook or LinkedIn and we were able to read up on their personality, interests and likes?

What does it matter where people are anymore? What we need to do is find the best people for the 'job-in-hand' and engage with them.

Could this be labelled ... Multi-Sourcing!

In the new Multi-Sourcing environment, each role is clearly defined and the compensation agreed for each business in which an individual operates. Success is measured by the performance in their capacity within the business.

The responsibility now passes to each individual to deliver... there are no corners in which to hide, remuneration is based on results. This model will be difficult for those who already have an existing business this is why the period of 2010-2020 will be such a challenge. It is not because the existing businesses are bad... but because the competition, young start up organisations will be working so very much more efficiently, where everyone is **'pulling their weight in the same direction'**, and corporate politics a thing of the past.

It will be as much a challenge for regular businesses in the coming years as it was for Microsoft to move from a 'Client / Server' model to the Internet model, or for IBM to have gone from Hardware to the service model... both required a revolution in the way the business was organised, functioned, who worked for them and with what skills.

In such a collaborative and open market, the power of Social Media platforms and online networks will become highly important as a method of building credibility and personal branding. Those with a demonstrable track record and high profile will become very desirable hot property.

There will clearly be winners, but there will be large scale losers too, Recruitment will be replaced by online outsourced services with those having vast lists of connections on social media sites seeking out the best people for a task. Office accommodation will require a drastic overhaul to meet a different style of needs and the demands on transportation networks for business will reduce.

... Where will it all lead?

What this amounts to is the potential for increased earnings from multiple revenue streams, interesting and diverse work which can be undertaken at a time and place which suits the individual.

Innovative new ideas unlikely to have even been given a passing thought in years gone by suddenly become exciting business propositions. **ClickFix World** (http://www.clickfixworld.com) is one such example. A simple single telephone service to report a computer or technology fault, and someone will either fix it on the phone or come to you, check it out and then get it fixed.

ClickFix a franchise business harnesses people with technical knowledge and enjoy working with IT and provides an opportunity for them to earn a living in their local area sorting out IT problems for people… as we know there will be millions more working from home, who just want the problem Fixed… simple but effective…

Job security in the traditional sense depicted by lifelong roles within a single company is long gone. Welcome to the Digital Age where job security will be delivered through multiple revenue streams and working with likeminded people in a digitally connected network.

Existing businesses like many in similar situations before e.g. the Printing industry where pre-production went computerised in the 90's may choose to ignore the advice, carry on as they are… but never before has a change occurred that will affect EVERY business… some sectors have been singled out in the past, on this occasion there are no real exceptions, everyone faces change and needs to understand the implications.

The Results - Labour mobility, Global resources

The Digital Revolution will empower people to change their lives. Not only with whom they work and what services they provide but in what environment they want to live. No longer constrained by the need to be close to the office or dense areas of population we are free to choose any location which has good internet connectivity. This could mean living in more remote areas of the country or a completely different country entirely. Perhaps an opportunity to go and live in a Greek island by the sea in the warm rather than stuck in a cold miserable climate… any takers?

The Internet however allows us to reach well beyond country borders and Business Collaborations involving international participants will become a reality for many emerging micro companies.

International Mastermind groups teleconferencing weekly are springing up which can influence business decisions based on local market conditions and peculiarities in the different countries.

New JV partners in different countries can accelerate speed to market, with a vested interest in the success, translation services on tap and local knowledge things can move pretty fast.

As international collaboration grows so new ideas on how to deliver services will emerge... Service provision in local time zones is one great example. Staff can be trained online using Webinars or online videos anywhere in the world making operating a 24/7 support service globally a cost effective reality.

The Technology

Collaboration tools to enable individuals and disparate working units that are spread across the globe are already in use. MSN, Skype and other collaborative tools enable us to communicate and work together as never before. But times are changing again. Google has been working on a new set of products that are set to provide Outsourcing resources and people that use them with a whole new range of powerful tools...

*** Say hello to Google Wave

What is a Wave?

A wave is equal parts conversation and document. People can communicate and work together with richly formatted text, photos, videos, maps, and more.

A wave is shared. Any participant can reply anywhere in the message, edit the content and add participants at any point in the process. Then playback lets anyone rewind the wave to see who said what and when.

A wave is live. With live transmission as you type, participants on a wave can have faster conversations, see edits and interact with extensions in real-time.

- When would you use Google Wave?
- Group Projects
- Document Sharing / Image sharing
- Meeting Notes
- Brainstorming

Of course all participants would need to have accounts on Google Wave. Once accounts are set up, then finding people and including them on a wave would work in a similar way to MSN and Skype users, but with lots of collaboration technology build in.

Powerful API's (Application programming interfaces) that will enable other software developers to hook into Wave will mean that Waves can be embedded within Blogs and other web based systems in the future.

*** say goodbye to Google Wave... ***

Prior to this book being published, Google disbanded the Google Wave group. Many things which were Learnt here may feature in future products and services, but for now the uptake by the general user was too poor for it to be considered viable... This is an interesting lesson... Perhaps Google Wave was ahead of its time? One step too far in the integration of web services into our current modus operandi.

The Effects - Taxation and Government

These changes will not only affect Businesses in the coming years but will also change the profile of our economy. Governments are already facing challenges when confronted by businesses trading in a country different from where the owners live, where the taxes are paid? And where the income earned? Are already difficult questions to answer in a global economy.

Corporate tax revenues, Business registrations, Business rates (in the UK) will all be severely affected by the changes being introduced by the Digital Revolution. Governments already provide many of their services electronically, but have they seen yet the dramatic changes on the Taxation, Finance and infrastructure heralded by the Digital Age?

The importance of Web based systems

As we have seen things are about to change, not instantly but we cannot implement the changes we will need overnight either. In order to accommodate the longer term plans and move to a more Multi-Sourced model in the future, what can we do today that will put us on the right path?

The Cloud computing Web based business platform outlined in Step 3 is a crucial step in helping us 'get in position'. By placing the business information and management systems into the 'Cloud' this effectively opens up the potential to engage with any Outsourcing service or, Integrate with other web applications.

A good example of one such development has been the integration of two web based solutions, the i-Tr@der Business Platform and the **Truckcom** Proof of Delivery system (http://www.truckcom.co.uk/). The POD (proof of delivery) system extracts the Despatch details from the i-Tr@der system and then transmits them to the driver's handset. The driver receives a signature and name on the handset and then presses the Delivered button. The image and associated information is the transmitted back to the Truckcom system which then updates the i-Tr@der despatch details with a web link and POD available indicator. Staff can then look at the delivery note and view the web page with the signature image and the receiver's additional details.

Without the business management systems being web based the complexities of systems integration in the example above would have been far more challenging.

Growth with Cost Control

Outsourcing provides us with the capability to expand our enterprise without incurring large up front incremental costs. Work can be farmed out to our pool of external outsource resources on an as needs basis. This gets the work out of the way which…

Is very important to maintain service levels and continue progress

- Doesn't force existing staff to work even longer hours
- Enables us to synchronise new staff with sufficient work load

Utilise External Resources

Having adopted the 'Cloud computing' external resources can effectively 'Plug and Play' into the business systems. Using the same approach that software vendors developed in the 1990's where new equipment could be connected to our PC's and then just worked (perhaps with the installation of a bit of driver software), similarly with outsourcing, a little education about the process (driver) and then operational.

N.B. Some important points here :-

- The Outsource service provider can only perform the function that has been allocated to them. Other parts of the system do not feature as available options
- Access is switched on / off under the complete control of the Business

- All input is performed on the same business system, so there is no need to transfer data back and forth

- Activity is recorded for monitoring outsourced performance

Two great examples of how this can work really well for an organisation are in the areas of Bookkeeping and Contact Data Cleansing.

Historically Bookkeepers have worked on systems for the clients and then provided monthly management report, or received backup files, worked on them and then returned these once updated for the business to continue.

In both the situations above the business is 'out of action' with the data whilst the accounts are being worked on, and neither allows the management team to get up to date accurate information 'as of now'.

In the Data Cleansing example, one of the main issues for any business today is the quality of data. It is so simple to add contacts (with an email address) to our email contact list these days it is easy to get into trouble. With everyone using their own contact lists, private and business all mixed together as well, things can quickly get out of hand. It is not too bad when a single person is involved, but once more than one person is in the business things can get in a horrible mess quite quickly.

Quality of data is vital for any business and the ability to outsource this function and have the data cleansed by someone dedicated to the task is likely to get the job done more efficiently. Then after the task is done, just switch off the function and business as usual with up to date accurate data.

The same principle above can be used in a direct marketing role. A business associate in the UK, **Yellow Pig** (http://www.yellowpig. co.uk) is already generating great success with sales growth using outsourced resources based in the Philippines! Access is provided via a web based Business Platform and so all the information is held centrally in a common place. Once the campaign ends access is removed by disabling the login credentials.

Flexibility for growth

When growing a business it is important to have options. Cloud computing future proofs the business and opens up flexible choices for employment, sales growth and administration.

Open systems that are web based can often extend to provide customers and suppliers with information from your business. Deliver Net a distribution company in North Yorkshire are providing their customers with login credentials to generate their own reports on what products are being bought by each location. Suppliers working closely with them are also given access to see their product sales and who is buying what. This is all additional to full access to the audit trail of the commercial transactions i.e. Invoices and payments and outstanding accounts.

These added value services help to strengthen relationships and increase the potential for sales growth.

The future potential for Outsourcing

Escaping the Rat race

Those who have 'done their penance' in Corporate life and now choose to adopt a more 'life friendly' approach to work offering their knowledge and experience in a more agreeable location can now do so with ease. Similarly those in 'Later Years' who may have effectively become unemployable in the normal corporate world can now rejoin the workforce providing valuable guidance and assistance (in a Virtual Non-Exec director style) to younger business people going through the issues of 'building a business'.

An explosion in Micro businesses such as those above will in itself generate huge demand for 'Digital Services' as the only way anyone is going to find out about these valuable resources is either via Searches or Networking.

There has to be a huge retraining of labour to help take businesses on this road through the 7 steps as described in this book. Some of the step are taken care of already, but step 4 is wildly under resourced and as demand steps up Digital Coaches (outsourced service providers will be in huge demand)

Time and Control

Outsourcing both from the perspective of providing the work or on the receiving end as an outsourced resource, the concept works for clawing back time and returning control.

Outsourced resources manage themselves and their time; they are specialists in their field. They are capable of using their expertise and connections to complete the task in as shorter time as possible with the highest quality. As a supplier they're also well aware that every business has a choice and therefore seek to provide the best possible service.

When businesses outsource, they weigh up the in-house knowledge and skills available to complete the task, the resources available to work on the project, the tools available to do the job and how that fits in with the project timescales.

If we are going to change the brake pads on a car, we need tools, we need knowledge, we need parts and we need time... if this is not our passion and we are not comfortable being cold, wet and dirty then an auto servicing garage might be the right choice. Similarly without artistic flair, good image manipulation software and a marketing background we might do a less than professional job on artwork (and spend 5 times as long on the task).

If the outsource cost is less than the perceived pain of us doing it ourselves then often Outsourcing takes place.

Choose your working partners

You cannot choose your family... and often (if you are not the boss) you cannot choose your work colleagues either. A few readers might remember a few work colleagues they would rather not have had?

The other issue with staff is that very often you do not know what you are getting until 6-9 months down the road. The opportunity cost of getting it wrong is huge. In my experience if I hired 3 salespeople for whatever reasons only 1 would perform. So the business costs are huge if someone doesn't work out :-

- Recruitment Fees (if Applicable)

- Salary, guarantees and additional taxes to the government

- Desk space and overhead costs

- Training and Education

- Management time and effort

- Opportunity cost of the job being done poorly and rework

This can be $10's of thousands of dollars. People can sell themselves very well and the truth is we know nothing.

Outsourcing cuts through all of the issues shown above. Even if it is slightly more expensive it will still provide top value for money.

Outsourcing then enables us to pick the people we want to work with. Even now if there is an individual that we really think highly of but they are working in another business it is unlikely we could afford them as we wouldn't necessarily want them full time.

With outsourcing, we are able to find very good people either by referral or through networking who are already in position to operate in the engagement mode that we want. We can also talk to other satisfied users and take the guesswork out of the results we can expect.

In the context of our own Business and in relation to Step 5 in this book, Outsourcing is a key component in recovering a great deal of time back. Having implemented the 'Cloud Systems' we have opened the gates of potential, having introduced 'Digital Marketing' we have established a foundation for sales growth using the Internet to work for us… and as the demands on our own resources exceed our capacity we now have available to us an easy and cost effective method of Outsourcing tasks. Outsourcing is then perhaps the secret to future growth and prosperity without all the 'Red Tape' and bureaucracy that accompanies a business with a large number of employees.

Step 6

Ideas

A long while ago in the 6th year at School I remember being asked to write an essay on the subject of Ideas. One word was written on the Black board in white chalk... and whilst my fellow students and I hushed slowly for the patiently waiting tutor. He pointed at the board. Today and your homework for next week is to write about that word on the board.

I think I could write a pretty good essay now on this very subject but way back then an idea had less importance to me than it does today.

Most readers of this book will be reading it because of an idea, an idea that perhaps the information within it will be useful in creating a series of thought processes which in turn will result in something beneficial happening... some change or other for the better. The results will be varied depending on the reader and their background and how they perceive the information contained within this book.

If the first 5 steps have been implemented already or... are on their way then a few noticeable changes should have happened in the business. We should have good efficient processes in place and a cloud based system to manage the business flexibly from anywhere. Business Sales volumes should be increasing through Digital Marketing strategies and new outsourcing partners in place to cost effectively manage the growth. Steps 1 through 5 have been about putting the business into a state under which it can continue with or without you. This means you should at the very least got some of your time back!

Time... that rarest of commodities, which, first of all is in finite supply, and secondly we never know how much of it we have. Consider once again the goals we set in Step 1, was time on the list? What did we want the extra time for? Family, Travelling? For leisure purposes? Or might it to have perhaps taken up another passion which has been 'Parked' through lack of time?

The goal may have been to take the business to this position, sell it for a profit and then take time off, perhaps permanently... if so? Then congratulations, you are almost there! If on the other hand it was to maintain involvement but to manage in a more 'CEO / Chairman' type capacity? Then other projects more than likely beckon to compete for the newly acquired precious time.

One thing is sure... Entrepreneurs are never short on ideas! The problem is staying focused until time is available to develop these ideas. Start too many projects and effort is diluted, nothing gets finished or done well and… the money never arrives, or the time either. A common problem, we've all been there and those that are serial entrepreneurs are suckers for new and exciting opportunities!

The chances are that there are a multitude of 'Ideas' waiting in the wings just waiting to get activated, if this is so then time to bring out the first one. I would hazard a guess that during steps 1-5 if you hadn't any opportunities waiting then an opportunity will have emerged by now which looks interesting. The next step of course is to get things moving, but before we do, let's take stock on a few thing.

Existing Business Management

The 4-hour Work Week by **Timothy Ferriss** (http://bit.ly/96FABc) has had a huge readership, why? Because we like the idea of doing what we really want to do with our lives and spending an acceptable amount of time on our business; keeping it ticking over and our money coming in. 4 hours a week, about an hour a day, with Friday off is what Timothy recommends!

So now we have got our business into the position that it should only take a part of our time not, all of it (and then some) what should we spend the hour a day in our regular business doing?

KBI (Key Business Indices) – Keeping a hand on the tiller

Make sure that the team know how to prepare the necessary information for review, daily, weekly and monthly. Each business will have different criteria for keeping it on track. Working with your team define and create the key reports which will determine the status of the business. This might be Orders per day, turnover, profit margin or products shipped… it could be registrations for a newsletter or it could be non sales related like how many orders shipped today had a backordered item… or total number of products out of stock that clients have ordered.

Once these key reports have been identified then a business dashboard should be set in place to provide this information at a glance. There are numerous products on the market, but it is important that the information can be collated from many sources.

Business Dashboards are web based software tools that accept input from Spreadsheets, manual feeds and also other business applications like i-Tr@der , Sage line 50 and ACT!. Services such as these can be set to collect data at regular 30 minute intervals to ensure that the data being looked at is as up to date as possible.

Once the reporting is in place 'minding your own business' becomes a simple point and click task... anomalies and issues can be quickly picked up and executive decisions taken immediately.

Evaluate the market (Existing products and services)

As the person who started the business initially, there is no one better placed to keep an eye on the market place for the business.

Part of the time allocated to the 'Automated Business' must be to check out the competition... evaluate what is happening in the marketplace with competitive analysis and ensure that the products and services stay ahead and relevant in the market.

Role as a leader (Where are we heading?)

As a CEO (Chief Executive Officer), Chairman or even Managing Director the role comes with the responsibility of future proofing the business. Everything should be running smoothly now... effectively the railway line has been laid and the professional managers are driving the train along the track, so apart from keeping a watchful eye on the numbers and the competition, what do you do?

The railway track might be laid, but what is coming around the corner? Is the marketplace changing? Are there complementary activities that would consolidate and strengthen the position in the market? The role as Leader is to ensure that the business is positioned for the future, has the right products and services in development (R & D) and the mechanisms are in place to integrate the changes.

If the above items have not been happening before it is no surprise because very often there is little or no time to do them.

What Next?

Above we have discussed the 4-hour work week... now we have time perhaps we want to turn our attention to something else as well... Most Entrepreneurs love the buzz of business and 4 hours a week isn't going to satisfy the need to be at the coal face, being challenged, and building something... it's a bit of a drug and with the main business working well and with a strategy to keep it there we are now seeking our next Business Fix.

Anyone who has read the book, **The 7 Habits of Highly Effective People – Stephen Covey** (http://bit.ly/b5fYln) (one of my favourite books), will find the subject of Independence and Interdependence. Running your own business looks a lot like Independence (although there is dependency on others… staff for example). Entrepreneurs who do eventually win through have struggled against the odds to victory in most cases through sheer grit and determination.

Having served the apprenticeship and survived stepping into the next idea or opportunity does not have to be so painful.

New Projects

There are two main types of new ideas, those that are complementary to your business and those that are an absolute change. Whichever it is there has to be passion.

Personally I am a keen Table Tennis player and although nothing to do with the main business interests I am privileged to be part of an initiative to develop table tennis in the UK, this project is **Urban Progress Table Tennis Club** (http://www.urbanprogressttpro.com). I am also heavily involved with the local amateur Table Tennis League and we sponsor and maintain the **Watford & District Table Tennis League's Blog** site (http://www.watford.tabletennisblogs.com). This has been a tremendous success and generated positive debate about a whole raft of different topics. Historically Table Tennis has received very minor representation in the local newspaper and now for the first time people can actually participate in making and reporting the news, even watch themselves online, and has evolved into a real community, which is even starting to transcend from Table Tennis.

Clearly the items above are part hobby, part business but nothing to do with the main SME7 thrust. Interestingly lessons learned, products used and all the knowledge gained in existing business activities can be brought to bear on new ventures and speed up time to market. There may be connections which span the activities above but they are quite tenuous and definitely making financial gains is not the main focus.

Synergistic businesses or those where one project is a subset of another can be the most rewarding. In effect the success of one business can provide a continuous stream of prospects for the another. Extending the product or service offerings can leverage off existing resources, systems and collateral and present a quick return on investment.

Joint Venture opportunities

As we have worked through the 5 steps already completed with our SME7 Practitioner and/or Digital Coach discussion will inevitably have lead to ideas for other opportunities which will dovetail into the existing business or complement it. We have discussed joint ventures and the different flavours in an earlier section, but let us look at the Joint Venture option from where we are right now :-

Experience and Self confidence

A joint venture can come to be when there is mutual respect and understanding between 2 or more parties. When looking at a joint venture it would always be more desirable to form a relationship with those that have a proven track record.

Two minds are better than one

Or three or four! Being in business as we have mentioned before can be a lonely affair, done that, been there got the T-Shirt! Shared responsibility and decision making will often result in a much more considered direction, although avoid delays through inability to agree on certain elements.

Other people have complementary skills

A few years back... fixing a car which had gone wrong could be undertaken by someone with a few spanners and a basic understanding of the combustion engine, brakes and electrics. Today you need a specialised computer to analyse the car to diagnose the problem.

Like car mechanics, running a business has got a lot more complicated than it was of old. No longer a pen, paper and a basic business plan! Computers, Software, Internet, websites, Digital marketing, Social Media, Mobile technology, and all that before we decide what it is that the business is actually going to do. This requires a myriad of disciplines rarely found in one individual. The basics could be there but to affect a comprehensive marketing campaign today in itself might require 2 or 3 specialists. Building a team that have the right mix of Networking, people management, finance, research, creativity and most important communication is essential.

As businesses tend towards becoming more disparate over the coming years, management teams will rarely operate out of one location, often spanning countries as well. Outsourcing will have already fuelled the move to flexible task orientated working this is applying the same principles at the business owner level. Communication, the use of technology and clear well defined roles for each participant will become highly important as face-to-face contact becomes less frequent. Each member will need a thorough understanding of the overall picture and how their contribution blends with the other team members.

A great example of a joint venture that I have recently become involved with is in relation to part of the SME7 process.

Matt Purser (whom I met through networking... More on this in the next chapter) has access to a large number of technical and creative people. The SME7 Business (specifically at step 4 - Digital Marketing) has need for an all embracing service that can handle any requirements that may emerge from this part of the process.

We Do Web Stuff (http://www.wedowebstuff.co.uk) has been set up to deliver on exactly this objective. Matt has all the technical connections required and the capacity to project manage both building online collateral and handle ongoing tasks such as Blogging, Tweeting or Article creation. The good news is that this service can be tapped into directly by the SME7 Practitioner community who can then offer this as a Plug 'n' Play service to clients.

This is a prime example of how complementary skills can be combined effectively to solve a business challenge. There is almost no cost in setting up this kind of entity, and it is therefore no surprise there has been a huge surge in new business formations over the past months as people awaken to the attractions of doing business this way.

Shared contacts and resources

The wider the variety of expertise covered the greater the chances of being presented with an opportunity. Like with hiring people the more substitutable a person is the more valuable. Those with the ability to wear many hats can contribute in many ways.

Apart from the partners personal contribution other great assets maybe a huge following on Twitter, Facebook fan or group page owners. A large list of opt-in subscribers (but what did they subscribe too... might not be relevant in this case)

Halve the workload halve the lead time

Ok... taking an idea and sharing it with someone else means dividing the proceeds in half... or at least in proportion to the work being done. This is time to bring up the old quote...

I'd rather have smaller percentage of a larger cake than 100% of nothing.

So true, with partners, each individual's percentage might be a lot less, but the value of it could well be a lot more!

Sharing the workload will reduce the time to market, improve the end result and not consume all of your hard earned free time. Remember to sort out all the percentages right at the start though... **When the business is worth nothing it is easy to divide up, once it has a value attitudes change!**

Accountability, Enthusiasm and Energy Levels

What is good about having partners? If chosen well then bringing other people into the venture or setting up with a few select people you've had your eye on working with can be extremely rewarding.

Working with others brings accountability into the equation. This not only ensures the tasks get done but improves their overall quality as no one wants to let the team down.

Enthusiasm is infectious. We have all been around someone who is so positive, so convinced about their product or solution that it is transferred like a magnetic force on to us. How good is it to have people around us like this? Pick partners well, this is an essential component... not everyone is of this ilk and certainly there needs to be people who offer the voice of sanity and reason (the dismal Desmonds as I fondly name them) ... these are important roles too as overzealous positive people can get into hot water without some reigning in.

Energy levels... If like me you have been to these huge conferences and listened to the positive, fantastic motivational presentations and been taken to that almost fever pitch where anything is possible? How high are the energy levels and how good does it feel at that moment? If we could bottle that we would be sorted!

Unfortunately back at the office the next day with all the Customer issues, Suppliers letting you down, Sales not happening... Internet is down... the downward spiral can be as fast if not quicker than the rise the day before... Questions like... What on earth is this all for? Why am I slaving like a dog and going backwards? Is it worth it? If I knew running a business was this hard I wouldn't have bothered...

Sound familiar? This is where Business Partners earn their weight in gold... none of us are up on a high all the time... some of us more than most... but being able to support each other through thick and thin is essential to keep the project on the right path.

The Virtual Board

Looking back to the early 1990's to suggest that a business could be run, managed and effective without an office (in the traditional sense) would have been met with scepticism at best and complete disbelief more likely.

As with Flexible working practices however (working from home), the business management team are changing their attitudes. With new businesses forming either Joint Ventures (JV's) or individuals leaving the corporate world and setting up new 'life style change' companies then this process can only accelerate.

Quite simply what is the point of paying out for Offices, Staff, and travelling, when with all the right connections, business can be written and delivered using associates, partners, and outsourced services?

Books such as 'Think and Grow Rich - Napoleon Hill' discuss building the dream team around us... imagine the 'movers and shakers' in industry either now or in earlier times in our minds; discussing ideas with them and listening to what we think those individuals might have to say about our business. Of course when the book was written to imagine our dream team might have been the only solution, and that still has value even today, but fortunately we do have other options in today's highly connected world.

If we take a look at some of the huge companies out there today Facebook... Google, Microsoft, and in other industries as well... the person at the top has always done one thing really well... surrounded themselves with good quality people. It's not about knowing everything yourself it's about creating that mastermind group of likeminded individuals who together can assist in creating an entity which is greater than the sum of the component parts (Synergy).

The Internet gives us the power and the opportunity to seek out those we respect and who we would like to welcome into our virtual dream team... money might need to change hands, but how much value could be contained within a 1 hour session with one of the best brains in your business area? That could convert to $1000 every month!

Today we can reach out and find the best... Mastermind groups can and are springing up literally all over the world... Who would you like in your dream team?

Establishing a well connected network is fundamental in not only developing your own ideas but being in position to pick up on ideas of others and using the contacts in place to accelerate business. The TV program Dragons Den and other similar reality shows make good TV but are also providing those with money and connections access to new entrepreneurs and ideas. The entrepreneur gets money and great connections and the Business Angel gets a good idea, a willing excited partner and a diversification of their own portfolio. So the arrangement is a win / win.

A recent initiative that I have also had pleasure in being part of is providing assistance and guidance in setting up and establishing JV businesses from just an initial Idea. This can include registering the business, setting up bank accounts, configuring the online Business Management platform, establishing the online strategy (and creating it) and even finding the appropriate JV partner to accelerate the business development... http://www.jv-ing.com for further details.

A great Japanese Proverb that I heard just the other day sums up this concept very beautifully :-

"one of us is smart, but NOT as smart as ALL of us."

Read on now into Step 7 where we explore the 'art of networking' and how vital this is for both growing the existing business today and presenting exciting options for the future.

Step 7

Support groups & Business Networking

Now that we have completed Step 6 we have essentially created an automated business and revisited what we want to do going forward.

Step 7 is not really a step in its own right more of an approach that can be applied at each or any of the previous steps but one which should continue on into the future as well.

Networking is an 'Art', is it? Many business owners including myself have at some time become disgruntled with Networking. Not because meeting new people is necessarily difficult (although some find this in itself daunting) but because we come away thinking 'what was the point of that?'

Maybe there was no one in the room that fitted our target profile, maybe we weren't comfortable with the meeting format or it could've been that we got the feeling that people in the room were being nice and talking to you just to find out how they could sell something to you… do these strike any chords with readers?

If we look behind the bad experiences described above and the poor outcomes we can perhaps begin to understand the secret to Networking.

- Anyone going to a Networking meeting expecting quick sales will be disappointed

- If we believe we are going to stumble upon a room of people just queuing up for our products and services we're seriously over-optimistic

- If we're there to sell sell sell then why should we surprised that others are there trying to do the same to us?

Meeting new people and 'breaking the ice' is never easy so the meeting format might just take some getting used to

What we can see above is that what we have taken to the meeting as our objective, our expectation, and in our desire to find customers has created the very opposite result… therefore quite rightly Networking doesn't work! .. But, oh yes it does… how then can it work?

Great Networkers understand that every single person in a room is important. Everyone can contribute to your network, as either a Supplier, a Client or probably the one that has most impact but is least understood, be an Advocate for you. By building Rapport with people you meet you are developing the concepts of 'know, like, trust' and by providing a simple and clear statement of your proposition (what you do) you empower others to introduce you when you are not around... this can change the dynamics of any business, and it will happen, but you must give it time... no less than 6-12 months! How would you like 100 people or more, talking about your business, when you are not around, this is the real powerhouse of networking!

Six degrees of separation (also referred to as the "Human Web") refers to the idea that, if a person is one step away from each person they know and two steps away from each person who is known by one of the people they know, then everyone is at most six steps away from any other person on Earth

The above is the Wikipedia definition of the Law of Six Degrees of Separation. So in just 6 simple connections we could talk to any other human on the planet. That is quite an amazing concept to comprehend, but behind which lies one of the secrets to Networking.

When I look at networking today, I never ever go there with the intention of saying much about our business at all. Listening is the best tool in our kit bag and we have two ears and one mouth and we should use them in those proportions.

For myself and for a great many others, Networking is about finding jigsaw pieces to a puzzle. We all live complex lives and at some point in our life we will need a range of services and products so varied that anybody we meet would have been able to help us at some point. So it is just a question of timing as with all business. I would much rather give an order and do business with someone I have met and chatted with over coffee and got to know a little bit better than a complete stranger.

Now here is the important point... if I communicate with 200 people on a regular basis and those people also have complex lives... at some point they will need the same varied set of products and services as me... and their timing will be different to mine.

So what I am doing when networking is really trying to complete a Jigsaw puzzle of people who can provide every different conceivable product or service that might be needed. Then, when a requirement arises, either for myself or an acquaintance I have the solution available in my list of contacts.

Networking can deliver quick business sometimes (if we're lucky) but it is more often slow burn, reliable, and continuous business that comes out of it which will yield business on a consistent basis long into the future.

There are many ways to Network today. The Networking concept has spawned many Breakfast clubs and other specialist groups which we will come on to later, but there are many online groups as well which can be used to complement these or even substitute for, in some instances.

But networking is not the same everywhere… read on…

Now here is an interesting observation and I was discussing this with my lad the other day on the way to a **4Networking** (http://www.4networking.biz) meeting. Many moons ago I was lucky enough to spend some time working in the far east… specifically in Bangkok, Taiwan, Seol, Singapore and also Hong Kong. In Taipei as a visitor to DEC (Digital Equipment Corporation) I was looked after by a guy who basically went to work Monday morning (5am) and finished work Friday night (7pm). The whole time between this he was at work including the evenings, he never actually went home during the working week at all, only at the weekends.

Now we had business meetings in the Sauna, Sushi bars, huge Chinese restaurants serving Dim Sum and every conceivable Chinese delicacy… in fact we were doing business in most places except the office. This style of business was ubiquitous throughout the far east region.

Actually in reality it would be true to say that the majority of business was done in the evenings socialising with prospects and hosting clients. So much a part of business life was entertaining that at the time 50% tax relief was given on all such expenditure! Night life was booming as you can imagine.

Now here is another interesting discovery… it didn't matter whether you had the best product in the world in the Far East… if the product or service could be provided to the prospect by a friend, relative, relative of a relative, or friend of a relatives relative… if there was a connection the business would go to them. Business which is undertaken between people who are friends or relatives generally means the provider will go the extra mile… they won't want to lose face and cause disharmony within such a tight knit community (network), so there is an inbuilt guarantee that comes with doing business in this fashion.

In the West we have been detached from doing business like this for a long while relying on Broadcast advertising to sell our products into a cold marketplace. But as our businesses go through the transitions outlined in this book, as business units become individuals working as a collective, collaborating in business so we will witness two things happening :-

Work hours becoming far less defined moving away from the traditional 9 – 5 office model, to a much more flexible way of working

Business and social activities becoming more closely linked as we start to work with those people we like and trust rather than being thrown together in 'normal' business.

The net outcome is that perhaps relationships and our standing within our networks and the community at large will become much more important to us, without it, we become effectively outcasts. It is an interesting concept and puts a big onus on us to be fair, reasonable, and provide value for money, and, at the same time, accept responsibility for our actions. Remember bad news always travels much faster than good.

Respect can never be demanded it has to be earned, and our reputation is only as good as our last transaction.

Perhaps the spread of networking has much greater and far reaching consequences than any of us can imagine today?

Why are we Networking?

There are two ways in the future that business will be generated for regular 'Typical' businesses (there will always be exceptions, local pizza establishments, take outs, clubs etc.) and these are online and offline networking, that is it! If we are not participating in either of these then it is going to be extremely tough out there.

Online searching is cold market, we can use tools available to us and over time nurture our 'Optin-Lists' as we have seen to cultivate them into our 'warm market' space, but, Networking allows us to get up close, meet people and develop rapport face-face. It goes something like this... smile, chat, like, trust...

Networking works! there is no question, the only question is... are you doing it? And doing enough of it? And going with the right attitude?

So what can we get out of it?

New Sales Opportunities

The number one reason why we network is that we want more business. We all know it, but this is a by-product of the activity. The business will come, don't take my word for it… it's a fact.

Below is an example of how networking works :-

A local company in a networking group I belong to provides Telephone answering services. Now she, 'Katie' (from *Jam*) (http://www.jam.co.uk) has built up a great reputation… amusing, good rapport, helpful and generally a nice person. At this moment, at this time, for our business, we aren't in the market for a telephone answering service, however if and when we are? Or a business associate of mine mentioned to me that they were looking for someone, who would I recommend? Katie of course! during our conversations Katie has already demonstrated her credibility, built up the trust and I have even spoken with a few of her happy customers.

So it becomes an easy sale, at some point… it is just a question of time!

New Supplier Opportunities

Probably the biggest headache for me (and perhaps everyone reading this book) is when we need a job or task to be done, but we don't know anyone directly that can solve our problem.

The thought processes then follow this trail… who do I know that might know someone who could do this? Who do I know that has lots of contacts? … failing that then we might search on the Internet and narrow down the results (if possible) to someone fairly local (if this is important).

We might think we'd go straight to a search engine but if it was a product like a digital camera… we already know where we could buy it, so this is just a question of price and service… this is shopping rather than business to business or a more service related requirement.

Networking provides us with three fantastic opportunities :-

To become the popular person with all the contacts (Suppliers), become the first point of contact for people looking for solutions

To be seen as a problem solver

To quickly solve our own issues as we have a wide and diverse contact list of Suppliers

What is even more fundamental here... if you give other people business freely, what will they do for you? Return the favour of course!

New Referral Opportunities (be an advocate)

There is nothing more rewarding in business than giving other people referrals. How much time and effort does it take? And what are the effects of our actions? Let us look at these two for a moment.

How much time does it take to give a referral? Answer... a few sentences... how much time did it take to discover the requirement? ... as we are now the person with all the contacts and people contact us because normally we can solve their problem, maybe... all we had to do was just answer the telephone? Worst case we are chatting with an existing customer / supplier or business associate and a requirement comes up in the conversation. So the bottom line is that it doesn't require much effort.

But what are the effects of passing on a lead... and remember this is not just a lead... this is a qualified, warm contact introduction between trusted parties... You have inherited the trust of the person passing the referral when you talk to the potential customer... they already believe you are the best in the market, their all knowing, wise confidant has recommended 'the best' to them...

What has actually happened is that by referring someone there is a 80% plus chance that the business will happen. It is almost money in the bank! How happy will this make the person receiving the lead? But remember passing a referral (unsolicited) is based on the fact that credibility and trust have already been built and developed over time.

Communicate your story

What do you do? And why do you do it? All networking meetings provide the Members to broadcast to the group what they do. This can often lead to establishing a quick connection as there may be a latent demand in the room for exactly your products or service.

What if there are multiple people in the room 'doing the same thing'? Actually in some instances, some Networking groups do not allow this, but in others there is the abundance attitude (the only way forward in my opinion, applying rules to networking doesn't really work). Accountants and Bookkeepers are often at networking groups, and it is not uncommon for 4 to be present in a meeting of 30 or so. I'm not going to go into why Networking attracts so many Accountants and Bookkeeping people but the point is that it doesn't matter. There are millions of companies out there and everyone needs to file tax returns... there is enough work for everyone, and the ability to select the person that you 'get on with best' is often a great advantage that Networking offers.

Networking also gives us the opportunity to tell our story. Everyone has a story to tell. I'm not saying repeat you life story verbatim, but we all have some interesting stories to tell.

I always find the time to find out what people do for a hobby or leisure pursuit... my big thing as I mentioned is Table tennis which is quite an unusual sport, normally it is soccer, golf , tennis or perhaps going to the gym. For some it might be Photography, Acting or even Wine collecting!

The objective of this book is not to teach 'how to build rapport' but people love to talk about their passions... make it a personal goal to find out what each person's passion is when you meet them and get it recorded in your Contact Management System.

Advice and / or guidance

I wonder if you could help me? This short sentence does it for me every time. If these words are uttered to you? It sends a few messages straight away from the person asking... I think you can help me, I respect your opinion, you have already demonstrated good values and credibility.

As the recipient of this question, we are put in a mode of listening, thinking and taking on board everything being spoken to us, all with a simple few words, how good is that?

Of course Networking harnesses so many people from different backgrounds that getting advice and guidance is normally just a few metres away from you... people love to help and in these circumstances to develop rapport and make a new contact asking for help can be a great 'ice breaker'.

Learn

I can't remember the last time that I went to a networking meeting and didn't learn something.

Often there is a guest speaker or one of the Network Members can present for an 'extended' period to the assembled audience. These often last no more that 10-15 minutes and offer a deeper insight into a specific persons area of expertise.

New ideas

If you are looking for inspiration this can often be found Networking. Almost every facet of business will be catered for by either those in the room or people that they know.

Networking meetings are a hotbed of enthusiastic positive people and this releases energy, enthusiasm and thought processes. I have had many an idea that has resulted from what someone has said or is an extension of a service already being provided.

Strangely enough the days following on from morning Networking meetings are always more positive and more enjoyable as we come away with new ideas, new contacts and new opportunities. The only way that this isn't the case and don't get these feelings is to not turn up... to not be there... so which is better for business would you suggest?

Find new Business Partners

As we open up and speak with people perhaps over many weeks or months deeper levels of understanding develop. Who people really are... how business is developing, challenges, success stories and the reality of what is going on rather than the business sales pitch, we all deliver at the start.

Whether it be a new venture, the bringing together of businesses, assistance in branching into a sideline or an additional profit centre... working with someone who is an active member of a networking group brings with it certain reassurances that would not be there if the relationship were developing in the 'outside world'.

Find a new life Partner

Stranger things have happened... and it might not be the primary objective of Networking, but it is certainly a possibility.

I'm not suggesting networking is a dating environment, nor should it be, but if it happens then it happens. Networking permits us to 'get to know' people and that can have repercussions, so be aware!

Networking it's not new

If there are so many benefits to networking, then why hasn't it happened before? Well the answer is that it has happened before, it is just that business is evolving and in the new world, new styles of Networking are needed to address todays requirements. The Internet has opened up business turned it into a global phenomena where we can literally buy anything from anywhere… so to compete we need to build personal contact and relationships at a local level. This can't be done as effectively over large spatial distances. Networking is like an antidote to Globalisation!

Below I have listed some of the types of Networks that we can find

Chamber of Commerce

The grand daddy of Networking is the Chamber of Commerce. This is a little bit like the story of Wimpy and McDonalds.

Wimpy just didn't see the bigger picture on the scale of standardisation of a fast food product in the same way that McDonalds saw it… Then MacDonalds realised they were in the Real Estate business not the Beefburger business and now have more prime real estate than any religious denomination in the world. The vehicle of course was Burgers, the marketing aimed at pleasing kids… the rest is history. Wimpy of course make good burgers!

The Chamber of commerce have been in existence for decades and still organise lunches and evening networking events with an excellent range of speakers. The Chamber of Commerce has representation from all different sizes of businesses from very small to very large.

Business Link

A government funded institution put in place to act as a conduit for SME's to receive business advice, training, consultancy and a range of other services, some paid for and others free.

Business Link as part of their portfolio offer a range of 'networking' type events where business owners can learn about a particular topic such as 'Guides on Tax filing requirements', 'Employee Law', 'IT and the Internet', 'Sales & Marketing' and many more. These events present opportunities to not only learn but network with other business owners attending the event.

Institute of Directors

The IoD is an organisation has been representing businesses since 1906. The IoD has 44,000 members and operates from 44 different locations around the UK.

The IoD hosts 50 regional networking events across the country each month, has a LinkedIn group that members can participate on for free. The IoD's roots are in the more traditional business model and have members from International Blue Chip companies right down to the family business.

Breakfast clubs

Without doubt the emergence of the Internet, the Digital Age and the Digital Revolution that is taking place this sector has experienced the biggest growth of any Networking model.

Affordable, accessible, flexible and with few rules and regulations, breakfast clubs deliver for the Micro and Small business owner exactly what they need.

Breakfast clubs have experienced amazing growth by harnessing the low costs of Internet technology and streamlining business administration. These clubs also lead the way in terms of Online / Offline interaction. With online forums that both members and non members can participate this provides an opportunity for people to interact and 'get to know' each other and then arrange to meet-up at regular breakfast meetings.

Most breakfast clubs also provide an online database of members with all their profiles and their business category. Members looking to find a product or service can then use a search tool and then introduce themselves with a direct message.

Some of the more well known Breakfast groups are listed below :-

4Networking (http://www.4networking.biz)

BNI (http://www.bni.eu/uk)

BRX (http://www.brxnet.co.uk)

Women's Networking groups

There has also been a rise in women's networking groups that have been started to cater for the differences in lifestyle challenges between Males and Females. There is absolutely no difference in the power of these networking groups from any other. Women in Business meet at lunchtimes which is often more convenient for Women who are running homes and businesses.

Athena (http://theathenanetwork.com)

Women in Business Network (http://www.wibn.co.uk)

Industry lead Organisations e.g. **BPMA** (http://www.bpma.co.uk) (British Promotional Merchandising Association)

There are types of Networks which as yet we haven't discussed in this section and these are Industry specific networks. The members of these Networks would actually be competitors to each other and so although they may hold annual conferences and industry events they are not aimed so much at networking but rather supporting their members with information and resources to assist business.

Online Networking

So far we have discussed the very many benefits of local, physical networking for business building. What about the Global Network? The Online world... Globalisation? As we have seen in earlier steps outsourcing and the location of the service provider is having less and less impact. There is an inevitability about this, however the actual work might be outsourced but the responsibility for delivery, quality and the contract may still reside with a local business, one that might have been introduced through a regular network meeting.

People travel, people talk and people share connections. Those who have travelled further afield may well have contacts on different continents and these in turn are passed on. There are some fantastic tools out there in this Digital Age that allow us to pass on contacts, introduce people without involving us in any work. Below I have listed a few of the more popular ones, although we have mentioned these many times elsewhere in this book it is worth understanding their importance in terms of 'getting connected' and 'networking'. I'm using my own profile examples.

Business Networking – **LinkedIn** (http://uk.linkedin.com/in/chrisogle), **ecademy** (http://www.ecademy.com/account.php?id=149131)

Tools like Linked in and Ecademy allow us to extend our networking activities beyond the local area.

Integration of these sites using 'Mash-ups' or linkages between different online services such as Blogs and twitter accounts enables us to communicate with a single post automatically with this extended network with little or no extra effort.

Today we can throw open the challenge... I am looking for... can anyone help with... does anyone know someone who... and communicate this to thousands of people instantly.

There are no guarantees of business anytime soon... but the ability to reach out across the globe, build and communicate with a truly world wide audience represents an opportunity not to be missed.

Social / Business Networking – **Facebook** (http://en-gb.facebook. com/oglechris), MySpace

Everything stated in the section above also applies to these global social networking sites. The difference is in the roots of why and how they came to be in the first place.

LinkedIn and ecademy started life as Business Connecting networks, whereas Facebook and MySpace started as friends connecting together. Much has changed since those early years... 2004/5 and the applicability of all of them to Networking is now pretty much the same.

LinkedIn asks more questions about relationships when connecting to other people, this reduces the speed of building contacts but each connection has more meaning. Facebook is more relaxed about the establishment of a connection in the first place.

Facebook has been working hard in the area of building Business elements to their site and introduced Business Pages and greater levels of individual customisation. Our own page **SME7** (http://bit.ly/ SME7) is an example of how facebook can be configured to work more for your business.

The creation of Groups highlights profiles as does participating in groups set up by others and helps to increase visibility and extend the 'Reach' of the global network.

Communication can be broadcast to Groups (in LinkedIn, Facebook and ecademy) and Fans of Business pages (Facebook), the larger the list the greater the impact.

You Tube Social Network

At the very least You Tube is a place to host and allow play back of video for your business at the other end of the spectrum it could be the website... depending on the nature of the business. Video is becoming incredibly important as the preferred means to 'get the message across'. What can be said in a single 5 minute video would take pages of written text, and not interpreted as succinctly as if by video.

Video can be used in so many ways, education and training, customer updates, staff announcements, previous webinars, promotional events, introductions, business announcements... even advertisements!

Combining video and placing onto Global social networks such as LinkedIn and Facebook brings another dimension, improves communication and accelerates the connection building processes.

Remember You Tube is about real regular people making video not great productions teams... and its purpose is to communicate a message not whether the lighting is spot on or not. That being said, we should attempt to make it as good / funny / enjoyable and as good a quality as possible.

Open Networking – Forums

Forums present us with a chance to Network in the open but focus in on people with a common interest. We have discussed in Step 4 how this can be part of your digital marketing programme, but by default it opens up a chance to build credibility, get our names and that of the company's in the Public domain.

Networking groups such as **4Networking** (http://www.4networking.biz) have cleverly combined Forums with their physical meetings which provides not only a means to start online contacts but to take them offline as well. A little later on we will explore the offline element and its importance.

Membership Sites – **SME7 Community** (http://www.sme7.net)

Business Referral network

So far we have discussed using other people's online communities and bending them to suit our online networking requirement.

Depending on our business we can however use standard membership products to build our own online networking communities. **SME7 Community** (http://www.sme7.net) is our own online membership site. Being independent, the community consists of members from any networking community or background, some will not be networking at all. The purpose of the **SME7 Community** (http://www.sme7.net) is to provide a common place for all the businesses that we have spoke too and are willing to recommend to others, so an accredited SME7 referral database. All members will therefore be able to search and find details on other members, and their businesses.

It is easy to get carried away and start to set up a whole host of Social Network profiles. The recommendation is to work with a few no more that 2 or 3 initially and start to build the online presence. Updating and taking care of a few Social Networking accounts will bear much more fruit that 10 badly managed ones.

It is interesting to note that although many networking activities started online such as LinkedIn, ecademy and BNI and that we have truly global connections, there is now a big move to real physical meetings again.

LinkedIn members have now started to invite members to local 'Net Linked' Network' meetings, these are offline meetings involving people who are part of the LinkedIn Community. Ecademy have now started 'Boardrooms' which are offline meetings between ecademy members to discuss face-to-face their business challenges.

It is reassuring to note that in this era of globalisation and the Digital Age there appears to still be the need for us Humans to want to meet up in person and experience networking for real rather than just in the ether…

SUMMARY

That is it... the 7 steps completed! In this book we have gone from a business which was not delivering in terms of Money or Time or perhaps not meeting other criteria for the business which were identified early on in Step 1 to a business which is on autopilot and will continue to function whether we are there or not.

The steps in this book are working for myself right now in a variety of business ventures and have worked for many of my customers over the past 7 years, and they will work for you too.

What happens next is not within the scope of this book... but the details and the content within it can be applied to any business either in existence or yet to be.

If you have got to this page then there are possibly three outcomes which can now take place :-

Nothing changes and the book is placed on the shelf or filed electronically next to others and will never see the light of day again.

The book has been read from cover to cover and it is time to go back and start to work through it as an exercise book, enlisting the help of an SME7 – Practitioner as necessary.

The book has been worked through and you have arrived at this page having carried out all the 7 steps. If this is the case congratulations are in order and enjoy doing whatever you wish with the rest of your future.

I implore everyone who reads this page to not choose option 1 above... do something with the knowledge that you now have in your hands and make a decision to have a different future.

I wish you all the best in embracing the challenges of the Digital Revolution and look forward to hearing of your successes in the coming years.

Best Wishes,
Chris Ogle http://www.public-cards.com/chrisogle

TESTIMONIALS

"Chris Ogle's Into 2 The Clouds is a must read 7 Step guide into how SME's face the challenges of adapting to the very modern Digital Age. Engaging and relevant. Cuts through the jargon to help you deliver the business you want."

Zoe Palmer – Chirus Limited

"In 2 the clouds is a truly inspiring read that is a real must in any business owners growth strategy. Written in an endearing way that maps out the way clearly so that businesses can understand what they need to do to survive in this challenging Digital revolution! Based upon the 7 steps in this book, I am now establishing a worldwide network of SME7 Practitioners with the same code of ethics and understanding to guide businesses through their exciting transition into the Digital Age!"

Scott Dwyer - Business Coach and Mentor

"Following, and putting into action, the steps in the book has allowed me to increase my sales through the Internet and work from anywhere in the world."

James Morley, BlueAutumn.co.uk

"I wish Chris had written this book when I first started with creating my on-line business. By following the 7 Steps I would have had a much more methodical structured approach and would have eliminated the overwhelm. With this book I can now formalise my business processes"

Suzanne Barnett – KISS Training

WHAT NEXT?

If you are excited about applying this 7 Step process to your business and would like to 'get the ball rolling' then contact the person who introduced you to this book or alternatively you may find the following information helpful.

To provide high quality and consistent services to business owners working through the 7 steps as described in the book, we have created a programme called SME7. The website is http://www.sme7.com/, please visit the website where you can find an enquiry form to 'Fast Track your business' under the what next section. Complete the form with as much information as possible including your website address and full contact information.

Once your enquiry is lodged then an SME7 Practitioner will be in touch within 24 hours to discuss your exciting lifestyle change project.

SME7 Practitioners are professional business specialists with experience in NLP, Sales, Business Management, Business Processes, Finance and Digital marketing. An SME7 practitioner will project manage your journey through the 7 step process and ensure that all the necessary resources to achieve your goals and ambitions are available as and when required.

LIVING BOOK

In 2 The Clouds is not just a static book, much of the content refers to web and Internet technologies, and as we know this subject changes constantly.

The website http://www.in2theclouds.co.uk has a 'live book Blog' which will be updated as new information and relevant products and services become available. The Blog will be broken down into categories one for each Step in the book making it easier to locate items of interest.

Make the most of your investment with In 2 The Clouds and get all the updates absolutely free!! Check back with the site regularly or why not subscribe to the blog feed and receive email updates automatically when additions to the book are published.

CONNECT WITH US ON

Twitter (Chris Ogle) (http://twitter.com/chrisogle)

Twitter (in 2 the clouds) (http://twitter.com/in2theclouds)

Twitter (SME7) (http://twitter.com/sme_7)

Twitter (DirectorsWeb) (http://twitter.com/Directorsweb)

Twitter (WeDoWebStuff) (http://twitter.com/wedowebstuff)

Facebook (http://en.gb.facebook.com/oglechris)

LinkedIn (http://uk.linkedin.com/in/chrisogle)

Ecademy (http://www.ecademy.com/account.php?id=149131)

4Networking
(http://www.4networking.biz/members/view.htm?UserID=37113)

BECOME A FAN

Facebook - SME7 (http://bit.ly/sme7)

Facebook - In2TheClouds (http://bit.ly/94w61R)

Facebook - Directors On The Web (http://bit.ly/directorsontheweb)

SUBSCRIBE TO OUR BLOG FEEDS

SME7 (http://www.sme7.com)

In2TheClouds (http://www.in2theclouds.co.uk)

Chris Ogle (Daily Diaries) (http://www.chrisogle.com)

Chris Ogle (Internet Power Systems Ltd) (http://www.ips.co.uk)

Lightning Source UK Ltd.
Milton Keynes UK
02 November 2010

162256UK00001B/7/P